Comrades

Comrades

Alan Bookbinder
Olivia Lichtenstein
Richard Denton

BRITISH BROADCASTING CORPORATION

To our parents and
to Vicki, Jonathan and Valya

Published by the British Broadcasting Corporation
35 Marylebone High Street, London W1M 4AA

ISBN 0 563 20416 8

First published 1985
Text and photographs © Alan Bookbinder,
Olivia Lichtenstein and Richard Denton 1985

Set in 11/14 Baskerville by
Wilmaset, Birkenhead, Wirral
Printed and Bound in Great Britain by
Butler & Tanner Ltd, Frome
Colour separations by Bridge Graphics Ltd, Hull
Colour illustrations printed by Chorley and Pickersgill, Leeds

Contents

IC OCEAN

• PREOBRAZHENKA

LAKE
BAIKAL

IRKUTSK
•

MANCHURIA

MONGOLIA

VLADIVOSTOK
• • NAKHODKA

PACIFIC
OCEAN

SEA OF
JAPAN

TOKYO
•

INA

Acknowledgements

We would like to thank all those who have been involved in the making of the television series *Comrades*. To our production assistants Sara Fletcher and Sue MacGregor, without whom we would probably still be lost in some remote corner of the Soviet Union. To the cameramen Derek Banks, Alex Hansen, Rex Maidment, Colin Munn, Kevin Rowley, David Swan and their assistants John Deeble, Terry Doe, Eric Fever, Chris Kochanowicz, Robert Pascall, Steve Plant, Mary Routh and Mike Shelton. To the sound recordists Fred Clark, Morton Hardaker, Ron Keightley, Christopher King, Richard Merrick, Ian Sansam, Robin Swain, Michael Turner. To our film editors Tony Heaven and Andrew Willsmore and their assistants Alice Forward and Gillian Hill who put it all together. To Roger Mills who guest directed 'The Trial of Tamara Russo', to executive producers Peter Pagnamenta and George Carey and to head of department Will Wyatt for their support, and to Peter Ruff, 'our man in Moscow' who has always been ready to help.

Thanks to Vitaly Sufan and Pavel Tsarvoulanov, our colleagues at Gosteleradio (State Commission for Television and Radio) who have travelled and worked with us for the past two years, and thanks to Leo Feigin, Mark Frankland, Alexei Konovalov, Margot Light, Valera Lobych and Leonid Melamud, who have always been on hand to help and answer questions.

And to Hilary Duguid and Anthony Kingsford, our editors, who gave us the encouragement and help we needed to write this book.

Introduction

The Iron Curtain serves a purpose only to people of ill will. It helps to keep Soviet citizens out of the West and Westerners out of the Soviet Union. The ignorance that has grown up is evident in the opinions expressed on both sides. When we think of the Soviet Union we think first of repression, of the lack of political and individual freedom, of dissidents and labour camps. While all of these exist, there are a great many other things that we should know about if we wish to understand the Soviet Union. When we were asked to make the BBC television series *Comrades*, we felt that it would give us the opportunity to explore and depict what life was really like for people who lived and worked in this vast continent. Two of the authors of this book had already spent a year in the country and spoke Russian fluently. The third met and married his Russian wife during the making of the series.

The Soviet Union is made up of fifteen republics, each with its own language, culture and traditions. Our research and filming took us from Leningrad in the north facing Finland to Samarkand on the border with Afghanistan, from Lvov next to Poland to Nakhodka on the Sea of Japan. The three of us spent a total of twenty-one months travelling in the Soviet Union meeting people and listening to them. Never before has a Western film crew had such freedom in the Soviet Union. We have lived in army barracks, feasting and drinking with generals of the Red Army, we have survived in sub-arctic conditions, sleeping nine to a hut in the depths of the Siberian forest, we have witnessed courtroom dramas and intricate eye-surgery, attended fashion shows and football matches.

Our choice of candidates for the chapters is based on the films in the television series. We wanted to find a wide variety of characters, different in age, sex and occupation, and in the time we spent in the Soviet Union we built up a large circle of both official and unofficial friends and acquaintances. Thus, although we were working with the cooperation of the State Committee for Television and Radio, we were well enough informed not to be fobbed off with people the Soviet authorities considered to be suitable candidates. To take just one example, when selecting collective farmers to film, we ourselves chose a farm from the three offered to us. Of the two suggested individuals, we found neither suitable for our purposes and asked to meet some more. The farm director then called some twenty together and we spent a day interviewing them and visiting their homes before deciding on the Kulinich brothers and their mother Mariya.

Professor Fyodorov, Abdugaffar Khakkulov, Dinara Asanova and Sergei Kuryokhin were specifically requested by us to be subjects for our films, as we had found out about them through our own contacts. Unlike resident Western journalists, who are usually able to spend only a very short time with interviewees, we spent a minimum of two weeks and often a great deal more time with each of the people and families described in the book.

The last three years have seen three changes of leadership in the Soviet Union (the first three leaders spanned nearly sixty years). We were there when Yuri Andropov and Konstantin Chernenko died. Now, with the arrival of Mikhail Gorbachev, the country has a vigorous and energetic leader for the first time in ten years and may well be on the brink of a new era. Certainly the mood of people in Moscow at present is one of optimism. The vast majority of the people, however, are indifferent to politics and more concerned with those things that everyone the world over concerns themselves with, irrespective of race or creed: a world without war, a comfortable home, good marriages and jobs both for themselves and their children, enjoying themselves and falling in love.

The time we have spent in the Soviet Union, the freedom with which we have been able to move about and meet people, and the endless conversations into the night both on and off camera, have left us with a wealth of experiences. This book is our attempt to share some of them. It does not purport to be a definitive account of such a diverse and impenetrable country. We gratefully extend our thanks to all those in the Soviet Union who made it possible and answered our questions and probings. We would also like to thank everyone here who helped us and a special thanks to our families and friends who put up with our prolonged absences – both physical and spiritual.

Alan Bookbinder, Olivia Lichtenstein, Richard Denton
London, June 1985

ONE

Educating Rita

Children are the only class who are allowed to have privileges.
V. I. Lenin

Rita Tikhonova is twenty-one, a student in her fifth and final year at the Moscow Lenin State Pedagogical Institute and, like virtually all Soviet students studying in their home town, living with her mother and father. Home is a typical Soviet flat: two rooms, plus a kitchen and bathroom. Both rooms are sitting rooms by day and have none of the intimacy of a bedroom. Current Soviet taste dictates that wooden furniture be varnished to a high glaze, and the Tikhonovs' beds, tables and cabinets conform to this. The beds are covered with costly, Persian-style carpets – the latest craze if you can afford or find them. Housing is a major problem in Moscow and the other big cities: because Muscovites have so little space, they have become ingenious at putting every inch to good use. The small entrance hall is therefore lined with books and the lavatory doubles up as a tool shed. In spite – or perhaps because – of the lack of space, perfect order prevails. There is a carefully engineered place for everything and everything is in its place. Indeed, so accustomed have Russians become to living, eating and sleeping all in one room that when Westerners describe their living quarters, they are asked, why do you need all those rooms? Comfort is an indulgence and Soviet values are based on having what you need; anything more is a luxury.

The Tikhonovs are perfectly satisfied with their flat, and with good reason. The two rooms command an enviable view of the Moscow river. They live in the heart of Moscow not five minutes from Tagansky Square, home of the famous 'Taganka' theatre whose director, Yuri Lyubimov, recently came to the West – and stayed. Rita is an avid theatre-goer and her mother has good contacts and is able to 'get' tickets from time to time. In the Soviet Union you rarely 'buy' things; you 'get' them. Most purchases involve a long chain of contacts, mutual favours and, most of all, time and energy.

By Soviet standards, the Tikhonovs are lucky. Their apartment building is enviable, they have been living in it for fifteen years and doubtless will end their days there. They rent it from the State at a nominal rental of fifteen roubles a month, about 10% of the average wage. Gas and electricity are extra, perhaps twenty kopecks per month, and a central-heating system warms the entire block throughout the cold winter months. According to official exchange rates a rouble is worth a pound, however the currencies are not comparable. The cost of housing and transport is minimal while luxury consumer items such as cars and clothing tend to be more expensive than in the West.

While the flat itself is kept scrupulously clean and tidy, the common entrance hall is dark, dank and depressing. Light bulbs are missing, the stone floor is broken in places, the windows are crusted over with dirt and obliterate the light. It is puzzling in a society that purports to concern itself with the well-being of the majority, as opposed to the individual, that the area shared by all is so squalid, while the individual flats are clean. Yet this is commonly the case.

Rita is an only child; in fact, she is the only child in the three families that make up the sum total of her relatives and she's always been perfectly happy about this. 'I liked the fact that everyone always looked after me.' Most Russian families are small and one child is the norm. This is a matter of some concern to the government as Russia's population will shortly be outnumbered by that of Soviet Central Asia where women customarily bear six or seven children, and this could jeopardise the Russian Republic's right to hegemony over the Soviet Union. The State encourages Russians to have children by awarding child benefit, four months paid maternity leave, crèche facilities and housing priority to couples with children. It is interesting to note the different policy in China where benefits accrue to you when you have *no* more than one child. The Soviet incentives, however, are not great enough: housing still remains a problem, money may be short, the woman will have to go on working and, as Soviet husbands rarely help in the home, a young mother finds herself with two jobs instead of one.

Aleksandr Tikhonov, Rita's father, is an exception and is frequently to be found in the kitchen. A thin, shy man in his late forties, he works in a factory teaching others to make school furniture. He suffers from kidney trouble and has to spend time in hospital. Medical care is free. Aleksandr is a shadowy, albeit amiable, presence in this flat which is dominated by the vivacity and volubility of his wife and daughter. They can do no wrong in his eyes. 'I think Dad's always happy with everything I do.'

Maya Tikhonova, Rita's mother, is plump and blonde. She is usually smiling and reveals the gold teeth that are the hallmark of Soviet dentistry. She is the secretary to the director of a factory and is equally devoted to

Rita. Children are indulged by their parents in the Soviet Union. Lenin, a ubiquitous form both in statue and precept, said that there were no first-class citizens in the Soviet Union except for children. Rita at twenty-one is still in many ways a child. Her mother proudly follows her everywhere, whether it's to watch her teaching practice at the school or to hear her sing at the youth club. Women in the Soviet Union belong to their parents until they get married, when they belong to their husbands. Westerners are always asked if they are married; if they are not, it is assumed that they live with their parents. Single people who live alone evoke first astonishment and then sympathy.

If Soviet parents spoil children, they in their turn respect their parents, and behave politely and considerately towards their elders. Anyone who does not will be rebuked. 'Aren't you ashamed of yourself?' a stranger on a bus will say to someone who fails to give up their seat to an older person. Rita is charming and considerate to her parents: 'My mother's very sensitive towards me, she understands me, so I try to be equally considerate in return. Everything's based on mutual respect.' If her mother's eager need to know the details of her life irritates her, she does not show it. She smiles indulgently. 'It's absolutely impossible, I don't know when I'll be able to give my mum the slip.' Aleksandr and Maya's pride is not without cause. Rita is an excellent student and she sings beautifully. A contented and responsible member of Soviet society, she will soon be a teacher.

The Moscow Lenin State Pedagogical Institute is the oldest in the country. The main building, where Rita studies, is near the centre of Moscow, by Frunzensky tube station. It is an extravagant pink Palladian building, formerly used as a finishing school for young noblewomen. Now a statue of Lenin presides over its impressive colonnaded hall and the former chapel is an examination room. To qualify for higher education, applicants must have their secondary school diploma. They then enter a competitive examination and will be enrolled on the basis of their entrance examination points plus the mean points of their school leaving certificate. Some institutions are more popular and more highly regarded than others: Moscow and Leningrad universities are notoriously difficult to get into and cream off the best students, those who have consistently received 'fives' for their schoolwork and have distinguished themselves as members of the Young Communist League, the Komsomol.

From the age of nine to fourteen, Soviet children are Young Pioneers which is similar to our Cubs or Brownies, but instead of fledgling Christians, Pioneers are nascent Communists. Lenin is an avuncular figure about whom they sing songs, and Russia is the motherland they are taught to love. Membership is not an extracurricular option, but an integral part of school life. In summer most Young Pioneers go to holiday camps. At fourteen or later they will elect, or be invited, to join the Komsomol. One Soviet woman who came up for nomination in class at school was denounced by her best friend and refused admission. 'Natasha says anti-Soviet things to me in private.' She was the only one in her class not to become a member. It is rare to receive university education without membership. Natasha, however, managed to do so and is now a member of the intelligentsia, a clearly defined group that exists on the fringes of Soviet society.

The daughter of an 'intellectual' – the word carries no irony – came home from school one day: 'I was invited to join the Komsomol today and I refused.'

'Did anyone else refuse?'

'No, just me.'

'Why?'

'I don't want to join in with all that nonsense, it's stupid.'

'You brave thing, isn't she brave? Congratulations!'

This young girl has a difficult time ahead. Among other things, Komsomol membership opens doors to higher education and to foreign travel. Soviet society looks askance at individuals; it prefers dealing with groups and organisations.

Rita was an eager Pioneer: 'It's stayed as something sacred for me! Taking part makes you feel so responsible. While the State is large-scale government, the school was managed by us, governed by us. We decided who should be on duty at school on any given day, and what we would do after lessons were over. We decided everything ourselves. We believed in what we were doing so sincerely, we did it with our heart and soul.' The feeling of collective responsibility and the habit of self-criticism that the Pioneer and Komsomol organisations engender in Soviet youth is seminal to an understanding of Soviet education and society.

Membership of the Komsomol ends at the age of twenty-nine. Contrary to common Western belief, membership of the Communist Party of the Soviet Union is not automatic and only 9% of the 270-million population are card-carrying members. Rita's mother Maya is a member and her responsibilities are largely administrative. She collects Party subs in the factory where she works. Aleksandr isn't a member but he, like 'everyone' (Rita's word), follows the Party line. Rita does not know yet whether she will apply to join or not. 'It's something you have to be very serious about and I don't feel I'm ready to take the step yet.'

As a Komsomol member and good pupil, Rita has privileges. She easily gained entry to the prestigious Pedagogical Institute, has travelled to Hungary to teach Russian at a summer camp and goes regularly to Moscow's 'Interklub', a Komsomol-run organisation with its own discothèque that hosts meetings for groups from Socialist and 'Capitalist' countries.

The Institute has a Komsomol office. 'If someone fails their exams, or isn't attending lectures, or doesn't do any preparation work for seminars, then they ask to see him, they have a chat, try to find out why, whether he's having family problems of some kind or is just being lazy. Then they either offer some help or tell him off – after all, you have to be serious about studying.' Rita's account describes in microcosm the way Soviet society works: you have to be serious about being a citizen as well.

This may sound ominous. However, a lecture at the Institute is reassuringly like a lecture in any university anywhere in the world. Some students sit attentively and write notes diligently. But, in the back row, knitting needles flash and students read, whisper and pass notes. Rita, who is to be a Russian teacher, is in the department of Russian Language and Literature. Of the fifty students in the lecture hall only one is a man. Schoolteaching in the Soviet Union is almost exclusively a female profession.

Rita's department contains a branch for students from Uzbekistan. These students are taught separately as they may not be fluent in Russian, and they do not seem to interact with Russian students in other contexts either. With their black hair, broad faces and narrow eyes, the Uzbeks are easily distinguishable from the Russians. It is a matter of policy that the best students from the non-Russian areas of the Soviet Union are sent to Moscow or Leningrad in order that they can carry the dominant Russian culture back to their places of origin. Amongst the Uzbek group at the institute there are equal numbers of men and women. The women, like all Soviet Central Asian women, tend to be deferential and meek. Once they are wives and mothers in their home republic, fewer of them work. A long way from home, these students are housed in hostels on Vernadsky Prospekt near the Economic Achievements Exhibition where they live three or four to a room. By the end of their fifth year most of them are married, usually to each other, and are well on the way to producing the large families that they are accustomed to.

Panokhon Yegamova is twenty-two and comes from Samarkand Region. She met her husband Abdulbaki in the first year and they live in an Institute hostel for married couples. He comes from a family of twelve, she from a family of seven. When she talks, she keeps her pretty dark eyes demurely cast down to her hands neatly folded in her lap. The beauty of her face is marred only slightly by those inevitable gold teeth. She looks little more than a child herself and yet has a daughter of seventeen months and another child on the way. Her daughter is thousands of miles away with her husband's mother. This is not unusual – parents often bring up their children's children, and Panokhon and her husband will be returning to live with his family. Housing is far more spacious in Uzbekistan and they will have their own small wing in a building that houses four generations.

Graduates are allocated jobs by the State and are obliged to work a minimum of two years in the profession they have trained for. Because the Moscow Pedagogical Institute is so well-respected, many Uzbek students go on to do postgraduate work in Tashkent. Rita will be allocated a job in Moscow. There was a time when new teachers were sent to outlying regions of the Soviet Union to 'work out' the obligatory two years. The policy has now changed and, as Moscow needs Russian teachers, all graduating students are sent to schools as near as possible to where they live. If you want to go elsewhere you can. 'One girl wanted to work on one of the settlements along the Baikal-Amur Railway in Siberia. There are a lot of new schools being built there, so of course there's a shortage of teachers. So that's where she went.'

Rita gets a basic grant of forty roubles a month from the State; there are no tuition fees. She hands her grant over to her parents and they give her spending money. As a new teacher, she will receive a basic wage of 100 roubles a month and extras for duties like being form mistress and marking homework. Wages have just gone up, and Rita can expect to earn a total of 140–150 roubles a month which she feels will be enough to live on.

On a morning at the end of March, 1984, Rita dresses with more care than usual. Instead of her Western jeans, she dons a skirt that falls modestly below the knee, a jersey, high-heeled shoes and earrings. She is alive with anticipation. Today is job allocation day and although she is virtually sure of where she'll be teaching, it is an important ritual. In sheepskin coat and fur hat, for the weather is still cold, she travels the few stops by tube to the Institute. (Anyone not wearing a hat in winter is scolded by passers-by: 'Young lady, where's your hat? Go home and get it at once or you'll freeze.')

Russians love ceremonies and the erstwhile chapel, a beautiful round room with a gallery, is the scene of today's pageant. The students cluster round its doors chattering excitedly, and one by one they file in, now solemn, and sit before a semicircle of august figures: the Rector, the Dean of the faculty, a representative from the Ministry of Education, a Party representative and the head of their Komsomol branch. The Dean introduces the student to the assembly, underlining the particular merits of the individual student. Rita is offered a job at School number 397, a school she knows and wants to work at. She has no complaints and is asked to sign her contract there and then, undertaking to 'work out' her two years. What she does after that is up to her. She may stop teaching altogether if she wishes. If students are offered posts they do not want, they may object on the grounds that it is too far from their home or for some other reason. However, as so often with Soviet ceremonies, the job allocation is well-rehearsed and any objections will long since have been heeded or quelled.

Rita's last term is nearly over and with it her formal education. Saturday is the last day, the day of the 'last bell'. This too is ritualised; instead of the usual electronic buzz that signifies the beginning and end of classes, someone rings a handbell, students and teachers exchange thanks and good wishes, and it's time for a party. Soviets love parties. You have only to mention that it's your birthday, or your parents' wedding anniversary, and vodka and food appear in vast quantities from nowhere, the furniture is cleared and everyone dances.

Rita and her friends are more temperate than many of their peers and the party that Rita has to mark this auspicious occasion is a restrained affair. She and her mother work together making fish and meat salads and intricate pastry cases deliciously stuffed with chopped egg and sour cream – hors d'oeuvres are the mainstay of any Russian meal. Aleksandr prepares the main course, pork that he has carefully tenderised with a mallet. When the guests arrive he and Maya retreat, good-humouredly giving Rita and her friends the run of the flat. There are eight of them. Andrei is Rita's boyfriend, quiet, pretty and doting. She is literally pink with excitement and talks incessantly. Two of her classmates are there with their boyfriend and husband. Evenings start early and at 6 o'clock everyone has gathered. By midnight, they are replete, surprisingly sober, singing songs and reciting poetry.

Going to university for those living at home is like going to work. It is not the sort of campus or college life that we in the West are accustomed to with its obligatory trips for coffee between seminars and drinks in the bar. There are no common rooms; once you've attended your classes, you go home. The ten-minute break between ninety-minute classes is just long enough for a quick cigarette. Smoking is forbidden inside the building and the entrance to the Institute is always clustered with groups of people lighting up. Out-of-town students who live in the hostels have more of a student life as we understand it. Now all that is left for Rita and her classmates is to pass their course exams and the State exams.

The Soviet education system has a strong oral bias. During classes, students of all ages are taught to stand up and answer questions at length, and to deliver their essays and exam answers orally. This probably accounts for the astonishing composure with which they approach public speaking and for the ease with which they pronounce long and elaborate toasts at the table. Exams are nearly always oral. It would be a mistake to assume that this was a Soviet invention. The picture that Tolstoy paints in his semi-autobiographical work *Childhood, Boyhood and Youth* is as true of the exam system now as it was in the Tsarist Russia of the 19th century. The difference is that then it was a privilege accorded to a small group of people, the Russian nobility. Now everyone enjoys (or endures) it.

The State exams are the ones to be feared and, revision lectures now over, the day of reckoning is here. Rita and her friends stand outside the examination room. The examiners are inside and taking their places behind a long table. There are four of them – the Dean, two teachers from the Institute and an external examiner. The subject is Russian Literature. Finally all the students are told to enter the room. They each pick a piece of paper at random on which two questions are written and they have forty minutes to prepare their answers. One by one, they will then have to approach the examiners' table and give their answers. The last student to answer will thus have had far longer in preparation time than the others – a fact that does not seem to worry anyone except us!

Some way into the preparation time, the door opens and a grey-haired, hatted gentleman enters looking exactly as a doyen of Russian Literature should. And indeed this is precisely who he proves to be – a well-known expert in 18th-century literature. He is a second external examiner. Students take about thirty minutes to answer their questions and then leave the room to pace the corridor outside. Rita, pink-cheeked as she always is when nervous or excited, acquits herself fluently. When everyone has answered, the examiners, who have been noting down marks, are left to confer. Top score is 5, 4 is good, 3 is fair and 2 and 1 are best forgotten. Having reached agreement, the examiners invite the students back in and give the results. Rita's consistent habit of getting 5's has earned her the title 'otlichnitsa' (excellent student). This is not merely an accolade for a student's abilities: it carries material advantages of scholarships to the value of 100 roubles. This exam is no exception and Rita has scored 5.

There is one State exam that students of all disciplines are required to pass. This is Scientific Communism. 'It's in the syllabus of every college course. It determines our position, our general outlook, our view of the world. It's the methodological basis of our knowledge, of our whole education system, it summarises our philosophical ideas, our economic and political system, everything. You see, it's a question of your general outlook, your view of the world. For example, certain Western specialists in Soviet Literature would claim that Socialist Realism does not exist as a literary method, that it's a fiction. And they approach the work of modern Soviet writers from that point of view. Whereas our approach to the same work is based on Scientific Communism and philosophy.'

This is the window through which Soviet citizens are taught to view the world. For Westerners, the idea of a State overtly dictating to its citizens an ideology by which they must live is anathema, while to many Soviet citizens it is perfectly acceptable. They are very aware of their collective identity and responsibility, and devoutly patriotic. Propaganda may be a pejorative term in Western circles, but in the Soviet Union it is a fact of life and for most people nothing to be ashamed of. Buildings boldly proclaim themselves Propaganda Department. For those less at one with the status quo than Rita, the placards and red banners urging citizens on to greater productivity and labour have a different resonance:

'Do they write things all over the place like this in the West?'

'No, I bet they write less and DO more.'

The role of teacher in Soviet society is an important one. As citizens of a state committed to a particular ideology, Soviet teachers must be ideologically and politically 'sound'. It is no wonder then that Scientific Communism is a compulsory subject.

Rita has not always wanted to be a teacher. Until a few years ago she flirted with the idea of becoming an actress. Love of the theatre evolved into a love of Russian literature and language and her first teaching practice deflected her forever from the stage to the dais.

'I was taking the fourth year [eleven-year-olds]. They were so small with such big eyes, there's so much they don't know. I remember thinking it would be nice when they learnt something and you would know that you alone had been responsible and no one else, that it would be you who had taught them to recognise and appreciate beauty. I will always remember a teacher I had at school. She only taught me for two years, she was the person who taught me to love Pushkin. So, if one of my pupils remembers me in the same way, even if it's only one, it will have made my life and work worthwhile.'

Rita now has the equivalent of a first-class degree from the Institute. The graduation ceremony takes place in Moscow's Hall of Columns, where

Soviet leaders and members of the Politburo lie in state after their death. A spectacular room, dripping in chandeliers, it is designed for pomp and glory and ritualised mourning. 2 July is a celebration and the hall resounds with the Institute song, clearly composed in the days when students were sent to far-flung corners of the Soviet Union to 'work out' their two years.

> The dean has signed the last order, comrade,
> You're off to Lake Baikal, Sakhalin, the Caucasus,
> In May or March you'll look on a map,
> You'll remember the Insitute and with it us.

The graduates are free until the middle of August. Rita has been intending to go to Hungary to teach in the summer camp again and the mere mention of the fact that she will be away for thirty days is enough to make her and her boyfriend Andrei cry. This enforced separation is a taboo subject between them. Courtship is one of the things that Russians do best. The romantic Russian Spirit is not a myth. 'He loves beautifully,' they will say of someone admiringly.

In order to survive the torment of thirty days apart, Rita and Andrei have determined each to write thirty letters to the other before her departure. They were inspired to do this after reading a story called 'Tenderness' by the Russian writer Kuprin. A woman leaves her loved one and commits suicide, and for ten years after her death he receives a letter from her each year. In the last letter she tells him that she has done this in order that he may grow accustomed to his loss gradually. Russians live their literature. At the railway station, amidst the tears and the flowers, Andrei and Rita will each hand over their bundle of letters, and every day they will open one. Even in May Rita has started composing hers; each letter is pages long. About what? Love? 'Well yes, I suppose it all tends to boil down to it, yes.' To their mutual relief the trip is cancelled. She gives him the letters anyway.

At twenty-one this is Rita's second significant relationship with a man, and she and Andrei plan to marry. They met at a friend's home. Rita remembers, 'My friend said, "Come over and bring your guitar and sing, someone who works in the theatre with me will also be coming. He plays the guitar fantastically, he used to play with 'Time Machine' [a well-known Soviet pop group]." '

Russians are shamelessly superstitious, great believers in fate and premonitions, and Rita is no exception. The Russia that was steeped for so many centuries in folklore and infused with animism (each peasant hut was believed to have its own spirit) and natural remedies has left its legacy to the Soviets. 'I'm very superstitious, I believe in all conceivable omens. If something important is happening, like an exam, I always walk out of the door left foot first; I save lucky tickets and then eat them [certain computations of numbers on bus and tram tickets are lucky]. Black cats are unlucky. If you meet someone who's carrying an empty bucket, that's unlucky too. This year's a leap year and all weddings that take place this year are doomed to failure.'

The night she met Andrei, Rita 'felt' that it was no accident, their meeting was meant to be. There she sat in a smoky, candlelit, Moscow room: 'The first thing I noticed were his eyes. Maybe he noticed me because I was singing, I don't know, I just saw those eyes, I couldn't see anything else. I sang, he played, we talked. I felt as if I'd known him for ever . . . we saw each other the next day and the next and every day since. Since I've known him I think of my whole life in terms of before meeting him and after.'

They have known each other for five months. Andrei is twenty-five. He too lives with his parents in a three-roomed flat which is on the outskirts of Moscow. Rita has never met them. Andrei does not get on well with his father and lives a completely independent life. He earns his living as a set-designer at a children's theatre in Moscow. In the evenings he attends an institute where he is taking a degree in architecture. This is common and all institutes run evening degree courses. In spite of Rita's closeness to her parents, Maya and Aleksandr do not know Andrei well – they use the formal mode of address with him and he is shy with them. They think he's a fine boy and will do very nicely as a husband for Rita. She has not told them they are planning to marry. 'Will she marry him?' they wonder. 'It's time she got married.'

Andrei did not propose officially: 'Not like my friends tell me their boyfriends did. You know, the man arrives with a bunch of flowers, dressed up in a dark suit, shirt, tie. Terribly nervous, blushes, goes pale, cold sweat pours off him, his hands shake and he says, "I love you and I'm asking you to be my wife." I said to Andrei, "You know we're always talking about where we're going to live, but you haven't actually asked me to marry you." He said, "Do you want me to officially? OK, I offer you my hand and my heart." '

But 1984 is not the year they marry – it is a leap year. Also Rita is caught up with her new job and Andrei with work and studies. Most important of all, they have nowhere to live. The perennial housing problem has widespread repercussions. As everyone lives with their parents, it is hard for young couples to be together. Society frowns on unlicensed co-habitation and they are therefore forced into early marriages. Sex outside marriage is widespread, although little discussed, and impracticable. You may as well get married or life becomes an endless problem of where to go to make love. 'Tanya's mother's away this weekend . . . I've got the key to Tolya's apartment, but his grandmother will be back in an hour . . .'

Once married, couples generally live with their parents until they can find their own flat. This may take years. Andrei's parents will probably try to swop their three-roomed flat for a one-roomed flat for Andrei and Rita and a two-roomed flat for themselves. This exchange of one dwelling for another is common, competitive and unofficial. People nail notices on to trees offering or asking for accommodation. These notices are thoughtfully provided with tear-off strips bearing phone numbers, so that those interested can easily apply.

Many eighteen-year-old girls think it is terribly chic to have a husband. Not surprisingly, these young marriages frequently fail and in a country with a very high divorce rate, there is an even higher incidence of failed marriages in the seventeen to twenty-four-year-old age group. About half of Rita's class are already married and one twenty-one-year-old has taken her finals heavily pregnant with her second child.

Rita's lovely face glows when she talks about her feelings and emotions, but she is very embarrassed when she talks about sex and contraception. It is never a topic of conversation between her and her friends: 'We know about each other's personal lives, but we don't go into detail. Maybe it's just us who're like that, I don't know . . . we don't want to interfere in each other's personal lives, someone may not like it. Everyone has their own inner world which they allow only a few to enter.' Although strangers make personal remarks about one's appearance, there are areas where privacy is not to be infringed. Perhaps because there is so little physical privacy, emotional and psychological privacy is treasured.

Contraception is rarely available and for most women abortion is the only way to prevent unwanted motherhood. It is legal and free and treated matter-of-factly. It is not unusual for a woman to have had as many as nine abortions and it is rare to meet a woman who has not had at least one. Again, this is not discussed much but is accepted as a fact of life. If an unmarried woman decides to keep her baby, she will be praised and helped. Childbirth and motherhood, in spite of the smallness of Russian families, is generally acknowledged to be a woman's principal function.

Male and female roles are clearly delineated. Rita, who would not herself be content as a housewife with no outside job, says: 'The woman should be the homemaker and create a happy family atmosphere. She can soothe her husband and change his mood if he comes home from work feeling irritable. Women are born actresses. Actresses who can do everything.'

Women are chiefly responsible for bringing up children and Rita is not surprised that most schoolteachers are women – this is as natural to her as it is that most surgeons should be men. She goes on, 'It's no accident that lots of women want to hide behind their husbands. Nowadays, more and more women are working in industry and science and they suffer from having taken everything upon themselves. Those feminine qualities of weakness, defencelessness and tenderness are lost.'

But there is some ambivalence in the attitude towards women and their role. While Soviet women do enter fields traditionally dominated by men, they are expected – and expect – to fulfil 'the woman's role' in the home. Soviet husbands are lords in their own homes and usually to be found slumped in front of the television while the women are busy in the kitchen.

Russian women, Rita among them, are never overtly sexual. They are artlessly coquettish in the company of the opposite sex. This is true even of the Russian prostitutes who, although they do not exist officially, frequent the foreign currency bars of the hotels where Western visitors stay. They bear little resemblance to their Western colleagues and behave with prospective clients like young girls flirting at a party.

Russian men for their part tend to fall into two categories: those who are dominated by their wives and adore them for it and those who are rarely to be found at home, drink too much and are consistently unfaithful. There is little doubt that Andrei, like his prospective father-in-law Aleksandr, will fall into the first category, because Rita is a matriarch in the making, and in her words, 'Women should rule men.'

Rita spends July and August feeling dislocated and lost after the rigid structure of lectures and seminars. She is impatient to begin work and to feel purposeful. Finally, it is 1 September, a Saturday, and the first day of studies for every student in the Soviet Union. For the past week red banners have been proclaiming the 'Day of Knowledge' in all Soviet towns. Parents and children, mindful of the 'Back to School' posters that festoon every department store window, have been crowding the shops for exercise books and satchels. Commodities for those first-class citizens, children, are usually in plentiful supply. This is a day you cannot fail to notice. The streets are crowded with children in school uniform. The little girls wear black dresses and white lace collars and white pinafores (on ordinary days they are black), their hair is a mass of ribbons and bows. The little boys are in black trousers and jackets and white shirts. They are sporting the red kerchief of the Young Pioneer. Older boys and girls wear blue suits and white shirts.

Each child is preceded and partially obscured by the bunch of flowers that will be given to the teachers. Rita's mother is up by 5.30 a.m. cooking *syrniki* (fried curd cheese cakes) for the breakfast that Rita will be far too agitated to eat. At 6 o'clock Rita gets up looking as much a child as one of her pupils. The first time she went to the school for a staff meeting she was asked if she was a pupil who had come to enrol in the 10th class (for seventeen-year-olds), so she now has had a new 'sophisticated' haircut. She dresses in smart skirt and sweater, her bed is left unmade – it's bad luck to make it on important days. On the bridge she gets the trolleybus, puts four kopecks into the pay box and rolls off a ticket – the numbers are lucky and holding it up triumphantly, she waves to her parents who are watching her from their window.

School number 397 is only a few stops and a short walk away. A general secondary school, it goes from class 1 to class 10; classes 1 to 3 are the equivalent of our primary schools and 4 to 10 of our secondary schools. Complete secondary education is universal and compulsory. At the end of the 8th class (when fifteen years old), pupils may stay in the same school, or go to a vocational training school where they can learn a specific trade, or to a specialised school. For example, there is a special English school for those wishing to concentrate on English language. Other specialised schools emphasise other disciplines. Entry is competitive and proven ability in a particular subject is essential. Good contacts are a bonus too. A personal relationship with a teacher or a director at one of these special schools will often ensure your child a place. Special schools are most commonly entered in class 1, at the age of seven, and the education offered is felt to be considerably superior to that in the 'ordinary schools'. At the end of the 10th class of all schools, pupils must pass their school leaving certificate. They will then be in a position to apply for higher education or go to work.

Rita is to be form mistress, and bearing a sign saying '4B' (for eleven-year-olds), she collects her class around her in the flagged courtyard in front of the school which is already littered with the first autumn leaves. It is also a mass of flowers and ribbons. Parents look on and amongst them stands Rita's mother who, in spite of her daughter's entreaties, has come to watch her first day at work. The headmistress addresses the pupils as a general does his battalion. 'Stand to attention. Dress to the middle. At ease.' Soviet schoolchildren are very disciplined. The band plays, it is 8 o'clock and the school year has begun.

This school year is a particularly significant one as it sees the implementation of Andropov's educational reforms. The main thrust of the reforms is that school will now commence at the age of six and not seven and that children in all schools will receive more vocational training. They will be groomed for jobs in production. The Soviet Union is constantly in need of more manual labour. Teachers, too, are to be better prepared for their jobs and their wages have been increased by about thirty roubles a month.

Soviet education is criticised for its emphasis on memorising and rote learning. Rita welcomes the reforms because she feels the vocational emphasis will make apparent to pupils the reason for learning a particular subject. 'Our standard of teaching is far from perfect. It has paid more attention to giving pupils a great volume of information irrespective of whether they were interested or not. Now it's not enough that the teacher should teach – the pupil should understand.' She feels a school with a strong vocational bias is the ideal sort of school for pupils to receive not only knowledge, but the ability to learn for themselves. 'We weren't given much independence [as pupils] and when there's no independence – when the teacher chews the knowledge up and feeds it to you as though you were a baby bird and you diligently swallow it up – then where's the interest?'

The first lesson all over the Soviet Union this year by State decree is the 'Peace lesson'. Rita decides to get her class to sing songs on this theme and has invited a veteran of the Second World War to speak. The war veteran is an important Soviet symbol; he stands for the twenty million who died, the invincibility of the Soviet Union and the overwhelming desire for peace. The terror and ruin that they suffered must NEVER be repeated.

The school programme is drawn up by the State. It defines the material the pupil should learn, the order in which it shall be learnt, and at what time of the year. Throughout the country the same material is being studied at a particular time in a particular class. How the teacher presents the material, however, is 'entirely up to the teacher's own imagination ... This is precisely what makes up the peculiarity of the teacher, he creates the lesson with his own hands.'

The first lesson is over. Rita, in her form room, the Russian literature and language room (each classroom has a specific function and is decorated with posters and teaching aids relevant to the particular discipline), gives a lesson in Russian language. To illustrate the relationship of Slavic languages to each other, she uses an image with which all eleven-year-olds are familiar – the family. The languages are all related to each other, some are brothers, some cousins, some distant cousins. She has no trouble holding their attention.

At break, the young children are given juice and an individual container of jam to eat – the foundation for the gold teeth of later years is being laid. The little children are collected by their mothers and grandmothers at noon. School ends for everybody else at 2 o'clock. School dinners are not provided. Andrei meets Rita with flowers and takes her home, where her parents are waiting to hear every detail. Maya had not been able to get into the classroom on this occasion . . .

Rita is launched, a confident and secure member of her society. Is she happy? 'Everyone has their own idea of happiness. I would like everyone to be alive and healthy, because that's the minimum you need for happiness – life and health. All the rest is up to the individual's own efforts. And I'd like everyone to have what they wish for. I suppose that's all.'

[o.l.]

TWO

Hunter and Son

Even in Siberia people live.
Russian proverb

If you stand in the vast Siberian forest alone in midwinter the first thing you notice is the silence. A silence which envelops the brain, a silence made more complete by the knowledge that the nearest human settlement may be hundreds of miles away. Then, slowly at first, the mind adjusts and crystal-clear sounds emerge from the icy landscape. The tall Siberian cedars reaching in serried ranks into the shining blue of the sky begin to click and crack in the cold. The temperature may easily be −40° C or less and, as the heatless sun penetrates the trees, the wood is moving and you can hear it. A snowfall from a branch 100 metres away echoes through the spruce. A hare or ermine moves on the ground, a squirrel or sable stirs in the trees, but it is impossible for your untrained ear to judge its distance. At its highest the sun barely rises above the tree-line, but when it does its blinding white light reflects off the snow and bleaches the landscape of colour.

The Russians call this forest the 'taiga'. It is a place of stunning beauty and strange terror, stretching for thousands of miles east of the Ural mountains and north of Lake Baikal. To successive waves of convicts and political exiles sent to Siberia it was one great roofless prison, wild and sinister. To Soviet geologists, the latest band of pioneers to take on the taiga, it means boundless mineral riches beneath the snow. But to Mikhail and Yuri Kuzakov, hunters father and son, it is their home and their livelihood. They live in and off the taiga, up to four months of the year alone in a tiny log cabin from where they hunt and trap, the rest of the time in an isolated settlement of 800 people, all hunters and their families.

Each pair of hunters, for even these experienced men are not allowed to tackle the taiga alone, has the use of a cabin they call their 'zimovye' in the forest. 'Zimovye' literally means 'a winter place', and the hunting season runs from October to February, when larger animals like bears can be disturbed from their hibernation, and smaller ones like sables and squirrels are hungry enough to take the bait on the hunters' traps. The very best time for hunting, says Mikhail, is the beginning of winter, the prolific month between mid-October and mid-November when the snow is still shallow enough for his dogs to pick up scents and for his horses to trek through the forest after them.

Mikhail is nearly sixty, a hunter all his life and a healthier and fitter man than his somewhat shambling appearance suggests. His outdoor life – hunting the taiga in the winter and fishing the Siberian rivers in the summer – has given him a glowing complexion and a relaxed manner. He learned his skills from his father and passed them on to his son Yuri, who is a trained expert in furs with a degree from the Agricultural Institute in Irkutsk. Yuri is less talkative than his father, taller, tougher, and in the forest more impatient for action. Neither Mikhail's age nor Yuri's education has dampened their enthusiasm for winters in the taiga.

'I simply couldn't stop hunting,' says Yuri. 'I can't wait for the season to arrive. It's the contact with nature, the wildness of nature. Any young man wants to test himself against nature.'

Any old man, too, judging by Mikhail's almost mystical enchantment with the forest. 'I need to be there in the cabin, and go out and just see the taiga. You know there's an animal there, and you want to be after it. Your soul longs for it.'

From the high ground near their cabin it is possible to scan the landscape and see nothing but the endless taiga stretching away to the horizon. A tiny white smudge above the trees betrays the presence of a fire, and further scrutiny reveals a short horizontal collection of dark lines against the snow. As you approach, crossing a frozen stream and climbing past a barren tangle of broken and twisted trees, the cabin appears and disappears and then is suddenly before you, camouflaged against more trees on the edge of a clearing. It is a simple structure of wooden logs packed with moss for insulation. Behind it stands a miniature replica on wooden stilts, a natural fridge-freezer where captured pelts and food provisions lie frozen side by side, safe from foraging forest livestock and reachable only by a rickety ladder.

Thirty metres in front of the cabin is a makeshift paddock for the Kuzakovs' two horses, whose only protection from the elements is a mound of stale hay. The pack of half a dozen Siberian huskies are not allowed into the cabin, they must rely on their own fur coats and the overhanging cabin roof for warmth and shelter. A straw teepee hides the hole in the ground which serves as a toilet. Here the cold has two functions, first to freeze and disinfect, second to speed up your movements, for you don't want to bare flesh at −40°C for longer than is absolutely necessary!

The cabin itself is nothing if not practical. The overhanging roof leaves space for storing equipment, while all along the outside walls nails support a motley collection of tools, traps, buckets and guns. Inside the hut, the small door, no more than chest-high, is covered by a thick sack curtain to minimise heat-loss. A small window glazed in sheets of murky plastic is the only source of natural light. The stove is made of an old oil-drum with a pipe reaching through the roof to serve as an improvised chimney. Kettles of tea and pans of Siberian *pelmeni* (meatballs and onion wrapped in dough – like ravioli but without the sauce) are boiling here, while the dogs' diet of week-old squirrel stew bubbles away in buckets on the open fire outside. In all the zimovye is a mere four metres long and three metres wide. The furniture consists of wooden shelves for beds and sawn-off tree-stumps for chairs and table-legs.

Thirty kilometres away, Mikhail and Yuri's family homes in the settlement of Preobrazhenka look positively palatial in comparison with the zimovye. Mikhail's wife Darya lives in one, and three minutes' walk away is Yuri's house, which he shares with his wife Galya and their two children. The men are away three or four times during the winter, for a month at a stretch, with short breaks at home between trips. The family's log cabins are reasonably large by the cramped standards of Soviet housing, with three or four rooms in each. The internal walls are little more than partitions, which do not reach the ceiling, allowing heat from the wood-burning stove in the kitchen to circulate around the cabin. People who spend time outdoors in temperatures down to −50°C seem to know exactly how to keep warm indoors.

Darya has the stubbornness of character, the resilience and the mischievous humour characteristic of many Siberians. Unlike older women in the European part of Russia, she has remained fit and slim, but her worn face reflects the toughness of life in the wilderness. She was the twelfth in a family of thirteen children, her parents were too old and dependent on her to let her go away to study, so she stayed on the settlement where the family then lived. For thirty-eight years she was a vet's assistant, and animals are still an important part of her life – pigs and chickens to raise in the summer, dead dogs and squirrels to turn into fur coats and hats in the winter. Since hunters are allowed to keep back a proportion of their catch for family needs, most women on the settlement have become expert furriers. In her kitchen Darya removes any remaining tissue from the pelts and greases them with sour cream to soften them, then stretches them lengthwise and crosswise on wooden crucifixes. Only then is the fur ready for sewing. Out of all Darya's creations Mikhail's favourite is what he calls his *parkah*, a coat made of dog fur with an additional piece attached to the shoulders like a cape for extra warmth.

In midwinter, blanketed in deep snow, the settlement looks forlorn. The river running alongside the 200 or so cabins is the main supply route in summer, but by October it has been frozen by ice floes drifting down from the north. The whole environment will be held in an icy grip until May, when the thaw finally begins. Strung along one bank of the river is a strip perhaps 300 metres long. Preobrazhenka is made up of a main street of shops, a hospital, a school and kindergarten, a 'house of culture' for film shows and amateur theatricals, and of course the local Party headquarters.

But despite all appearances to the contrary, the settlement is no more than sixty years old, an unusual example of a relatively common Soviet phenomenon – a collective farm. Its main harvest time is winter, and its principal crop is fur. Instead of farmers, the workers on the collective are all hunters. Yuri's home belongs to the farm, for half of it is used as the collection point for the pelts which hunters bring in from Preobrazhenka's allotted share of the taiga. This share stretches for hundreds of miles in every direction. Depending on the distance to their zimovye the hunters go into the forest by horse or helicopter or ski-scooter. They are licensed by the collective farm to shoot and trap wild animals: sables, squirrels, hare, fox, ermine, and, if they're lucky, moose and bears. It is Yuri's job to check their catch, gauge the quality of the fur, and settle on a price. 'We have all sorts of government standards, according to the warp and colour of the fur. But there are no technical means for assessing a pelt. As the buyer I decide – if it's got lots of fur and looks pretty, it'll be worth buying!' There is a special premium on wolves, for though their coat is worth nothing on the international market, they are predators of other more valuable animals.

Yuri was posted to Preobrazhenka after finishing his studies, and he brought his new wife Galya to live here in 1971. Like many Soviet couples they met and married as students. Galya is now director of the small kindergarten on the settlement. Mikhail and Darya decided to leave their home in another village to be closer to their grandchildren. 'What would become of them, with both their parents at work?' says Darya, voicing a common Soviet fear. 'Anyway, it's better to be all together. They belong to us, after all.'

Living in the same settlement also gave Mikhail and Yuri the chance to go hunting together again. 'When Yuri was a boy he liked to come along with me. He wouldn't be left behind. I taught him how to handle a gun, which animals he could shoot, and which ones he mustn't shoot. That's how the boy got the bug.' Thirty years later, as Mikhail's health starts to weaken, part of Yuri's reason for carrying on hunting is to keep his father company. 'There's no need for him to do it, he's well enough looked after,' Yuri says. 'But he just can't stay at home when the season starts.'

So it is that the beginning of winter sees the two of them installed in their zimovye. Every morning they wake before dawn. At this time of year and this latitude the days are not long and there is much to do. Clothing is the first priority, and plenty of it. To survive ten hours or more in the taiga at these temperatures it is not enough to be a hardened Siberian, though it helps. They wrap layers of felt and fur around their feet and legs. High felt boots prevent any snow from penetrating the leggings; a huge coat made of dog fur covers more layers of wool around their bodies. During the hunt they will wear fur and leather hats and several pairs of gloves, but around the cabin they work bareheaded and barehanded at the fire outside and the stove inside.

A wooden box of frozen squirrel carcasses thaws by the fire; the dogs have shaken off the overnight frost and are pacing about in anticipation, lifting first one paw and then another to protect them from the icy ground. Two leather saddles, frozen rigid overnight, lean against the fire. In Siberia morning is not so much about waking up as thawing out. The horses are led down a slight incline to the frozen stream, where they slither nervously on the iced-over surface, hearing the water ripple tantalisingly past beneath their feet. Yuri hacks a hole through the ice for them to drink. The horses' nervousness is well-founded; already this season one horse has fallen through the ice and perished, a miserable freezing death. On that occasion Yuri had to struggle back to the settlement alone to fetch a new horse.

All over the taiga other hunters are making the same preparations. When they leave their zimovye they must make sure there is enough food for any of their colleagues who might pass their way. Equally, they know the precise location of each cabin where they can take refuge and find sustenance should the need arise. Mikhail says conditions have improved immeasurably since he started hunting. It is no longer a case of man fighting alone against the elements: now they have horses, helicopters, better guns, ski-scooters, all provided by the collective farm, and a network of zimovyes allowing them to extend the range of their hunt.

Soviet estimates put the amount of pelts caught in the wild by licensed hunters such as Mikhail and Yuri at about 10% of the total yield. The rest are reared in elaborate, mechanised fur farms. Yuri insists that the quality of wild fur is far superior to the scientifically-reared pelts. In any case sables, the most valuable of all furs, are virtually impossible to breed in captivity, and they alone constitute about a quarter of foreign currency earnings from fur. Yuri pays up to 200 roubles for a decent barguzin sable – 'the tsar of sables', as they call it – and by the time that sable has been resold at the Leningrad fur auction and joined a couple of hundred of its mates in a splendid fur coat at Harrods or Saks the price tag will be around £50,000. The irony of communist workers providing luxuries for the richest of Western capitalists escapes Yuri – or perhaps he doesn't care. 'I suppose it would be desirable for your ordinary people in the West to have fur coats, but they can't. For us it doesn't make any difference so long as our government makes a profit.' In any case, politics means less to the men of Preobrazhenka than the chance to continue doing what they, their fathers and grandfathers have always done – hunt.

As the sun begins to clear the morning mist and the curious purples and pinks of the dawn sky give way to the piercing blue of the day, Mikhail and Yuri are ready to leave. Horses watered, dogs fed, guns primed, the fires doused, they set off into the forest. There is little animal life in the immediate vicinity – they must ride sixteen kilometres, perhaps more, through the endless and apparently unchanging taiga to find their prey. To Yuri, hunting is a contest involving him, the animals and the forest itself: 'Some people think the taiga is monotonous, but no, at every step there is something new, new sights, many new and beautiful sights. I enjoy tackling animals. You have to learn an animal's habits. You chase and chase an animal, then it suddenly turns off and you've lost it. You've got to admire its cunning.'

A couple of hours from the cabin Mikhail and Yuri split up, each hunting his own section. Mikhail's dogs catch a scent. He is quietly guiding his horse along paths known only to him when he hears the dogs – a strange baying and barking, a brittle wailing sound ricocheting drily off the frozen trees, audible for miles. They are some way ahead. The horse quickens its step uncommanded as Mikhail reaches for the gun slung over his shoulder, an old Kalashnikov, an ancient army hand-me-down. They reach the dogs, who crowd beneath one tree then another as the luckless animal – squirrel or sable – tries in vain to escape across the treetops. A series of whistled commands and the dogs attempt to drive the creature closer to the hunter. Dogs, horse, hunter are now all working together. Mikhail rides with one hand on the reins; the other clutches the gun as he gazes up into the cedars trying to take aim. The squirrel is visible for a moment and then lost again. A pull on the reins and the horse stands still, Mikhail's one-handed grip on the gun stiffens, a moment's stillness, intense concentration on the darting creature twelve metres overhead.

Suddenly a shot splinters the tension, the dogs are quiet, the forest still again, except for the sound of the dead animal tumbling through the trees. More imperious whistling from Mikhail warns the eager dogs off the

Lenin presides over the lobby of the Lenin State Pedagogical Institute

Rita Tikhonova

Rita's apartment building in the centre of Moscow

Rita's new pupils get down to work

Mikhail Kuzakov

Preobrazhenka, the settlement in Siberia where the Kuzakovs live

Above Darya and Mikhail Kuzakov
Below Moose are among the hunters' most treasured trophies

The kindergarten at Preobrazhenka, Siberia

Nikolai and Lyudmila Krylov watch Valera swearing his oath of allegiance

Volgograd: Soldiers' Field – memorial to the sons of the motherland who perished in the Second World War

Valera and other recruits prepare to swear the oath of allegiance

Victory Day: veterans of the Second World War reminisce

carcass, and he dismounts to scoop up his prize. The bullet has passed through the squirrel's lower jaw and exited through the top of the head, leaving the pelt intact. It will fetch about twelve roubles when he sells it to the farm, but to Mikhail the sense of achievement is worth far more than that: 'What I really get out of it is something, well, spiritual. That's what makes you want to go back again, it's what you miss about the forest.'

The challenge of hunting, he says, is to be pitted against nature, to combine professional skills with the right qualities of temperament. 'Daring, that's the first thing. And reliability. A hunter must be determined, he mustn't be distracted by anything.' A hunter cannot hunt without knowing the taiga intimately and respecting its hazards. He has to know how to walk rivers and negotiate collapsed trees, to orient himself by day and by night, and to recognise nature's many signals. 'Take bears,' says Yuri. 'You've got to know when they're about. If it's been a bad year for berries, their basic food, that means the bears will be on the prowl late, right into the winter.'

For Preobrazhenka's hunting community, bears are the greatest challenge and the most treasured prize. Several cabins on the settlement proudly display bearskins on their outside walls, as if to show off the skill and daring of the occupant, whose trophy fetches more in prestige than it would in cash. Bears are deadly animals, especially at the beginning of winter, the very time when the hunters are patrolling the forest, for it is then that the bears are gathering food to fatten themselves up for their long hibernation. On one occasion Mikhail and Yuri arrived for the start of the season and disturbed a bear in the zimovye itself. 'When the animal sensed our presence, he ran away into the forest. We tied up the horses, took our guns and ran off after the animal, but it escaped. We had left food in the cabin, but when we went in we saw the bear had ripped off the door, torn off the roof, smashed the window and eaten all the food.'

The important thing, Mikhail adds, is for the hunter to be properly prepared, mentally and technically. 'Whatever a bear finds he'll kill. If he meets the hunter and the hunter has a bad gun or the hunter is afraid or the dogs don't bark to frighten the bear off, you're dead.'

It is hardly surprising, then, that Darya worries when Mikhail is away in the forest. For thirty-five years she has tolerated his annual excursions – in a hunting community her objections would be given short shrift anyhow – but now she tries to persuade him to stay at home. 'His health is poor, he has trouble with his legs. It's hard when you're hunting, very hard, so why should he risk ruining his health completely?' She sighs. 'Because he's a romantic, that's why.' Darya is no faint-heart herself, but she is not above putting a touch of moral pressure on her husband, telling him how hard it is to manage when he is away. 'I have to carry the water from the well, feed the animals, clear the dung, put out fresh hay. I'm a pensioner too. My hands hurt as well, and my feet.'

Mikhail dismisses her grumbles as if he has heard them many times before. He merely says that Darya has never been out to the zimovye herself, so she worries unnecessarily on his behalf. The argument dissolves into a joke about the difference in their personalities. Whereas she is impulsive, fiery and nervous, he is calm, stubborn and relaxed. 'I've got used to her tempers,' he laughs. 'You adapt,' she says, 'you have to respect each other.'

Yuri's wife Galya does not seem to share Darya's anxieties. She is sure nothing will happen to Yuri, as he knows how to look after himself in the forest. Nor does she mind being left alone in Preobrazhenka, though she is lucky, for unlike most husbands here, Yuri rarely spends more than a few weeks at a time away because of his duties as fur inspector at the settlement.

For Galya, who left the large town of Irkutsk to come here, conditions on the settlement have some advantages over urban life. 'We have certain privileges here, the government pays for our cabin and the electricity and firewood. Of course, it's harder to live here, it's not like it would be in a comfortable apartment in the city. You have to do everything yourself – carry water in buckets, water the garden from buckets, chop wood, and light the stove twice a day.'

While the menfolk pit their wits against the taiga, the rest of the community in Preobrazhenka carry on their normal routine. Overhead, if there is no blizzard blowing, helicopters buzz in and out of the tiny airport, and biplanes land on skis instead of wheels. The control tower-cum-terminal is distinguishable only by its two storeys and the nest of aerials on its roof. Nearby is what they call the canteen, another much smaller cabin where the pilots eat between flights and snowstorms.

Galya's kindergarten is housed in a more substantial, generously over-heated cabin catering for about eighty children. Inside it is little different from kindergartens all over the Soviet Union: the same songs and games, the same coloured ribbons and red Pioneer ties, and the same poems about kind old uncle Lenin. But a glance in the cloakroom, with its piles of chunky fur coats and padded helmets, tells you that the children are well equipped for the unrelenting Siberian climate. With some pride Galya says that they are physically tougher here than in other parts of the Soviet Union. Elsewhere children are not allowed to play out when the temperature reaches 25°C below. Here the limit is −32°C. As for her own children, Andrei, fourteen, and Olga, ten, Galya thinks they have gained from the chance to ski and skate and ride horses from very young. In this one community, at least, it seems that Siberia has been tamed.

But Preobrazhenka is a far cry from the wild and wretched Siberia that has confronted travellers down the ages. They came first as Cossack soldiers and adventurers, who conquered the Tatar kingdom called Sibir – from where the modern name comes – and annexed it to Russia. Then came fur trappers and merchants with newfangled equipment for hunting the precious sables. The native Yakuts and Chukchis and other indigenous groups were overrun. Many Russian peasants fled east from poverty and oppression in central Russia, for whatever else Siberia lacked, it had abundant land and no serfdom. These colonisers set up trading posts for fur, tea and, later, gold. In 1904, despite terrible working conditions, the two ends of the Trans-Siberian Railway were joined at Lake Baikal to make a continuous line nearly 9000 kilometres long from Moscow to the Pacific. Successive Russian and Soviet governments have since encouraged voluntary settlement in the rich agricultural and mineral lands of the East.

But though the Kuzakovs' forefathers came to Siberia willingly, many others before and since did not. Exile in Siberia is first officially mentioned as a punishment in the Russian Law Code of 1582, and the frozen wastes soon became a convenient dumping-ground for criminals and political malcontents. The latter included counts, civil servants, scholars and clergymen, the more privileged of whom resettled in towns like Irkutsk and Novosibirsk, where many established thriving businesses.

It was an exiled merchant called Grigori Shelekhov who discovered Alaska for the Tsars, before they rather wantonly sold it to the Americans for a song. Then there was Count Stroganov, who invented his famous beef recipe while languishing in Siberian exile. But for the majority of exiles conviction to the roofless prison meant a terrible journey in convoys and by foot along the Great Siberian Way. If disease or exhaustion did not claim them on the way, the regime of the mines and labour camps surely would. Many escaped to wander and thieve in the old settlements. Indeed, the escapees were known to the original, law-abiding settlers as Kukushkin's (General Cuckoo's) Army, because they would flee from their convoys every spring, just as the first cuckoo of the year was heard.

The Kuzakovs do not talk, and certainly not to Western visitors, about the appalling uses to which Tsarist and Soviet regimes have put Siberia. The labour camps – gulags – are a taboo subject for almost all Russians. Most people know they existed, though they are probably not aware of their enormity, nor of their continued existence on a lesser scale. Even those Soviets who long ago had relatives sent to the camps find it too painful, or perhaps just too risky, to dredge up their dreadful past. The very fact that Russians have visited such destruction on fellow Russians seems too agonising to contemplate. Far better to fill your glass and drink another toast to the memory of twenty million Soviets killed by the Nazis.

Ironically, it is the sense of freedom in the taiga that seems to inspire men like Mikhail and Yuri. All the Kuzakovs are resourceful, independent characters; their sturdy self-confidence seems to be born of the environment itself. For the very scale of Siberia is its wonder – no one could find you here, no one could control you with their rules and regulations and suffocating bureaucracy. Preobrazhenka is far from Moscow, detached from its metropolitan concerns, so detached that the Director of the farm could ask us in a quiet moment not to bring our film crew to the settlement for Revolution Day, because if we did they would be forced to celebrate the occasion for our benefit, and a day at the height of the hunting season would be lost. And when the log cabin housing the Party Secretary's office burned down in an accident, another official scoffed at our alarm. 'Don't worry, we'll find somewhere else for him.'

Modern Siberia continues to attract pioneers, men and women with the drive and ambition to take on this vast and forbidding land. As if the Trans-Siberian and the new Baikal–Amur line were not achievement enough, Mikhail told us proudly and with awe about the so-called 'Project of the Century', a massive scheme to reverse the flow of the River Ob from the Arctic Sea to Central Asia. Siberia's oil, gas, coal, gold and diamonds might one day make the USSR fabulously rich, but despite generous material incentives, European Russians cannot be persuaded to move here in big enough numbers to work the vast resources beneath the snow.

The Kuzakovs are well aware of their remoteness from the centre of Russia. Mikhail and Darya have visited Moscow only once, with Darya's sister. They joined the thousands of out-of-town Soviet visitors who flock to the approved sites: Red Square, the Museum of the Revolution, and the Exhibition of Economic Achievements. But the visit included an unusual episode which they vie with each other to tell. They had arrived at Red Square late, and as closing time at the Lenin Mausoleum approached they were well back in the queue. As luck would have it, the soldiers closed the gate just as they reached the front. Mikhail's sister argued and pleaded with the soldier in a way only Russians in queues know how – they had come all the way from Siberia, it was their last day in town, their last chance to see the great Vladimir Ilyich, and *please* could they go in? The soldier apparently relented, and the three Siberian tourists were ushered round the back, and into the great man's embalmed presence. 'We even had a chance to look at him closely. Most people have to walk past quickly to keep the queue moving,' says Darya triumphantly.

In the forest the hunting day is long. Mikhail and Yuri can expect to be out for anything up to fourteen hours, riding out to distant parts of the wood, hunting and travelling back. The taiga does not exactly teem with wildlife – on a good day they might bag a dozen squirrels and perhaps a single sable. Anything else is a bonus. Sables live in the hollows of cedar trees and spruce firs, or between the roots. Their light crimson and dark chestnut coats are hard to pick out in the wooden debris. Evil-looking mechanical traps left in low-hanging branches are more likely to catch the prized animal, who will swing by an ensnared leg until he freezes or starves. Does Mikhail think there is any cruelty in this? At first he misses the point. 'Cruelty? Not at all. On the contrary, we have all the facilities we need.' Any thought of the animal's welfare is so far from his mind that he thinks we were asking about cruelty to the hunters. He is still nonplussed when he understands the question. 'Of course animals get hurt. But why would you be a hunter if you're going to feel sorry about that?'

There are fixed quotas and controls the hunters have to abide by, minimums that fulfil the plan and maximums to protect the species and ensure a good yield the following year. Nevertheless, the sable population has repeatedly been threatened by over-hunting – it all but became extinct in 1912, and between 1935 and 1941 sable hunting was banned altogether. Poaching and black-marketeering have also depleted stocks. In 1972, even *Pravda* complained, in its laconic code language, that 'private sales have assumed considerable dimensions'. The state was forced to increase its purchase price to official hunters in an effort to reduce the incentive to poachers. Mikhail says the average hunter can earn about 2000 roubles during the season, not an extraordinary amount, though if the real figure is more than that – inflated by a touch of private enterprise perhaps – Mikhail is certainly not going to tell us!

Mikhail is keen for his grandson Andrei to maintain the family tradition of hunting the taiga. Yuri says he would welcome it too. 'It's a good occupation, it'll harden him up!' But the women are more circumspect. Galya wants him to go to college first. 'He'll most likely have some other profession and go into the forest in his spare time when he's on leave. He won't just be a simple hunter.' Darya says he might suddenly want to be a pilot, which she seems to think is a safer bet than hunting. Andrei himself is keeping his own counsel.

When father and son finally return from their day's hunting, they collapse into the zimovye in a haze of ice and steamy sweat. Removing the layers of gloves they try to touch their thumbs with each of their fingers in turn – the inability to do this is the first danger sign on the road to frostbite. There is one final burst of activity for the day, as they settle the horses, feed the dogs, light the stove and prepare their supper. The day's catch is simply left in the elevated storeroom outside to freeze. Later, on a day less conducive to hunting, they will thaw and skin the animals at leisure.

Even in the taiga one occasionally has guests, most likely a hunter travelling the last leg back to the settlement with his booty. For Mikhail it's a chance to hear news of other hunters and swap stories about fugitive bears – the ones that got away, no doubt. They have a custom in these parts that says the percentage of pure alcohol in your drink should match the degrees latitude of your location. The further north you are the purer your fire-water must be. Mikhail's zimovye is 61° North, and even hardened Siberians gasp and grunt as the drink scorches the back of their throat, before they reach gratefully for a hunk of bread and another spoonful of boiling *pelmeni*.

After each month-long stay in the taiga, the men return to the settlement. When they do, it is a cause for family celebration. Darya boils buckets of water which she leaves in the makeshift bathhouse in the back yard, for after a few weeks in the taiga without proper facilities Mikhail will not be fully welcome in the house until he has had a good scrub. It takes eight hours on horseback to cover the 30 kilometres from the zimovye back to Preobrazhenka. Mikhail and Yuri will follow separate routes to check the traps and trails along the way. Darya's anxiety does not subside until both are home, their arrival anticipated by the frantic barking of their dogs.

For the meal, potatoes and carrots are brought up from the cellar and Darya breaks into the family's supply of frozen meat and tomatoes. Wild berries in iced sour cream sit in tempting mounds at the centre of the table. Darya wants to know how deep the snow is in the forest, how the dogs are coping, whether there is any sign of bear or moose. Mikhail and Yuri answer between mouthfuls, and ask their own questions about who has returned from the forest, and who has caught what so far this season.

Mikhail's mood is rather subdued, the tip of his nose is red and sore, another tell-tale sign of incipient frostbite. For an experienced hunter the injury is not serious, but the blow to his pride is considerable. The taiga has wreaked a little vengeance. He eats on, munching his chicken and pickled peppers a touch ruefully, but grateful at last for a break from *pelmeni*.

[A.B. and R.D.]

THREE

War and Peace

The bayonet is a weapon with a worker at both ends.
V. I. Lenin

The Don flows quietly near Volgograd. Perhaps a little awed by the more massive presence of the Volga nearby, the river meanders through quiet backwaters and presents little picnic paradises to those Soviet families lucky enough to own a car in which to reach them. The Krylovs are one such family and it is to one such spot on the banks of the Don that they are coming on a sunny Sunday in 1984.

In fact three cars, two Volgas and a Lada, arrive and disgorge a positive cornucopia of families, friends, furniture and food. Eating, drinking and the open air are the three great pleasures that Russians can freely enjoy. The opportunity to indulge in all three simultaneously is not taken lightly. Nikolai and Lyudmila Krylov and their son Valera have brought everything with them, probably including the kitchen sink, certainly including a large inflatable dinghy. The two other families, who are old friends, will have brought as much again.

Like most Russians, Nikolai Krylov looks a little older than his years. Though only in his early forties he already has a somewhat battered and uncared-for look about him. Dark-haired and damp-eyed, with an ill-assorted clutter of teeth, he seems a lugubrious figure, thoughtful and melancholy. Lyudmila in comparison is almost vivacious. Once quite a beauty, she has retained the girlish flirtatiousness with which she once enchanted the young Nikolai and, despite her maturity in both fact and figure, it still suits her. Valera is smaller than average for his eighteen years, but has an aggressive adolescent masculinity to compensate for it. Unfortunately he also has a rather adolescent complexion to match. His pride and joy is a recently grown moustache but his hair is so blond that probably only he is really aware of it.

Almost immediately upon arrival, the families are deep in mutual and serious consultation to find the perfect spot for the picnic. This decided, preparations can begin. Soon Valera is swimming with his friends, diving somewhat inelegantly from the wobbly inflatable and dodging the snakes which glide across the surface of the river. At the water's edge bottles of

Georgian wine are cooling while the kebabs are cooking on the open fire.

In a society more environmentally conscious, the men might not have lopped branches off the trees to make the fire. In a society more conscious of the feminist movement, the men might also have helped the women to prepare the enormous meal which they were all about to consume. But this is Russian society and the environment is there for the use and convenience of man – and maybe the women are too.

It is only May, but a hot and beautiful day. The only cloud on the horizon is a metaphorical one, for this will be the last family picnic for two years. Valera is leaving home. Like Nikolai and Lyudmila, many Soviet parents must sooner or later contemplate this sad situation, but their sorrow after all is tinged with Soviet pride. Valera is eighteen and must now join the army and do his National Service. He had hoped to go to medical college after leaving school which might have deferred his army service. However, his academic work was not good enough to qualify him for higher education and anyway, to the Krylovs, as to many others, it is something of a sacred duty to serve. Few families were left intact by the Second World War, known in Russia as the Great Patriotic War. Valera's grandfather, for instance, never returned from the front. All Soviet citizens are constantly reminded of these sacrifices, of the fact that their entire history can be charted from invasion to invasion.

For the moment life's more serious obligations are set aside for the simple pleasures of the picnic. Nikolai, less formal than usual, is in lighthearted and expansive mood, telling of his plans to build a dacha not far from here. The meaning of the word dacha can be misleading, for Nikolai has no ambition to emulate the lifestyle of some idle rich Chekhovian aristocrat. Many modern Russians have dachas, though they might be more accurately described as allotments with a larger than average shed, and the Krylovs' dacha will be no exception. Nikolai and Lyudmila have already bought a small plot of land. In certain specified areas such private ownership of land is allowed. They have already planted some trees and soon the building of a simple wooden cabin will begin. Valera, however, will not be there to help.

Lyudmila is in her element. Surrounded by her family and friends, she dispenses the *kvas*, a bread-based and mildly alcoholic beer, and prepares what is in reality a farewell feast. Even Valera, happily and almost childishly playing in the river, seems quite unaware of the more serious obligations that await him soon after his return home.

Home for the Krylovs is Volgograd. They live in a typical two-roomed flat in a standard Soviet block, one of a five-piece set of apartment blocks just over the bridge from the railway station. Landscaping has never been a noticeable feature of Soviet urban design: the urgent and constant need for housing has apparently precluded such frivolous priorities. These five blocks simply sit there like discarded boxes, with a small area of swings, roundabouts and climbing-frames separating each. Hastily and shoddily built, they probably looked twenty years old the day they were completed, and now they have the scruffy and careworn look of most Soviet urban architecture.

Nikolai works for the Dockers' Union. Though Volgograd is inland the Volga river is a major working waterway and the town supports a substantial shipping industry. Lyudmila works in a bookshop, conveniently situated just across the road from their home. Convenient because, like most Russian wives, Lyuda must also do most of the work in maintaining the home and feeding the family. Valera himself, since leaving school, has worked in a small factory making medical instruments. With three incomes the family is comparatively well off, hence the car, but nonetheless their home is a simple one. Nikolai and Lyuda sleep in the only bedroom while Valera sleeps on the convertible sofa-bed in the sitting room. One majestic but absolutely standard article of furniture dominates this room: a vast, glossily veneered combination of sideboard, bookshelf, drinks cupboard and record cabinet. A garish but undoubtedly expensive rug hangs on the wall but there is little or nothing to distinguish this from any other Soviet home. Indeed there are several stories and at least one comic film based on the idea of people accidentally and unknowingly living in other people's apartments.

There is a hi-fi music centre although the 'hi' is rather 'lo', also a television, but few other electronic conveniences. In the kitchen an apparently old gas cooker and fridge suffice. There is no washing machine, tumble drier, washing-up machine, food processor, toaster, not even an electric kettle. No one else has these items so the lack of them is fairly painless. Indeed the Westerner soon begins to feel uncomfortable about the gadget-entangled life he leads, particularly when enjoying the sumptuous hospitality and the vast, delicious meals which any Soviet family seems able to conjure up at a moment's notice with almost no discernible effort, and yet with none of our labour-saving devices.

Volgograd itself is a 'Hero City'. Originally called Tsaritsyn, it knew greatest fame as Stalingrad when, along with Leningrad, it saw some of the worst suffering of the Great Patriotic War. During the Battle of Stalingrad in 1942 the city was so completely destroyed that even the few trees that survived now have plaques to commemorate the fact. In the first few days of the battle 40,000 people were killed by German bombs. The city was then evacuated and the battle continued for a further six months. Few other cities can have sustained such damage and survived. Stalingrad did survive, at least in spirit. Now standing as a witness to post-war Soviet persistence, the modern city is a vast urban sprawl hugging the banks of the Volga, after which it was subsequently renamed when the association with Stalin became politically unfashionable.

It is almost impossible to turn a street corner in Volgograd without being made aware of its past. Tank turrets litter the streets and parks marking the Red Army's front line. Ruined buildings, left deliberately untouched since the end of the battle, stand as mute but nonetheless articulate reminders of the terrifying brutality and futility of war. On the edge of the town is Soldier's Field. Here the statue of a young girl holding a flower stands looking over a Soviet Star carved deep into the ground. The Star is filled with discarded rusting weaponry. Next to the girl, also carved in stone, is a replica of a letter she received from her father at the front during the battle.

My black-eyed Mila,
I'm sending you a cornflower . . . just imagine, there's a battle going on, the enemy shells are exploding all round, there are craters everywhere and a flower is growing here . . . suddenly there's another explosion . . . the flower is torn down, I picked it up and put it in my pocket . . . it would have been trampled underfoot. Your Papa will fight the fascists to the last drop of blood so that they do not treat you the way they have treated this flower . . . Mama will explain if you do not understand.

It was the last letter she received from him, for he was killed in the ensuing battle. Now her statue stands, still holding the flower, forever watching over the field upon which her father died. All around her the metals of war have literally been 'Beaten into ploughshares' which mark the perimeter of the monument. The painful poignancy combined with an almost naïve sentimentality is typical of Soviet war memorials.

High above the town, on Mamayev hill, are some of the most extraordinary memorials. Here, alongside the massive fist that holds the eternal flame and alongside the almost endless list of Volgograd's war dead, is one of the few remaining representations of the Soviet Union's war leader Joseph Stalin. However, dominating the scene as it does the whole city is Yevgeny Vuchetich's spectacular sculpture of Mother Russia, all 52 metres of her, her 250-ton scarf flying in the wind, her solid steel sword, 30 metres long and weighing 14 tons, held high, and at its tip the ever-blinking light to ward off low-flying Aeroflot planes. Here she stands, proudly female and yet strangely threatening, calling her people to her defence should she ever be threatened. Twice a year, from an impressive square laid out at her feet, the young men of Volgograd are called to her service. On 17 May 1984 Valera Krylov is to be one of those young men.

The Soviet Union takes war, and peace, very seriously indeed. In the Great Patriotic War twenty million Soviet citizens were killed. It is an almost meaninglessly large number. It represents more or less the entire population of the United Kingdom north of Birmingham. This morbid statistic is a paradoxically vivid thread in the fabric of Soviet society. It is hard to sit at a table anywhere in the Soviet Union without being called upon to drink or propose a toast to peace. The slogan 'Miru Mir' (Peace to the World) is emblazoned across almost as many rooftops as 'Glory to the Soviet People' or 'Workers of the World Unite'. However, the Soviet Union chooses to represent itself as oppressed and always defensive, consistently invaded in the past and surrounded by antagonistic powers in the present. The Soviets find it as easy to believe that the Americans are poised to invade Russia as the Americans find it to believe the Russians are poised to invade the West. Both views would be simply naïve if they did not, within their mutual exclusivity, contain the seeds of some self-fulfilling prophecy. Therefore, alongside Lyudmila's natural maternal grief at parting from her son, and her patriotic pride in seeing him fulfil his duty, she is frightened for her son in today's political climate. 'Well, my reaction is like that of any mother. Of course he has to serve, I understand that. In my heart that is clear, but to see off one's only child, it's indescribable . . . as long as there's peace in the world, a clear sky, that's the main thing. Just let him serve out his two years – it's not such a long time, just so long as there's peace.'

However, dwelling on fears is not a national characteristic of individual Russians, particularly if they can be drowned in some justifiable celebration. Valera's departure is an excuse for a succession of farewell parties and valedictory vodkas. Family and friends gather round to toast and tease the new recruit, and by the last night there is an almost atavistic atmosphere as Valera prepares himself for this latest Soviet initiation. The women console each other. Some have sons yet to reach eighteen, while others have seen it all before. The men recall their own experiences, speculating on Valera's possible progress and frequently averring that this will make a man of him. Whether or not this is meant militarily, socially or possibly even sexually, is not clear.

All over Volgograd on the night of 16 May similar parties are being held, similar toasts are proposed, similar comfortings are murmured and similar innuendoes are exchanged. At one such party, in the gaunt flatlands on the outskirts of the city, the Shemet family gather to see off their son Igor. He and Valera will become friends in the weeks to come, but more through circumstance and proximity than through any personal compatibility. Igor is something of a gentle giant; while Valera's hobby is judo, Igor's is collecting chewing-gum wrappers from around the world. Both are the only children in their families and so the fast approaching day will be a difficult one for both boys and their parents.

17 May finally arrives and the recruits gather. Stirring speeches seem to strike a chord in the Russian soul but soon pride and patriotism are moved aside in the sadness of saying goodbye. Many of these young men will not see their families again for two full years, for leave is not a right enjoyed by all but a privilege earned only by a few. Despite the adolescent reticence of their sons, parents are unashamed of the tears and proudly physical in their embraces. Fathers and mothers positively cling to their children, unwilling to admit that this could be the last kiss, the last embrace, the last touch. Valera, having always known what he must do and by now well prepared to do it, finally breaks away from the parental clutch and with a self-consciously casual wave leaps on to the bus that will take him away.

After such long preparation the final parting is strangely sudden. Nikolai and Lyuda must now return home to a flat where, for the next two years, they may not have to convert the sofa into a bed. They will be alone for the first time in eighteen years. Valera on the other hand is not looking back. Together with a group of thirty other Volgograders including Igor, he will soon arrive in Lvov to take his place in the Iron Division of the Red Army.

Lvov is now in the Ukraine. It used to be in Poland but the redrawing of borders after the Great Patriotic War redefined these people as Ukrainians and Soviet citizens. The republics of the Soviet Union, though not independent in any meaningful sense politically, still maintain a fierce independence of spirit and language, and a Russian can feel as much a foreigner in the Ukraine, Georgia, or Estonia, as he might in Poland or Hungary. Maybe partly for this reason, the regimental headquarters of the Iron Division holds a commanding position overlooking the town. Like others the world over, the Iron Division is proud of its traditions, its military record and its current standing, and the new recruit is expected to spend a respectful amount of time in the divisional museum absorbing the history of his new home.

This is a good division and Valera and Igor are lucky to be part of it. Certainly the officers seem keen to dispel and disprove any fearsome stories the recruits may have heard of army brutality. Here they profess to be aware that a conscripted army requires a somewhat more informal approach than might seem appropriate if the new recruits were entirely volunteers.

At first the only obvious sign of the brutalising and chilling 'maleness' of the whole affair is the regulation haircut. Valera had in fact already cut his hair short in preparation for his army service but it seems there is a wide divergence of opinion on the subject of what is 'short'. Later on in his service Valera may be able to grow his hair to a casual, almost wayward two centimetres, but now he and Igor and all the other recruits are simply shaved – bald. Even the skull, it seems, must wear a uniform. The shaving gives them a convict-like appearance and the rest of the new recruits' uniform is also somewhat dated.

It is interesting to note that the post-revolutionary uniforms, in which it was (deliberately) difficult to tell the difference between the officers and the enlisted men, have gradually been phased out. Now they are replaced by uniforms much more reminiscent of the pre-revolutionary period. Valera, as a new recruit, will wear a thick khaki shirt with red and gold shoulder flashes marked CA for Soviet Army, jodhpur-like trousers, high black boots and classic Russian army footwear, two elaborately folded rags that can be washed out and hung over the bed each night. The whole ensemble is topped by a tiny folded peak of material that perches precariously upon the smooth bald head. It is not surprising, therefore, if the new recruits look more like confused, convicted, horseless cavalrymen than modern soldiers.

By the end of the first evening the Volgograd group have been split up and allocated to different sections. The forming of cliques or loyalties on the basis of nationality or local origin is thereby discouraged. As Valera settles down for his first night, only Igor from the original group remains. They choose adjacent beds in the dormitory section of the barracks. In any other environment the proximity of all these beds would seem positively intimate and perhaps there is some comfort in the fact that on this first night only a few centimetres separate the two boys from Volgograd.

The day begins early. Reveille is at 6 a.m. Recruits are expected to rise immediately and assemble outside for exercise. In May this does not seem too dreadful but come November their reluctance may be a little more obvious. An hour of running and fairly primitive PE is followed by an equally primitive breakfast of tea, bread and some stew-like substance of unidentifiable origin. Another type of PE forms the second major element of the recruits' basic training: Political Education.

Every morning Valera, Igor and the others must rote-learn the Soviet view of the world situation. Sitting in a small classroom surrounded by posters decrying the destructive influence of capitalist imperialism, they will be pumped full of propaganda, regurgitated Leninism and the words of their current leaders. Here they will learn of the Soviet Union's commitment to the complete abolition of nuclear weapons and the Americans' desire to colonise the world. Much of this they will already be aware of and, indeed, this is merely an attempt to haul back to the front of the recruit's mind the slogans with which he will already have been living for the last eighteen years. Alongside the political lectures, Valera will be expected to watch the Soviet TV News every night at 9 p.m. and the unashamedly propagandist programme 'I Serve the Soviet Union' every Sunday morning.

The boredom of the recruits during these classes and periods of enforced tele-viewing is palpable. They are not bored because they fundamentally agree or even disagree with what is being said. They have simply heard it all before and the ideas propagated are too straightforward to arouse any intellectual curiosity. In one sense the boredom is an integral part of the process. The whole environment and vocabulary of propagandised politics is so tedious and repetitive that the notion of debate is dull, the possibility of opposition uninteresting and the idea of an alternative viewpoint a bore.

The third major element of basic training is drill. This too should only be a refresher course. At school or in the Young Communist League (Komsomol), which all young Soviets are expected to join, most children will learn basic army drill. Yet one could be forgiven for forgetting this as the recruits seem to find it extraordinarily difficult. Red Army drill is still based on pre-revolutionary army drill. The origins of this lie in Peter the Great's admiration for, and wish to emulate, the skill and precision of the 18th-century German army. It is a complex and unnatural collection of movements, chillingly and ironically reminiscent of the goose-stepping drill of the fascist armies and yet irresistibly reminiscent of the stamping of bad-tempered toddlers. However, both the irony and the humour are entirely lost on the officers and recruits who struggle day after day to teach and learn these essential military skills.

However fit his body and sound his mind, a recruit does not and cannot become a soldier until he has a weapon. After a week or so of basic training, Valera, Igor and the others will be introduced to the basic weapon of the Red Army: the Kalashnikov automatic rifle. When Lenin was advancing the argument that the Russians should not continue to take part in the First World War subsequent to the revolution, he countered the point that their enemies would be the Imperialist armies by saying, 'The bayonet is a weapon with a worker at both ends.' If it is still the Leninist view that it is the workers who constitute the vast majority of fighting men the world over, then the Kalashnikov automatic rifle is not a Leninist weapon. It is equipped with a particularly efficient bayonet. Although this weapon is in use throughout the satellite countries and the friendly African states, it is by now a little ancient in design and will no doubt be replaced as soon as the various committees involved agree upon the design of its replacement. Meanwhile Valera will learn to strip, clean and reassemble it 100 times, though, due to ammunition shortages, he is not likely to fire it quite so often.

As the training progresses there is little if any time for relaxation. During the first four weeks the recruits do not even get one afternoon off barracks. A cigarette here, a ten-minute break there and then off to the next stage of the training. Only in the brief period after the television news and before lights out does any sense of relaxation emerge. Then the letter-writing begins, or the chess, or the chequers. Groups sit and watch the TV film or gather round a talented fellow recruit to sing old songs to the accompaniment of a piano accordion.

Drawing closer to each other through shared hardships, the soldiers grow more intimate physically. Russians are much less physically self-conscious about affection than their Western neighbours. They are on the whole more demonstrative even than the most effusive Mediterranean. The official bear hug, commonly practised by Soviet politicians, is, in fact, a formalised version of affectionate greeting. Men often walk arm in arm with each other and kissing is not a token reserved solely for lovers. Here in the barracks the new recruits sit around in relatively contented exhaustion, arms around each other and occasionally holding hands as they allow the rigours of the day to evaporate in an atmosphere of growing camaraderie.

Final inspection and lights out at 10.30 p.m. complete the recruits' day. Sleep comes quickly partly through exhaustion and partly through practice; they know that another day, only too painfully like the last, will begin at 6 a.m. tomorrow.

Apart from these personal glimpses into the way of life of a new recruit, little reliable information about the modern Red Army is available. Actual statistical information is an official state secret and anyway would not probably reveal a great deal. The intelligence forces of the West do their best to discover what they can but even the Pentagon and the CIA cannot agree amongst themselves on such a basic fact as whether defence spending in the Soviet Union has been steadily rising or has been static over the past ten years.

Internal Soviet propaganda portrays the armed services as a happy-go-lucky bunch of dedicated young men proud to serve their country. This may sound unlikely, but it is probably more true than you would imagine.

The most obvious sign of life in the armed services in everyday Russia is the sight of somewhat disgruntled young men in uniform working on road clearing or on building sites. Much of what has been written by emigrant Russians is lurid in its portrayal of cruelty and deprivation in the Soviet armed forces, but emigrant Russians are fast learners. Such portrayals of their country of origin are an effective way to please their country of adoption.

Without doubt, life in the Red Army is tough; life in armies tends to be so. The vast majority of all Soviet males over the age of twenty have served in the army but even the most articulate and discontented members of the young intelligentsia tend to shrug it off as a hard but irritating irrelevance in their lives rather than a major scarring trauma. National service cannot be a suitable occupation for everyone. Some would say it isn't suitable for anyone, and it should be remembered that for all its protestations of commitment to peace the Soviet Union is at present involved in a war – in Afghanistan. This messy conflict, whose origins are ironically similar to the Vietnam conflict, is promising to have an equally disastrous effect upon the morale of the armed forces. While Lyuda is hoping that Valera will be able to serve out his time in peace, she must have known that it was a possibility that her son might have to fight for his country's aims in that seemingly endless war. Conscripts do find themselves in Afghanistan, and a very disillusioning experience it is.

In this context some will, of course, find army life much harder than others. Valera was reasonably well prepared, though not as prepared as his adolescent arrogance might have suggested. Igor was less so and was therefore more obviously confused by the environment in which he found himself. By the end of their four weeks basic training both had lost some of their uncertainties, both were more confident in their new role. That is the purpose of the training period, for only after that four weeks will they officially stop being recruits and become soldiers.

New uniforms are issued for the passing-out parade. Jackets and peaked caps, trousers and conventional boots, are proudly and carefully carried from the quartermaster stores back to the barracks. Although brand-new, the recruits immediately re-press the uniforms and hang them carefully in the communal cupboard.

Both Valera's and Igor's parents have the money and, perhaps more significantly, the time to make the journey from Volgograd to Lvov to watch the parade. It will almost certainly be the last time they will see their children until their army service is completed. It is also a kind of Soviet masochism that drives them to replay the agonies of saying goodbye. They can, however, bring treats from home: cakes and fresh fruit or any other delicacy their children have asked for. It is a chance too for them to look over the barracks, to see what until then they could only imagine. Finally, it allows them an opportunity to retrieve the pride that they felt at the induction parade in Volgograd. Here again they will see their sons willing and ready to serve their country and, on this occasion, by the time the band strikes up the national anthem, Nikolai and Lyuda will have heard Valera speak out confidently the words of the military oath which every recruit must pronounce before he can call himself a soldier of the Red Army.

I, a citizen of the Union of Soviet Socialist Republics, on entering the ranks of the Armed Forces, take this oath and solemnly swear to be an honourable, brave, disciplined and watchful soldier, to guard firmly military and state secrets, to observe all military regulations and to obey the orders of my commanders and leaders without question.

I swear to study conscientiously the art of war, to protect all military and national property and to my last breath to be faithful to my people, to my Soviet Homeland and to the Soviet Government.

I am always ready to come to the defence of my Homeland – the Union of Soviet Socialist Republics – at the command of the Soviet Government, and as a member of the Armed Forces I swear to defend it manfully, skilfully and with dignity and honour, not sparing my blood and my very life in order to achieve complete victory over the enemy.

If I should break this, my solemn oath, then may the implacable punishment of Soviet law and the hatred and scorn of the whole working class be visited upon me.

Now Valera is serving somewhere in the Soviet Union, grappling with that strange Soviet concept of 'fighting for peace'. He will constantly be reconfirmed in his belief that the Soviet Union represents everything that is good and hopeful in the world and that NATO represents everything that is evil and destructive. In short, apart from the switching of the Communist and Capitalist labels, his life will probably not be profoundly different from that of any soldier in any army east or west.

[R.D.]

FOUR

Master of Samarkand

Empires perish, religions dissipate like a fog, but the work of learned men lasts forever.
Ulug Beg, ruler of Samarkand, 15th century

It's a special day for master-craftsman Abdugaffar Khakkulov. His first grandchild, a baby girl, is home from the maternity hospital. She is just a week old. Abdugaffar is normally a quiet man who keeps his feelings hidden, but on this occasion he smiles broadly and can hardly contain his delight. When he comes too close to the baby his wife and daughter-in-law shoo him away. 'A man has no business fussing over a child.' Abdugaffar is not discouraged, he wants everyone to share his enthusiasm. 'Here in Central Asia we have a superstition. When you start a family, if the first child is a girl, the family will be a happy one.'

This is Uzbekistan, one of five Soviet Republics in Central Asia spread along the border with Iran, Afghanistan and China. Though they are Soviet citizens, the Khakkulovs are not Russians, but Uzbeks, descendants of the Mongol armies who invaded the area in the Middle Ages. About half of the Soviet population is made up of the 120 or so non-Russian nationalities that live in the Soviet Union. Abdugaffar has the round face and flat cheekbones of a Mongolian and the dark, coppery complexion of a Turk. He also has the unmistakable gold teeth of a Soviet. He is fifty-four. Like most Uzbek men he wears the traditional *chebutika* – a skull-cap made of black cotton with white embroidered trimmings. He is usually dressed in a grey cotton suit without a shirt, the jacket fastened tightly over his vest. At work he exchanges this for an old lab coat, for the dirty work that his job as a restorer entails. He smokes occasionally, but only, he claims, 'when I'm anxious'. Uzbek men and women tend to have dark eyes and straight black hair. Abdugaffar, however, is bald.

His new granddaughter is the latest addition to an Uzbek population which is increasing rapidly – too rapidly for Moscow's liking. In the over-crowded Russian cities, families restrict themselves to one child, but in

Muslim Central Asia big families are normal, especially in the countryside. There a woman is expected to bear at least seven or eight children. It comes as a shock to arrive in Uzbekistan from Moscow and see so many prams in the streets, mothers surrounded by toddlers, and overflowing kindergartens. In Russia the rare women who have more than five children are given special prizes as a reward for providing labour for the Motherland. Among the Uzbeks they are commonplace. In this Muslim culture abortion is virtually unheard of and, though practised by some city couples, contraception is not widespread. It is an alarming prospect for the Kremlin that non-Slavs like the Uzbeks will outnumber the Russians in the Soviet Union by the year 2000, more so as there is very little that can be done about it.

This latest child makes ten in the Khakkulov family, which now extends over four generations. Abdugaffar's elderly mother, his wife, Kumushoi, their three sons, one daughter and two daughters-in-law share a traditional Uzbek home in the old part of Samarkand. From the street a door in the high sandstone wall opens into a large courtyard. The family owns rather than rents the house which Abdugaffar's grandfather built more than fifty years ago. It is a single-storey building in the shape of a large square with the courtyard in the middle.

By the standards of Russian cities like Moscow and Leningrad, the family has a lot of space: eight rooms in all, with a shared kitchen. 'As we had the right skills,' says Abdugaffar, 'we modernised it and arranged it according to our own taste.' The modernisation included a gas-stove in the small dark kitchen and a stand-pipe in the courtyard. But the pit toilet, hidden away behind a wooden door in one corner, is still in its original, very rudimentary state.

Although this is September and the heat of the long Samarkand summer is still intense, the baby is kept indoors, tightly swaddled. Uzbeks are no different from Russians in the way they encase their babies in layers of soft blankets and spoil them in every way they can. The older women take charge, as this is the mother's first child. The baby will spend her first days at home in the most comfortable room, surrounded by beautiful silk cushions with colourful woven rugs hanging on the walls around her. There is no furniture except for a low table for the teapot and cups. The room has a raised floor with space for storage underneath. All the children were nursed here once.

Everything the family have they share, but the rest of the world is kept at a discreet distance. It is no accident that all the doors of the house open inwards into the courtyard rather than out into the street, for the courtyard is the focal point of family life. Under the awning of the house stands an Uzbek couch, a sort of raised platform where people sit on rugs and cushions with their legs crossed drinking tea. A tapestry of vines provides shade – and temptation, for the translucent green grapes are deliciously sweet.

Here the family eat and talk and entertain guests. As each member of the family returns home from work they are called to account by Abdugaffar's mother Hanuda, the focal point of the family's domestic life, who is installed on the couch. No one has to stand in queues for hours at the shops as they do in Russia, or travel long distances by public transport to get home. Life has a slow, measured pace here, so they have time to share a cup of green tea from the old lady's white pot, and tell her the news of their day and the world outside. In any case Uzbek tradition calls for respect and deference towards the old. While Abdugaffar's youngest son Adughani splashes buckets of water over the yard to keep the dust down, daughter Raisa tries in vain to wring an interesting tale out of her ordinary day as a secretary to a shop director in town.

When we ask, Raisa protests against being filmed at work. She is shy and does not want a fuss made of her. But she is a good example of how Soviet rule has changed women's position in this traditionally Muslim society. Although Uzbek women rarely reach important positions of responsibility in the Republic, they are no longer expected to remain at home unseen. Like many young Uzbek women Raisa wears silk dresses with dazzling striped patterns. They are a rough compromise between Islamic and Soviet fashions – shapeless enough not to offend Muslim sensitivities, yet fashionable enough to stand alongside the mass-produced Moscow designs worn by Russian girls in town.

Old men still tell, with an amused mixture of horror and admiration, how Muslim women triumphantly burned their veils in the main market square when Soviet power was finally established in 1924. Did it really happen? The Soviet authorities would like us to think so. It is an appealing propaganda image: Muslim women welcoming the new government by brushing aside outdated religious customs. But such a scene is hard to conjure up now as you watch today's old women, bundles on their heads, cotton shawls tied round their chins, trying to negotiate heavy traffic near the same square. History seems to have passed them by.

In men's company women seem docile, even in the Khakkulov household. When guests stop by, the women sit with Abdugaffar's wife and mother on their couch under the verandah. The men join Abdugaffar in another part of the courtyard. At each table there is the same ritual exchange of greetings that marks every Uzbek meeting. 'How are you? How are your children? How is your house?' 'Very well, thank you, Allah be praised.' Abdugaffar says we should not pay too much attention to the separate tables. 'In our country women have equal rights. They work under the same conditions. But if women sometimes wish to be independent and talk among themselves, we do not object. Then men and women sit separately.'

Abdugaffar speaks Russian, but poorly, like a foreigner. He reverts to Uzbek when he wants to say something complicated or intimate. Russian is not needed at home or at work, where everyone speaks Uzbek. He would only use it when dealing with any of the 10% of Uzbekistan's population who are actually Russians. Nevertheless, Russian is taught as a compulsory second language in all schools.

Russians first came to Central Asia as Tsarist soldiers, colonisers who brought the huge area of Turkestan under a Russian protectorate in 1867. The Soviets inherited the Russian Empire after the revolution. Now Republics like Uzbekistan are nominally run by Asian party bosses, but the number two is always a Russian. It is usually with this proconsul that power really lies. The authorities promote Russian culture through special libraries and youth clubs, and select bright Uzbek students and specialists for training in Russia, who are supposed to return home with a new allegiance to Moscow. For all that, the failure of Russian culture to penetrate Uzbek life is evident in the fact that, although Abdugaffar's children all studied Russian for ten years at school, only Raisa, who works for a Russian, speaks it fluently. The problem of Uzbeks and other Central Asian groups not being able to speak Russian well is most acute in the army. Abdugaffar's oldest son Abdukahhar, who has done his military service, says that young recruits, especially those from rural areas, fail to mix with Russian soldiers or even to understand orders correctly!

Each morning the family gathers together for Abdugaffar's mother to read a brief passage from the Koran. She asks for Allah's blessing on their day's work ahead. Strictly speaking, the Khakkulovs are not practising Muslims. 'We have only one law,' Abdugaffar says. 'This law is the Party law, the Party programme. But if someone wants to go to the mosque, he can. If in a family there is an elderly father or mother, he or she prays.' He admits to going to the mosque himself from time to time, 'but not to pray – to listen'. He enjoys the atmosphere and the architecture. 'It helps me to think.'

But if he is not a believer in the orthodox sense, his life is clearly influenced by Islamic culture and customs. It is not simply out of indulgence that he lets his mother read verses of the Koran to the family, he too derives some comfort from it. When he takes the first mouthful of a meal, he says the Arabic word *Bismillah* – 'in the name of God the merciful' – and draws his hand over his face in a symbolic gesture of Muslim cleansing. When he greets his friends he crosses his left arm over his chest and extends his right to shake hands, a customary sign of respect among Uzbek Muslims.

But more than all this it is the work Abdugaffar does as a restorer and craftsman that links him with Samarkand's Islamic heritage. There are more than 2000 archaeological sites in and around the city, including 203 architectural monuments – most of them Islamic mosques, mausoleums or *madrasahs* (teaching institutes). In his thirty-five years as a restorer Abdugaffar has worked on all the major sites. He says he is happy to have them under state protection and in good condition, even if it means their original religious function is denied. 'It doesn't matter that they're mosques and *madrasahs*. We don't restore them so they can be used, but so they can be handed down to our descendants in their original form. They'll be used as museums for people to visit.'

In 1917, as news of the Russian Revolution spread to Central Asia, the Emir of Bukhara, one of two remaining Islamic kings outside the Russian Protectorate, launched a holy war against the Russians. He had the railway lines to Russia torn up in an effort to slow down the Russian advance. His Emirate was only finally overrun in September 1920. The Soviets then recruited local support and built up local Party organisations. They divided old Turkestan into Soviet Republics. Uzbekistan, Tadzhikistan, Kirghizia and Turkmenia were invented, to be run by officials loyal to Moscow.

Since then the vast majority of mosques have been closed or turned into museums. The sound of the *muezzin* calling the faithful to prayer no longer rings out from Samarkand's minarets. You have to travel 250 kilometres to Bukhara to find a *madrasah* that still trains new mullahs. The working mosque where Abdugaffar occasionally goes to sit and think is on the same site as the *madrasah* he is restoring. But the handful of men who pray there are frail old greybeards, bent over their walking-sticks. They are live museum exhibits for tourists from the European parts of the Soviet Union who are brought to the mosque by state guides. Islam, the guides say, is part of the region's outworn past. It is dying out, and this generation of believers is the last. Like the Russian Orthodox Church it has no relevance for the new Soviet generations brought up on scientific socialism.

Abdugaffar himself talks without irony about 'the genius Lenin', whose decree on the preservation of monuments made all his work in Samarkand possible. Soviet rule also meant the end of Islamic laws, and isolation from other Muslim countries. So few are the contacts between them that Islamic fundamentalism has no chance of crossing the Soviet border from Iran or Afghanistan.

Instead, the faithful are subject to strict controls. A regulated number of 'approved' clerics are allowed to make the pilgrimage to Mecca, and only a handful of mullahs qualify from the *madrasah* in Bukhara each year. The official Muslim Board of Central Asia is, by common consent, a tame and toothless body. Limited autonomy to run the few remaining mosques has been exchanged for political quiescence.

Present-day Samarkand has two great squares, one medieval and one modern. Registan, holy place of pilgrimage, is the site of the finest ensemble of *madrasahs* in Central Asia. Lenin Square houses the city's Communist Party headquarters, together with massive mounted photos of Politburo members and empty parade stands. Smiling pictures of Lenin in his flat cap look down on the city's ancient treasures. Local craftsmen like Abdugaffar are encouraged to explore their cultural heritage – so long as they do so under the Party's guidance. They are expected to regard their monuments as part of a glorious but outworn past. To stress the point, the local authorities organise folk concerts in the mosque courtyards, and fill Registan with batteries of floodlights and loudspeakers to entertain tourists with *son et lumière* spectaculars. Abdugaffar shrugs his shoulders at the suggestion that this is inappropriate – the most important thing to him is the buildings themselves. What use the authorities make of them is their business. After all they are paying the bills.

In the same way that it cultivates 'official' Muslim leaders, the Soviet state also rewards 'official' artists and craftsmen. A whole collection of awards and subsidies are available to them: People's Artist of the Soviet Union, Merited Artist of the Republic of Uzbekistan, membership of the prestigious Union of Artists, foreign travel and precious exhibition space. Abdugaffar has received none of these official honours, nor is he a Party member, so his position is vulnerable. Tact is required when he talks about the authorities. 'We can never adequately express our gratitude to our Party government for creating these conditions for us,' he says earnestly. As a token of his gratitude he has pledged to finish his current project in time for the 6oth anniversary of the Republic of Uzbekistan, just a few months away. A shrewd move – but the sincerity of his gesture should perhaps not be investigated too closely.

For Abdugaffar the link with past generations of master craftsmen is all-important. The skills of his trade have been passed down over the centuries from master to pupil. Before a pupil has a right to the title 'master' – *usta* in

Uzbek – he must serve a long apprenticeship, anything up to fifteen years. Abdugaffar's own father was a bricklayer. Abdugaffar drew well at school, and his drawings caught the attention of master-restorer Shamsi Gafurov. 'He asked my father to let me be his pupil, saying, "This boy will be a great craftsman in the future." I learned everything from my master. He was a perfectionist, he would not allow any work to be done without the utmost care.'

Most of Abdugaffar's work as a restorer has been on the Registan ensemble, which he calls his 'university'. 'I learned so much just by looking at each of its walls.' When he first saw Registan its three *madrasahs* were virtually in ruins. After decades of neglect most of the majolica tiles had fallen off. The minarets were leaning at dangerous angles and had to be levered back into position. Apart from structural work – strengthening the foundations and relaying the courtyard floors – Abdugaffar's problem was to reconstruct the tile designs used by the original craftsmen. This was no easy task. He had to retrace their steps and make the same geometric calculations to reproduce their original mosaic patterns. Books and engravings were not much help. He relied instead on small fragments of the original work, which he calls his 'passport'. Like an archaeologist who reconstructs a skeleton from a single bone, he rebuilt whole structures from tiny bits of ceramic evidence.

The magnificent portals, arches and domes of Registan are largely the result of his work. Its rich blues and greens are a beautiful sight in the sun. The Arabic inscriptions and the two storeys of 'cells' for Muslim scholars betray its old Islamic uses – but the images of stars, suns, flowers and fire suggest a pre-Islamic, pagan celebration of the natural elements that sustain life of every kind. It is an evocation of beauty and majesty, grace and power combined to impress and inspire mere human beings.

After Registan, Abdugaffar worked for shorter periods on two of Samarkand's mausoleum complexes. According to legend, the Gur-Emir mausoleum houses the tomb of Tamerlane, the warrior-emperor who vowed to make Samarkand the centre of the universe. Shakh-i-Zinda, Arabic for 'the living king', is said to be the place where the city's ageing rulers built themselves mausoleums while they waited to die. Not unlike the Kremlin wall today, a leader's prestige was measured by the prominence of his final resting-place.

Abdugaffar delights in the legends of medieval Samarkand. Emperor Tamerlane, he says, once decided to use the loot from his conquest of India to build the greatest mosque that Allah had ever seen. The best architects in the Empire were called in, and Tamerlane set off on another long campaign leaving orders that the mosque, called Bibi-Khanum, be finished for his return. Bibi-Khanum was indeed a magnificent creation, its grandiose dome was said to 'eclipse the sky itself'. But Tamerlane's joy turned to rage when he discovered that the chief architect had 'kissed the cheek' of his beautiful wife. The architect was executed, but as his head fell from the chopping-block, the great dome started to crumble.

That, according to Abdugaffar, is the end of the fairy-tale. The rest, he says, is a history of failed attempts to restore the mosque properly. Huge cracks are still visible in the main dome. Worse, the restorers have introduced modern designs into the mosaic work: authenticity has been sacrificed to Intourism. In Abdugaffar's private complaints there is a sense of violation. 'How can they have failed to be faithful to the original masters?' Publicly he will only say rather enigmatically that 'whoever has made a mistake at Bibi-Khanum will have to correct it'.

In 1976 Abdugaffar left the project at Bibi-Khanum, unable to persuade his fellow-restorers to change their work methods. He then did an extraordinary thing. He went freelance. He picked a site five kilometres outside Samarkand, the *madrasah* at Nadi-Devan-Begi, that had not been worked on at all, and set about persuading the Ministry of Culture to provide him with funds, materials and a small team of young apprentices. It was a long process. The very idea of setting up on your own is anathema in the Soviet Union. The State plans where you work and provides you with the wherewithal. Individual enterprise is suspect. But Abdugaffar argued that he wasn't a budding capitalist, he had serious plans for his new project. He knew the site well, for he had worked on the nearby mosque and decorated tombs in the attached graveyard some years earlier. Nor would he need to take experienced restorers away from any other projects – he would use his own sons and would train new apprentices from scratch.

Work started at Nadi-Devan-Begi in 1978 but there was one condition: a Party commission would visit the site every week to monitor progress. They meet on Saturday mornings, Abdugaffar and his team leaders, a man from the Party secretariat, the head of Samarkand's restoration programme and a representative from the collective farm which owns the land. Green tea, bread and grapes are spread before his honoured guests, as Abdugaffar in his dirty white lab coat gives an account of the week's work. Someone wants to know why a door has not been replaced as promised. Abdugaffar's manner at first seems deferential, but suddenly he launches into a plea for much-needed bricks for the courtyard's flooring. His implied criticism of erratic deliveries is couched in Asian understatement and courtesy. 'Our dear comrade Akhmad Dzhan has been of great help. First he supplied us with square bricks. Now we hope he will spend his valuable time to supply us not only with square bricks, but also with the standard ones we need.' The right ones were delivered the next day.

It seems Abdugaffar has learned a few tricks from his direct dealings with local officials. When he needs something – an earthmover or a few extra hands – he might drop in at the Communist Party secretariat to mention the problem and remind the comrades how anxious he is to complete the work in time for the Party's anniversary celebrations. We even suspected that he was using the presence of a BBC film crew to chivvy the authorities into sending new apprentices to him, shrewdly reckoning an eager bunch of new recruits would impress the foreign audience and ease his workload. His overall success in winning over the powers that be shows that even in the Soviet Union it is sometimes possible to play the political system to your own advantage even if you are not a Party member.

At work Abdugaffar is in his element. He is every bit the 'master', firing questions and instructions at his underlings as he makes his way across the site. He wants to know why three lads are lolling in the shade rather than taking their shovels to the heap of earth that is piling up as the floor is being evacuated. Suddenly he leaps onto the ladder and up the makeshift scaffolding to examine a mosaic panel that his son has been fixing to the front portal. His office-cum-workshop inside the *madrasah* is the scene of frequent arguments, requests, problems. One day the water supply has been cut off because of a burst pipe and the boys mixing alabaster cannot continue; another time Abdugaffar finds that the latest section of original flooring is not where he expected it to be. But when he is hunched over his designs or is cutting mosaic patterns, he wears glasses and frowns furiously with concentration – his sons and apprentices recognise the signs when he does not want to be disturbed.

Nadi-Devan-Begi is a daunting project. Abdugaffar's black and white photos of the site before restoration started show cracked portals and crumbling archways, bare bricks where decorated mosaics should be, and a rubbish dump in the central courtyard. Now it looks like a combination of building site, architectural dig and precision-machine workshop. The discovery of an original 16th-century floor beneath a foot of earth has increased Abdugaffar's workload – and his excitement. The most intricate work, which father and sons do themselves, is reconstructing the mosaic panels. These are made up of hundreds of tiny ceramic tiles glazed in different colours. Abdugaffar designs the shapes himself and the tiles are placed face down in an elaborate jigsaw puzzle on the workshop floor. White alabaster is then poured over the whole panel. When it is dry the panel is lifted in sections and fixed with cement and steel wires to the outer *madrasah* wall. The rickety scaffolding sways in the breeze but the young apprentices scramble up and down without a second thought. The technology of restoration is basic: a cradle winches the panel sections up the scaffolding, and a grinding wheel turns the tiles into exactly the right shape. Otherwise, the techniques Abdugaffar uses are little different from those of the ancient craftsmen he so reveres. His problems are more likely to be with modern specialists.

'When I studied the portal I found there should be a picture of a lion and a deer that were not in the architect's plan. The architects worked on it twice, but the results were not satisfactory. The third time we worked together and it came out well.' So well, in fact, that Abdugaffar allowed himself a touch of uncharacteristic vanity – he had an Uzbek inscription put on the main portal saying the project had been 'restored to its original form by A. Khakkulov'. Credit would go where credit was due.

Quality and authenticity are two words that recur frequently when Abdugaffar talks about his work. A restorer starts with the surviving fragments of old masters' work. These, he says, provide clues, riddles to be solved in puzzling out the original designs. 'Our greatest problem is that old craftsmen have not left us their formulae. It makes it difficult to achieve 100% accuracy. A craftsman has to learn all about the master who built the building. His work method should be learned, the glazes he used and all the secrets of his job. This is the most artistic task.'

Abdugaffar's true heroes are the skilled architects of antiquity who built the monuments he so admires without the technology available to modern-day restorers. The greatest of these, in his view, was a man called Ulug Beg – astronomer, architect and ruler of Samarkand in the 15th century. Part of the sextant Ulug Beg used is preserved in a memorial complex on a hill outside the city. Abdugaffar used to bring his sons here. He told them how Ulug Beg founded a *madrasah* in Registan Square where scientists lectured on philosophy and astronomy; the arts and sciences flourished and Samarkand was transformed from a trading town to a centre of learning. But his free-thinking only disturbed the Muslim clergy. He was murdered in mysterious circumstances, some say by his half-wit son, and his observatory was torn down by an angry mob. It is Ulug Beg's devotion to learning and his aesthetic sense that still inspire Abdugaffar. 'We are the apprentices of Ulug Beg,' he says. 'We are continuing his work.'

Because of the sheer volume of restoration work going on in Samarkand, the glazed tiles Abdugaffar needs are mass-produced in kilns at a state-run ceramics factory. But for other tasks he prefers to use skilled Uzbek craftsmen, men he has known for decades, whose workmanship he trusts. Master-carpenter Said Nazarev carved the wooden gates. 'He's reliable, he learned his trade with a true master.' Abdugaffar is prepared to go to the small town of Urgut an hour away to buy tools from his favourite blacksmith. Usta Allakulov's workshop is in the market at Urgut. There Abdugaffar will sit inspecting new tools. Quality control, so lacking in state-manufactured goods, is best done personally. 'Anybody can make a tool, but making one suitable for a certain job with high precision is what matters.'

Abdugaffar likes the atmosphere in Urgut. The market-place is full of traders and travellers, and mounds of melons. Around the square is a row of small shops – family bakeries, knife-makers, potters and weavers working in silk of many colours. He greets a barber, an old acquaintance, and introduces him with a local proverb. 'The barber's wisdom is greater than the wisest and most powerful of men, for in his hand he has held heads of kings.'

Beyond Urgut are the mountains that stretch south across the Soviet border into Afghanistan. Above the tree-line, hamlets perch on the hillside. The land is dry and stony, only good enough for a little grazing. Relatives of Abdugaffar's wife live here in one of the shepherd communities. Life in rural Uzbekistan is different from that in the cities: people see far fewer Russians and are much less affected by Soviet rule. Central Asia is one of the few regions in the Soviet Union where the peasants are choosing to stay put rather than move to the cities. In the countryside they live according to their own traditions – raise large families, practise Islam, and take their animals and produce to market with a minimum of outside interference. The authorities have tried to discourage peasant families from elaborate traditional celebrations, such as their spectacular wedding-parties. But to no avail. It is not that the Uzbek peasants are nationalistic or anti-Soviet. They are merely living the way they always have done.

The mountain tracks, no more than dusty trails, date from the ancient Silk Route that once crossed the Asian steppe from China to the Roman Empire. It is easier to imagine caravans of camels with their silk and spices than convoys of Soviet tanks rolling south to 'support' the Afghan revolution. Both have passed this way. Less than 250 kilometres from the border Abdugaffar raises a toast to peace. 'We want the work we do to reach our future generations, even after many centuries. So we want peace in the world – we do not want war.'

Like many Soviets Abdugaffar wants to impress on foreigners his urgent desire for peace. Official propaganda portrays NATO and especially the Americans as the warmongers. Visiting Westerners are always being urged to tell their friends at home that the Soviet government and the Soviet people only want peace. But the same toasts that might carry some weight in war-torn European Russia ring false in Central Asia. For ordinary Soviets hear very little of what is going on in Afghanistan. With a million fellow Uzbeks across the border, you might think information would filter through, but even in a country usually rife with political rumours, surprisingly little is said in Samarkand about the war. The media are strictly controlled, so details of the military campaigns and casualties are rarely publicised. Afghanistan will never be the Soviet Union's Vietnam, and Moscow's television screens never filled with scenes of horror and humiliation at the hands of a Third World country, as America's once were.

Samarkand has itself regularly been the victim of foreign aggression. Alexander the Great conquered the city in 329 BC. Fifteen hundred years later the hordes of Genghis Khan plundered old Samarkand and founded a new city on its present site. More peaceful visitors include Marco Polo and Omar Khayyám. Pilgrims still come to Registan, but without the trading caravans the city is no longer the cosmopolitan place it once was. The market is full of exotic smells and rich colours, but it hardly compares with the Oriental bazaars of antiquity.

The food on the Khakkulovs' table at home would still make Moscow mouths water: grapes, melons, peaches, tomatoes, and fresh lamb cooked on skewers. The sweet green grapes that grow on vines in the courtyard are known locally as 'the bride's little finger'. 'For their delicacy,' Abdugaffar explains. The thick sweet wine which he ferments from these grapes makes a good companion to the unsugared green tea for which all Uzbeks seem to have a limitless thirst. They are as particular about brewing tea as the English. The first cup must be poured from the pot and back again three times before it is ready. Superstition or science? Abdugaffar cannot say.

He will meet his friends to chat and drink green tea either at home or in one of Samarkand's many tea-houses. Conversations are long and rambling, reflecting the slow pace of life. The traditional tea-houses have fountains running to cool the air and settle the dust. On special occasions performers will play his favourite Uzbek classical music. This consists of high-pitched wailing, accompanied by tambourine and *sato*, a cross between a sitar and a banjo. They sing historical ballads by ancient poets and seers whose bearded, turbaned figures are familiar to every Uzbek schoolchild.

The friends who call to visit the Khakkulovs are almost all Uzbeks. Social mixing between Uzbeks and Russians is still relatively rare, and there is little intermarriage. Fewer Russians have been moving into Central Asia, while Uzbeks have not been emigrating to other parts of the

Soviet Union, even to places with labour shortages and better job prospects. They stay for the sake of family ties and close networks of friends, upon which so much depends. Large, extended families have been known to take control of a district and run it as a family fiefdom. In Bukhara in 1984, for instance, corruption based on who-you-know was so rife that the first secretary of the Party, the chief of police, the head of the fraud squad, and the chief legal officer were dismissed. It turned out they were all related to each other, and 155 policemen and 56 other officials were sacked with them.

The exception among Abdugaffar's friends is Gosha, a German who was taken prisoner in the war and held in Russia. He was deported to Samarkand, married a Ukrainian woman, and liked the place so much he never went back. His common language with Abdugaffar is Russian. The Uzbeks seem to regard Gosha with special affection; they are flattered and delighted by a foreigner's decision to stay in their midst.

At fifty-four, Abdugaffar says he can only work on one more project before he retires at sixty. 'Yet I feel I've only just begun.' He has chosen a UNESCO-listed building as his last project. Ishratkhona, on the outskirts of Samarkand, is another *madrasah* in ruins, barely a skeleton of a building. The huge front portal is so badly damaged that it looks like an abandoned Roman arch. The work, he says, will be very complex.

Abdugaffar pins his hopes for the future on his three sons. They have been groomed since childhood to take over from him and become 'masters' themselves. Abdukahhar, the oldest, is already a graduate of the Institute of Architecture, a gifted restorer, and his father's most trusted lieutenant at Nadi-Devan-Begi. Abdurazzak and Adughani are still in their early twenties, but their father says they too 'have the craft in their blood'. All three are shy, especially in Abdugaffar's presence. They do not wear bright stylish shirts and blue jeans like their contemporaries. In their conventional Uzbek skull-caps they seem to belong to an older tradition. At work they appear distant from the other apprentices – perhaps being the boss's sons sets them apart.

There are other protégés, too. Abdugaffar's first pupil started as an apprentice nine years ago. He is now brigade leader on the site. 'This man is like my son,' says Abdugaffar when he introduces him. It was the desire to pass on his skills that moved Abdugaffar to set up a modest training school to supplement his apprentices' practical experience. He says he was appalled to discover that no programme of formal training existed for restorers. Bad habits were being passed on. Standards were falling. He wrote a textbook and devised a syllabus for teaching the principles of architecture, aesthetics and technical drawing. It is a simply produced paperback with a print run of 3000 copies. The text is in Uzbek. Like all educational books in the Soviet Union it is very cheap, about ten kopecks.

The training 'school' consists of a single classroom in a low building next to Nadi-Devan-Begi. Pupils attend for a couple of hours each morning and do practical work on the site the rest of the day. Eager to establish the professional standing of the school, Abdugaffar awards about twenty diplomas a year. They are recognised as a qualification for getting into the prestigious architectural institutes in Samarkand and Tashkent. He and Abdukahhar share the teaching. Khakkulov senior is a hard taskmaster in the classroom. He barks out questions and subjects his pupils to Socratic interrogation. He stands over them at the blackboard as they draw designs from memory, correcting their mistakes unmercifully. 'They must learn the secrets of restoration work.'

Abdugaffar is a private man with a strong streak of determination. Most of the time he likes to let the quality of his work speak for him, but he is not afraid to be outspoken. Life, he says, has taught him to set himself goals, and not let himself be distracted from reaching them. 'When a craftsman wants to create something, he has to see in his mind's eye how it will be in the future. He must make an aim for himself. If he achieves this aim perfectly, he will consider himself to be a happy man.'

[A.B.]

FIVE

The Leningrad Sphinx

Of all the arts, for us the cinema is the most important.
V. I. Lenin

It is June in Leningrad, the season of the White Nights. The sun scarcely sets, so it never gets fully dark and there is always enough light to read a newspaper on the street. School is over for the year and the banks of the river Neva are lined with school leavers celebrating the end of an era. They stroll along the banks, singing and laughing. Groups of people down by the water's edge have guitars. They are waiting for the bridges to open and let the waiting ships through. If you don't watch the time, you may find yourself stranded on the wrong side of the city with a long wait for the bridges to close again. Not too far away, the sound of Mozart floats across the white night air from the windows of a pre-revolutionary apartment building.

Dinara Asanova, her husband Kolya (Nikolai) and their thirteen-year-old son Anwar are relaxing at home. They are entertaining, and Dinara, who is from the Central Asian republic of Kirghizia, has made a traditional Kirghiz dish, *manty* – huge dumplings stuffed with meat. Dinara is small and slight. Olive-skinned with short black hair, she has the high, wide cheekbones and slightly narrow, dark eyes of the oriental. She is a self-contained person who expresses herself with an economy of words and gestures. The music comes from three musicians playing in the next room, one of whom is Felix who plays every wind instrument imaginable. He also makes them and has supplied musicians and museums all over the world. Tonight he is playing the flute. Of the two friends that he has brought along with him, one plays violin, the other cello. 'We always phone each other up if we're in a bad mood or need to unwind,' says Dinara. 'Felix comes over with some friends and plays music and, all at once, we all start to feel better.' Certainly, having your own trio is an unusual luxury.

Dinara and her friends concern themselves less with material goods and more with spiritual food. She, Kolya and all their friends form part of the

Samarkand: the dome at Bibi-Khanum

Above left Abdugaffar Khakkulov
Above right Samarkand: the dome of the Tillya-Kari mosque, Registan
Below Traditional Uzbek festivities – music, melon and green tea

Samarkand: an arch at Registan, restored by Abdugaffar Khakkulov

Shakh-i-Zinda, the place where Samarkand's ancient rulers built themselves mausoleums while they waited to die

The mountains of Uzbekistan, 250 kilometres from Afghanistan

Dinara Asanova at work

A young actress auditions for a part in Dinara's new film

Leningrad: the Neva thaws – view from the Kirov bridge

Leningrad: the Summer Gardens. The statues are boxed up for the winter

Leningrad: a city street

Leningrad: Venice of the North

Soviet intelligentsia, a tight-knit group of artists, writers, musicians and actors. Everyone knows everyone else. It is enough to meet just one writer to find yourself with an entrée into this world. These are people who sit up into the small hours drinking tea and discussing ideas. They read whatever they can get hold of and pass on any new find to friends as soon as they have finished it. Kolya is a graphic designer by day, an artist by night. His paintings are vivid and disturbing. He uses the bright colours of the icon painter and images from the Bible figure largely in his works. 'My grandfather was an icon painter, my father an artist. It's in my blood.'

His largest painting dominates the room where Felix and his friends are playing. This room serves both as a second sitting room and as Dinara and Kolya's bedroom. The painting is Kolya's vision of Margarita on her night flight to Satan's ball. *The Master and Margarita*, by Mikhail Bulgakov, is the handbook of the Russian intelligentsia. Written during the 1930s, the years of Stalinist terror, the book tells the story of what happens when Satan pays a visit to Moscow. When he leaves, the city is in chaos, mental hospitals and prisons are full and the population is reeling from the impact of his visit. The book also tells of the trial and death of Christ. It is a mystical, weird and wonderful book and until a few years ago was not officially published in the Soviet Union – but all the intelligentsia had read it.

This is the world of samizdat, where work that has no hope of official publication is typed laboriously by hand and distributed among friends. Someone had brought copies of *The Master and Margarita* from the West and it too was retyped and passed around in this way. It is Bulgakov's mysticism as much as his humour and satire that appeals to the intelligentsia. Tibetan philosophy and Eastern religions are all the rage now. Kolya is deeply interested in mysticism and feels happier expressing himself with brushes and paints than with words. 'I'm an artist, our medium is silence and colours.' In fact, he probably talks more than Dinara. She does not waste words. But she is no meek, subservient Eastern wife. Dinara Asanova is a film director. At forty-two, she has already made some ten films for television and cinema. She is putting the finishing touches to her latest feature film, *Dearest, Darling, Beloved, Only One*, and has time to unwind a little. She works extremely hard, no sooner is one film finished than another is under way.

Dinara Asanova's home is round the corner from Lenfilm Studios where she works. It is an old high-ceilinged apartment with four rooms plus kitchen and bathroom. The furnishings reveal that there is a class structure of sorts in the Soviet Union: workers buy new furniture, highly-glazed wooden and glass fitted units, new tables and chairs. The intelligentsia favour the old. A high-backed lumpy sofa has an exquisitely carved surround, the sideboard is antique and handcarved and in the corner is a stove which has been there from the day the building was built. Golden beige in colour with a delicately tooled surface, it extends from floor to ceiling. It would originally have been the source of heat and is still in use, but central heating keeps the apartment warm in winter.

Everyone is relaxed tonight, enjoying the music, eating the delicious *manty* and chatting. Later the musicians come to the table and eat the supper they have sung for so beautifully. Those around the table are close friends, people who work with Dinara. Her team is like a family and the same names appear again and again on the credits of her films. Natasha is one of Dinara's closest friends and designs the costumes for all her films. She is also costume designer to the Bolshoi Theatre and recently won an award for her work. Natasha is from Tadzhikistan, another Central Asian republic; her aristocratic features confirm her ancestry, for there is the odd prince and princess concealed in her family's history. She is due to go to Czechoslovakia shortly, but has stayed in Leningrad to do some sketches for Dinara's next project. 'I don't really do films any more. I only do them for Dinara because I love her.' Natasha sits at the table quickly dashing off sketches of those around. She captures the person's main features and presents them with a kind caricature of themselves.

Lenfilm Studios is housed in a pre-revolutionary building not far from the Peter and Paul Fortress where the city was founded in 1703 by Peter the Great. Lenfilm was the first Soviet film studio, founded in 1918 some six months after the revolution. The studios have produced over 900 films. 'Of all the arts, for us the cinema is the most important,' said Lenin. Cinema was quickly recognised by the new Soviet State as being an effective way of indoctrinating the masses. Trains were sent to the countryside, slogans and banners decorated their sides proclaiming the new order. 'The sun of the Soviet republic lights up the path to truth and knowledge.' These trains, known as agit-trains, had cinema cars. 'Soviet Cinema is the theatre of the people' pronounced agit-train *V. I. Lenin number 1* as it travelled about the countryside in 1918.

The agit-trains were of great importance in the years of war communism from 1917–21. With a high percentage of illiteracy, the only means of communication with the masses was by visual images and the spoken word. This led to great innovation in the arts with the development of the cinema and the emergence of theatrical groups calling themselves the *Blue Blouses*, who acted out skits based on actual socio-political events and became 'living newspapers' for the illiterate peasantry. The early 1920s saw a period of exploration in the arts; in 1930 they were annexed by the Soviet State and put to the exclusive service of the Party.

The cinema had, and has, a definite didactic role in Soviet society. Indeed, all art, according to Soviet theory, has a specific didactic function. It should reflect reality in a positive way, its heroes should be positive and optimistic and encourage emulation. If, in the 19th century, art was seen as an imitation of life, it became, according to the tenets of Soviet Socialist Realism, a model for life. It represents the reality towards which one should strive. Socialist Realism is a distinct policy that evolved in the years following the Revolution and became orthodoxy at the first Soviet writers' congress in 1934. It applies not only to literature, but to all the arts, and states quite specifically that art has a duty to educate its audience in the spirit of communism. Revolutionary romanticism was the order of the day, its function to depict both the heroism of the builders of socialism and their dreams of the communist future. One early product of the Lenfilm studios was the film *Chapaev*, based on a Socialist Realist novel by Furmanov which tells the brave story of a hero of the Civil War.

Nowadays, although it is possible to criticise society, the criticism should be constructive, the answer to the problem should be given in the film. Much of Soviet cinema is sententious. Goskino (State Cinema) is the organisation that makes films in the Soviet Union. Mosfilm, Lenfilm, Gorky Film Studios, etc., all fall under its jurisdiction. There are no independent film-makers. The film studios employ full-time directors and technicians to serve their needs and have a stable of actors and actresses they can call on.

Dinara is a staff director at Lenfilm studios. In order to graduate as a director from the Institute of Cinematography, the student is required to make a short film. Dinara made hers at Lenfilm studios in 1968. It was a short children's film called *Rudolph*. She then went back to Kirghizia and worked as a film editor. 'I think it's absolutely essential for a director to have worked in the cutting rooms, to know how to piece the film together. I cannot imagine how anyone could do the job without that experience.'

Kirghiz cinema itself has the reputation for being original and interesting in the way it presents not merely national Kirghiz life, but human life in general. 'Film directing isn't woman's work,' says the head of Lenfilm studios, 'but Dinara does such interesting work that I think she's probably the envy of many men.' Female film directors are few and far between. In Soviet society, male and female roles are clearly defined and film directing is for men, film editing for women. It is, therefore, all the more surprising that Dinara has succeeded in this male domain. Lenfilm studios were so impressed with her diploma film that they gave her a full-length feature film to direct.

Making a film in the Soviet Union is an entirely different business from making a film in the West. There is no need to raise money, Goskino provides the budget. The screenplay writer presents his script to the editorial section of Lenfilm studios. The editors will usually be Party members or loyal servants of the State. They will judge the script according to various criteria: is it ideologically sound, well-written, worthy of being made into a film? The editors will then meet with the governing body of the studios. Once a script has been approved, it will either be shelved for a while, or, if a suitable director is available who is keen to take it on, it will go into production. The director will hold auditions for parts and some filming of various scenes may be done. This will then be shown to the studios' Artistic Council, made up of directors, producers, editors and the higher echelons of the governing body. The council will now have a clear idea of what the film will look like. Dinara, when listening to comments, is usually silent. She smiles, says, 'Thank you all, I'll think about what you've said,' and leaves. This has led to her being dubbed the 'Eastern Sphinx', and she takes full advantage of her reputation for being inscrutable.

Firm control is kept over the films. If the end result is deemed anti-Soviet or unworthy, the finished film will gather dust in an old vault and may never see the light of day. This may sound impossibly rigid, but it is possible to play the system, and while you may not get exactly what you had hoped for, you will be able to bend the rules. Dinara goes quite some way towards getting what she wants. She has early consultations with the screenplay writer even before he has written the script. She usually works with one of two writers: Yuri Klepikov or Valery Priyomykhov. They are both her close friends as well as her colleagues. *Dearest, Darling, Beloved, Only One*, the film she is putting the finishing touches to at the moment, was written by Valery. He is also playing the male lead, and his wife Olga Mashnaya the female lead. Neither of them had done any acting until they were 'discovered' by Dinara. This is another of her talents. She finds amateurs whom she feels will be right for the part and turns them into actors. Valery, a writer, had never thought of acting until Dinara persuaded him to. Olga was found while still at school. They met while working for Dinara and married, and have now both acted in several of her films.

Dinara frequently changes the script while filming. For her it is not graven in stone, but a rough outline to be changed at will. It is interesting to watch her work; she is much more involved with the theme of the film and the actors than with the technical side, and more concerned with spontaneous action than well-rehearsed lines. Often she doesn't allow any rehearsal at all and her films rely heavily on pure improvisation.

People who have worked with her stay with her. The unknowns she has turned into actors and actresses feature again and again both in front of the camera and behind the scenes. A baby was needed for this latest film and was provided by Masha, another schoolgirl 'find' of Dinara's. 'Even our babies are having babies,' smiles Dinara. On a night shoot for the film last winter, Dinara needed a chase scene the length of Nevsky Prospekt, Leningrad's main street. The street was closed for her and a police escort – vital for the scene – provided. There are some advantages to working for a State organisation.

Dinara comes to the studios early and makes her way over to her 'group'. The group is her production team and they have their office across the courtyard in another of the many buildings that make up the Lenfilm complex. 'The main building used to be a café and cabaret bar,' says one of her team, 'but that was before the events.' 'The events' are those of the Great October Revolution of 1917. This casual reference to them is symptomatic of the intelligentsia's attitude to the Revolution. They are rarely given to the deification of Lenin or adopting the usual awed tones when recalling his life and work. To them, this is history, a fact of life, and there are many more interesting things to discuss. However Sasha, an editor at Lenfilm studios, is a model Soviet citizen. 'It's a good thing Lenin had no children,' he proclaims. 'Geniuses ought not to bear progeny.'

Dinara's group say of Sasha, 'He is our comrade, but not our friend.' The Russian word for comrade has a particular Soviet meaning. The implication here is clear: it is far better to be a friend than a comrade. Dinara is quiet and restrained with comrades, more expansive with friends. Life exists on two levels in the Soviet Union and the Soviet citizen learns to play the game from birth, differentiating early between friends and comrades and having a different persona for each group. The official persona is, alas, the one the casual tourist is most likely to meet: those dour unsmiling people on the streets and in the shops of every Soviet city. These same people, once in the sanctity of their own homes, will prove to be the warmest, most hospitable people of your acquaintance. Soviet society with its rigid dogma and mass of rules has engendered this dual personality.

With the group in their small office you are among friends. People are in and out discussing things with Dinara and tea is always on the go. Someone has brought a cake and everyone is gathering round, sitting on the arms of chairs, taking a few moments to relax, eat a piece of cake and drink a cup of black tea. The tea is usually Georgian, or Indian, if they can get it. Dinara is very thin and never seems to eat. She drinks cup after cup of tea and always has a cigarette in her hand.

Lyuda, short for Lyudmila, is Dinara's first assistant. She is never far away. A plump, bespectacled, seemingly lugubrious woman, she exudes warmth and friendliness. 'I met Dinara just after her first film *The Woodpecker Hasn't Got a Headache* came out. I'd been wanting to meet her for ages. We talked and talked about the film, the script, life in general and I instantly felt as though I'd always known her. Since then we've made eight films together.' Lyuda has a daughter the same age as Anwar, Dinara's son. *If You Could Choose* starred the two children and explored the world of the nine-year-old. 'They are already people, future adults. Even at nine they have their own dreams, their thoughts, their opinions and their own relationship with the outside world.'

Dinara returns again and again to the theme of childhood and youth in her films. Much of contemporary Soviet cinema is sentimental, particularly when dealing with the theme of childhood. Dinara avoids sentimentality and faces problems of modern-day society head on. Her films are frequently peopled with badly-behaved, quasi-delinquent children and adolescents, but she believes that when children are badly behaved it is not their fault. 'There's no such thing as a "difficult child", all kids are the same. But there are difficult parents. Lots of kids may seem difficult, usually they're just lonely. In fact it's their parents' fault, they don't pay them enough attention.' Her treatment of the problems of youth strikes a chord in her audience and Dinara receives thousands of letters from children and adolescents asking her how to live one's life, what one should do, how one should behave. Some use her as a confessor, pouring out their wrongdoings and asking advice. She also gets letters from parents and teachers asking for her opinions and suggestions. 'I have to try and answer them all through the press. It would be a full-time job answering all the letters individually.'

Alcoholism and the unusually high divorce rate are two major problems in the Soviet Union today. Indeed, alcoholism is frequently cited as grounds for divorce. To find a man who does not drink is rare and teetotallers are at a premium as potential husbands. In her film *Misfortune*, Dinara shows how a husband's alcoholism tears his young family apart. The person who suffers most is the small child. In *The Wife has Left*, Dinara shows a child's hurt and bewilderment when his mother leaves him with his father. One is accustomed to thinking that Soviet art reflects only the positive aspects of Soviet life and propagandises them. Dinara shows that it is possible to make films about the negative aspects of Soviet life. 'I suppose I want to make people think about the problems and the shortcomings, make them think how they can put things right.'

Dinara's latest film is also about young people. Olga plays a girl who has stolen a baby to try and make her boyfriend marry her. She persuades an unknown man in a car, played by Valery, to give her a lift. Most of the action takes place in the car at night. Valery is twenty years older than Olga and the film deals with the generation gap by showing the irresponsibility and selfishness of the younger generation. This is not one of Dinara's best films. The plot is unnecessarily complicated and technically the film is rather poor. Dinara likes to employ the techniques of documentary film-making in order to capture those moments of real life, the conflicts and emotions that open her characters up and provide the drama. She is less concerned about the perfect, well-framed shot.

Her greatest triumph to date was a film made in 1983 called *Patsany*, badly translated as *Tough Kids*. *Lads* is a better translation. 'I think it is my own favourite film. It was very special for all of us who worked on it. All those little hooligans became so dear to us.' *Lads* is about a group of difficult children – truants, petty criminals – who are sent away to a special summer camp where the camp leader, played by Valery in his first performance, tries to teach them to behave by bestowing the love and understanding on them that their parents have denied them. It is a surprising film, starting as it does with a court scene where a young boy is being tried for pick pocketing. Antonov, Valery's character, comes to the courtroom, but the boy's father fails to appear; in spite of a summons he has apparently gone fishing. Antonov takes the boy off to his camp for the summer. Some of the children who appeared in this film have subsequently taken an interest in film-making. Vitya, the clapper boy on Dinara's latest film, is an ex-*Lads* 'hooligan'.

'Dinara has this amazing ability to make these kids feel at home. At first they think that it's a joke seeing themselves up there on the screen. But then they start to think about it all and it makes a big impression on them. They take it seriously and learn something from it,' says Igor Karakoz. He has been the producer on a couple of Dinara's films, responsible for the administration and for making sure that she brings the film in on budget. Karakoz is the archetypal producer. He is burly with a loud booming voice that carries across several rooms and you feel that if he had a cigar in his hand he would be just as much at home in Hollywood as in Leningrad. 'You know what I admire about Dinara, she always knows what she's after. She's never capricious and she's always ready to show you her material, doesn't try and make a big secret of it like some do.' Dinara has worked out a way of appearing to play the game. She never hides anything and her apparent openness means that material that might otherwise seem too risky, too outspoken, too critical, is accepted. 'Of course she fights with the bosses,' says Karakoz. 'What are bosses there for if not to fight with? Wouldn't be any point in having them, would there? I'll bet you fight with your bosses too.'

Dinara spends a few hours in the cutting room with Tamara, her editor of ten years' standing. 'We fight and fight about things and often work through the night together. We don't seem to tire at all. Dinara loves being in here, she always says, filming is filming, but now let's get down to the real business of cinema.' Dinara usually shoots too much material because she likes to use a lot of improvisation. In the cutting room, she makes the agonising decisions of what to take out and what to keep in. Tamara is about Dinara's age, small, plump and pretty. Like all Dinara's colleagues, she is devoted to her.

The cutting rooms are in yet another building. Plans are afoot to modernise the interiors of the buildings and the main building is a mass of rubble with rooms being completely gutted and transformed. No one knows when it will be ready. 'Remont' is an ubiquitous Russian word, it means 'repair'. Buildings, shops, restaurants, streets can close quite suddenly and a sign bearing the single word 'remont' will then appear and may stay for some time. 'Sanitary Day' is another popular sign that signals the cessation of all activity. This is a day put aside for cleaning the premises. It is often difficult to find out in advance when such a day is likely to occur. The puzzling factor is that when such signs appear, there is rarely any visible evidence of any work being carried out. The builders carrying out the 'remont' at Lenfilm studios, having wreaked havoc and left rubble lying everywhere, are never in evidence.

Among the devastation, photographs of past films still line the walls. One wall is given over to the faces of all those who have played Lenin in films made by the studio. These are many, all virtually indistinguishable from each other in their Lenin make-up. Recently a party was held for all those who had ever played Lenin. 'It was held in The Hall of Columns in Moscow,' says Dinara. 'They all had to go wearing full make-up. Just imagine a hall filled with hundreds of Lenins. Everywhere you looked there was Vladimir Ilyich.' This is just the sort of irreverent remark that Dinara reserves for her friends.

Dinara spends the afternoon with Kolya and Anwar and a new and much-loved addition to their small family, Gina, a black silky-haired puppy. They go to the park and play football. Anwar on film is open and enchanting, in real life he is quiet and reserved, even somewhat troubled. This afternoon he plays with his parents and his smiles are rare. Gina follows Dinara's every step. Finally Dinara settles down on the grass to feed her pine kernels while Kolya and Anwar kick the football around. It keeps falling into the nearby stream and complicated manoeuvres are required to rescue it. Then it's home, swollen with mosquito bites, for yet more tea and some bread, cheese and fruit. 'Dinara and I still live like students.' Kolya smiles. 'We can't seem to live any other way.' Anwar sits quietly in a corner playing with Gina. Dinara is now deciding what her next project is to be. She has three films lined up and it's a question of which screenplay will be ready first. Klepikov is writing one, so is Priyomykhov, and Dinara also wants to make a film about jazz. Most Soviet jazz is unofficial at present. Dinara wants to use some of these unofficial Leningrad jazz musicians as the subject of a film.

Dearest, Darling, Beloved, Only One is now showing at the local cinemas and has had a reasonably good reception. Although the cinema is not the money-spinning commodity it is in the West and the budgets are extremely small by comparison, going to the cinema is a popular activity in the USSR and reviews do appear in the papers. On most main streets, a poster will tell you what is showing in every cinema in the city. Cinemas are usually spacious but not comfortable. The chairs are wooden and hard. Tickets are cheap, less than a rouble, and you keep your coat on. In most public places, theatres, cafés, restaurants, you have to take your coat off and hand it in at the cloakroom where you are given a number and berated by the attendant if your coat doesn't have a loop. For some reason, the cinema is one of the only places where you are allowed to keep your coat with you.

Most of the films on offer are Soviet. There are a few imported films from the West: *Tootsie* and *Absence of Malice*, for example, have been judged appropriate for Soviet consumption. The only way of seeing other films is privately on video if you happen to know someone who possesses a video recorder. Those few privileged enough to have them may have access to foreign films through well-placed contacts and will invite friends over to watch. A recent fad among the Soviet élite is pornographic videos. When passing through Soviet customs these days, the visitor is always asked whether he has brought in any videos. Frequently, non-pornographic films are confiscated as the customs officials have no way of checking the content of the video at the airport.

It turns out that Klepikov's script is ready first and has the studio's go-ahead. Over six months have passed, it is now February. Dinara and her team have been working on the new film for two months. Like all Dinara's films this one too will have a large cast. 'I like having lots of characters, crowds and movement.' Auditions are getting under way. The film is to be about schoolchildren and Dinara has advertised in the papers and on the radio for fifteen and sixteen-year-olds. She and Lyuda have spent weeks going from school to school scouting for new, fresh talent. The film requires classroom scenes and will need some thirty boys and girls. All the action is set in winter and, since principal photography is scheduled for April, the film unit will have to travel to Murmansk in the frozen north as the Leningrad snow will have melted.

The film is called *The Stranger* and, in keeping with Dinara's usual themes, is about a young girl, Zhenya, who is troubled and unhappy. Her parents are divorced, she lives with her mother in a small and shabby apartment to which she is too ashamed to bring friends. She is in love with Boris, a boy at her school whom she telephones daily and will only say that she is 'the stranger' and in the same class. The group in her class whose friendship she craves are spoilt, well-off children. Zhenya goes to stay with her father whom she has not seen for some time. She borrows her young stepmother's jewellery and clothes and finds herself accepted by the others in her class and now acceptable to Boris. A moral stance is adopted: the materialism of the children is wrong, however, it is their parents who are to blame for fobbing them off with goodies when they should be lavishing time and affection on them instead.

Dinara auditions and carries out screen tests. 'I'll probably use some of this material in the film if it fits in organically.' The auditions are carried out in two stages. Stage one is in the make-up room; the aspiring actors have to answer Dinara's questions while looking at themselves in the mirror. Stage two is the enactment of fragments from the script. In the make-up room, the camera films the teenagers' responses. Dinara will not reveal what the questions are in advance. She wants spontaneous answers, and quizzes each of the twelve boys and girls in turn. 'Do you know yourself well? Do you like yourself? What do you want from life?'

Later Dinara explains, 'I ask these questions because young people often get lost. Little children always want to do everything for themselves and they ask questions constantly. But somehow, with age, they become lonely. I want to know how this loss comes about, when this severance from oneself occurs. Why are they bored on their own. There are children who love to play and fantasise alone. I thought it would be interesting to try and grasp how they felt inside. I can immediately see what they're thinking by their expressions. You can always tell on film who's lying and who's telling the truth.'

Olga Shukshina is among the girls auditioning. She is the daughter of the late Vasily Shukshin, someone else who extended the boundaries of Soviet art. A 'village writer', best known for his short stories about people and life in the countryside, Shukshin himself wrote, made and starred in a daring film in 1974 that illustrated the beauty of the Russian countryside while highlighting the growth of crime in the modern city. He died ten years ago, in his early forties. Dinara is a fan of his and a close friend of his widow.

A pretty girl with strawberry blonde hair is almost chosen for the part of Zhenya. At the last moment Dinara chooses a small mousy girl who, although you would never have thought it, instantly seems an obvious choice for the main role.

The film has an early sequence where Zhenya's mother visits her father to collect her daughter's birth certificate. Zhenya is about to turn sixteen, the age at which all Soviet citizens are required to obtain a passport. The screenplay states that the ex-husband is an office boss and that the action takes place at his place of work which is some sort of administrative building. Dinara ignores this entirely: the ex-husband is to be an artist. Kolya's paintings will line the walls and the action will be shot in a studio belonging to some artist friends of hers. Kolya's work as an artist is not officially recognised and this is a clever way of exhibiting his work.

Furthermore, the part of the husband will be played by a friend of hers, Andrei, who is also an artist. Knowing that the BBC would be filming her at work, Dinara had written us into the script and created a scene where the artist husband is showing us his work. We are interviewing him about it while our cameraman is filming. At the same time, Dinara is filming us filming them. Dinara has taken advantage of every opportunity.

Klepikov is used to Dinara changing his script. 'When she changed the husband's job and work-place, I must admit that I did get rather a shock. But maybe she's right. Her own husband is an artist, she knows a lot of artists, it's her world. She's not really interested in the written words, but in that piece of real life that's hidden in the action. That's what she's after.'

Kolya has drawn a sequence of sketches entitled 'Flying Boy', which act as a leitmotif to the film. As children we all know how to fly in our thoughts, but as we grow up we forget. We must relearn.

'Do you understand the secret of Asanova?' Kolya asks us later.

'Isn't this good?' says Dinara. 'I can sit here saying nothing while my husband tells my secrets.' She laughs.

'Well, what's the secret?' repeats Kolya.

'Is it something to do with her relaxed approach to following the script?' we ask.

Kolya wags a finger excitedly. 'You're getting close.'

The artist's studio scene takes place in a big studio shared by three artists on Krasnaya Street near the centre of town. The equipment takes some time to set up and everyone sits round a big table doing what they like second best after filming: drinking tea and exchanging jokes and anecdotes. Everyone roars with laughter and unwinds. Katya Vasilyevna is to play Zhenya's mother in the film. She is a leading actress at the Moscow Art Theatre and Dinara's 'talisman': she has appeared in virtually all of her films. Katya spends a long time with the make-up artist having her nose taped up so that it appears a little shorter than it is. 'You must only film my left profile,' she tells the cameraman, 'not my right, on absolutely no account my right.' Russian stars are vain too, but Katya is not grand about it and laughs at herself. She is an excellent actress, very natural and wholly convincing. Katya and Andrei improvise around their lines. The material shot today will be used in the final cut of the film.

Dinara works without pausing. She never has a meal break, nor indeed do the crew. No one complains. The following day sees an early start. 'Little Switzerland' is forty-five minutes' drive from Leningrad, so called because it is skiing country. Cross-country skiing is common in the Soviet Union; everyone can ski competently. In some frozen parts of the country it is the only way of getting about. In 'Little Switzerland' or Kavgolovo, it is possible to do some gentle downhill skiing. The film is to end with all the characters skiing down a hill. All of Dinara's films end in movement: people running to meet the train or plane that carries their loved one and failing. In *Lads* the small criminal of the beginning has run away, in all probability to commit another crime. The film ends with the whole camp running after him to stop him – we never find out whether they manage to catch him or not. 'You mustn't give a ready answer,' says Dinara. 'People should not just be fed solutions, they should learn to work them out for themselves.' This is most un-Soviet. In a society where answers and modes of behaviour are constantly dictated, such licence is rare.

It is −14°C in 'Little Switzerland', the air is damp and the wind makes it feel much colder. On the director's script there are typed notes in the margin which tell what equipment is needed for the various scenes and what film should be used. Soviet colour film is generally recognised as being of poor quality, so, where possible, Dinara uses East German film and for a few select scenes she uses Kodak film that she has managed to buy. The scene shot today in the dazzling white snow under vivid blue skies is deemed deserving of Kodak. The problems with film and with equipment in general is a constant one for Dinara and her colleagues in the film world. Camera lenses are poorly ground and make it difficult to see focus, filters are only obtainable from the West and most of the equipment is old and outmoded. After several hours filming, everyone returns to the lodge gratefully, opening their thermos flasks and gulping down hot tea. A few indulge in a quick and warming vodka – 'for medicinal purposes only'!

Dinara spends the next couple of weeks in the cutting room with Tamara as they piece together the material that has been shot so far. Dinara plans to show this to the Artists' Council to give them some idea of how she is working on this film. Much of the improvised audition material is included and Kolya's pictures form the opening titles. The result is an intriguing, impressionistic collage. The film promises to be interesting. The music she uses here is strange and evocative. Music is very important to Dinara's films. 'I always try and say with music what I cannot say with words or pictures.' Boris Grebenshchikov, a Russian David Bowie, sings a song that he wrote for Dinara some time ago. He is an 'unofficial' musician.

Dinara and her team leave for Murmansk. Dinara never returns. In April 1985 she suffered a heart attack and died in a hotel room in Murmansk.

In Leningrad the news has a shattering effect. The studios are strangely quiet. 'The family has been orphaned,' says Lyuda. 'How are we going to live, let alone work without her?' The studios hold a memorial service and there is barely enough room to accommodate all those who come to pay their respects. The funeral itself is held in Frunze in Kirghizia, Dinara's home town. Kolya, Anwar, Lyuda, Tamara, Valera Priyomykhov and some others make the journey.

Dinara's body lies in a room, a portrait of her hangs in the courtyard outside and her close family sit outside and receive guests who come to pay their last respects. Later she is taken to be buried and the whole town turns out to throw flowers along the route. This is the Muslim way of death and Kolya finds it difficult to bear. 'It was very difficult,' he says in Leningrad a few days later. 'They're very clannish there and they do things differently. My religion is Old Church Slavonic, theirs is Muslim. I need to come to terms with Dinara's death in my own way.' Anwar, always withdrawn, is quieter than ever. Their grief is palpable in the Leningrad apartment that is now to be Kolya and Anwar's home alone. 'You know,' says Kolya, 'Dinara and I, apart from being husband and wife, were such good friends. We'd been together for fifteen years and we sat up talking until 3 a.m. every night.' Always thin, Kolya is now gaunt. 'Dinara is one of these people that burn out too young like a shooting star. She gave everything and that's why she's gone so young. Others will talk about her work, will write books about her. That's not for me to do. I cannot yet comprehend that I have lost her.'

All of the group at the studio are subdued. Tamara cannot stop crying. She has a picture of Dinara up over her editing table. Everyone is keen for *The Stranger* to be finished and keen to make a film about Dinara herself. 'She was such a modest person,' says Lyuda. 'She actually didn't like talking about herself and I feel a bit awkward talking about her now. It's as if I can hear her saying, "Lyuda, what's all this talk about me, it's not necessary?" ' All of the group intend to keep Dinara's 'school' alive. They feel that they won't be able to work with anyone else, and the studio bosses are aware that they have lost one of their most talented directors.

There is an important moment in her film *Lads* where Antonov, the camp leader, is explaining to his colleague, a younger, less sensitive man than himself, that it is far better to discipline the difficult camp children with love than with anger. In Russian, as in French, there are two words for 'you' – the intimate *ty* (tu) and the more formal *vy* (vous). It is customary when addressing your elders to use *vy*. Antonov allows the children to call him *ty*. His colleague challenges this. Antonov replies, 'Everyone should have a man in their lives that they can say "ty" to. It's best if that man can be their father, but what if there is no father?' Dinara herself was fatherless from birth. Many of her friends and colleagues sense that she felt the absence of a father's love acutely and tried with her films to fill this gap both for herself and for others. The deep irony and sadness is that she has now left her own son motherless.

[O.L.]

SIX

Doctor in Moscow

And of the organs the gods first contrived the eyes to give light . . . to
minister in all things to the providence of the soul.
Plato *Timaeus*

On any weekday morning between 7.30 and 8.30 a.m., a horde of black
Volga cars crowds the entrance to an apartment building on fashionable
Dostoevsky Street, near Moscow's centre. The drivers use their waiting
time profitably: windscreens are cleaned, wings and bumpers burnished to
a high polish. In one or two of the cars a couple of drivers, clearly satisfied
with their cars' appearance, sit together exchanging a few words, while
others find time for a cigarette. A few yards away trams thunder and rattle
around the corner carrying people to work and the pavements bustle with
Moscow's citizens.

The cars and their drivers waiting so patiently are provided by the State
for people who occupy positions of power or authority. The Volga is a
substantial car and an expensive one, costing somewhere in the region of
15,000 roubles. It would take the average citizen seven to eight years to
earn this much. Notwithstanding, it is a common car: all taxis are Volgas,
as are many privately-owned family cars. When black, they are usually
official.

The apartment building looks smarter than the average Soviet block. It
is no ordinary building, it houses the élite. Rent in this block is no higher
than in any others, fifteen to twenty roubles a month, but these flats are
reserved for particular people – Party members, directors of institutions
and factories. At 8 o'clock, the door to the building opens and a short
stocky man in his late fifties with a distinctive 'hedgehog' haircut steps out.
His gait is a little uneven, as he waves to one of the drivers, 'Borya, bring
the car round here,' climbs in and drives off.

Svyatoslav Nikolaevich Fyodorov has earned the right both to inhabit
this prestigious apartment building and to have at his service a car and
Boris, its driver. Svyatoslav Nikolaevich, known as Slava to his family and
friends, leads a full and busy life. He likes to start each day with some
exercise; swimming and horse-riding are the sports he favours. And
hunting. This morning he has time for a swim at the Olympic pool before

he has to be at the Institute. Professor Fyodorov is an eye surgeon and the director of the Moscow Research Institute for Micro Eye Surgery.

When Fyodorov emerges from the swimming pool's changing rooms, the reason for his uneven gait is revealed. He comes out walking on his hands. One half of his left leg is missing, the result of an accident when he was seventeen. The uselessness of one leg is more than compensated for by the power of his arms and shoulders. He climbs the ladder of the highest diving board, does a handstand, springs off the edge and dives into the pool in a perfect arc. Boris, his driver, is with him at the pool and now stands on the diving board looking down doubtfully. 'Come on, Borya, dive in!' Fyodorov cajoles and Boris finally goes in. Fyodorov is proud of the way in which he has overcome his disability and has little time for faint-heartedness, self-pity or laziness in others. The music playing in the pool this morning is American singer Gloria Gaynor's 'I will survive'.

The Olympic swimming pool complex is impressive. It houses several pools of varying size. At this time of the morning it is fairly empty. This is not because people are unwilling to leave their warm beds, but because access to the pools is not straightforward. You cannot simply arrive, buy a ticket and enter; this sort of spontaneous approach to life has no place in Soviet society which is founded on a complex set of rules and regulations. In order to swim at these (or any other) pools, you will have to have purchased, in advance, a season ticket. There will be a limited number of these on offer and most will already be reserved – the director of the pool will have earmarked them for friends, contacts, people to whom he owes favours. So, although in theory anyone may swim here, in practice it will prove difficult for the average person to gain access.

Fyodorov will not experience any difficulty in gaining access to places or people since he belongs to the élite, a separate social class, known as the *nomenklatura*, with its own laws and rules of behaviour. Where the ordinary Russian finds himself ensnared by the complex web of bureaucracy, running hither and thither with pieces of paper and waiting endlessly in queues, Fyodorov and his confrères simply pick up a telephone and the matter is resolved. There are two worlds in the Soviet Union that exist contiguously: the world of the ordinary people and the world of the privileged. Soviet society has perpetuated the privilege and bureaucracy of Tsarist Russia. Nikolai Gogol, writing during the first half of the 19th century, fiercely satirised the crippling bureaucracy and the intricate system that prevailed then.

Bureaucracy is the bane of every Russian's life and the more influence and contacts you possess, the more power you have to circumvent it. A glance around the pool this morning reveals that those swimming are Moscow's powerful, but while Fyodorov purposefully sets about the business of exercising his body, they are content to rest in the water along the pool's edge, splashing each other playfully as they exchange comment and information. In the centre of the pool, some young girls are being trained in the art of synchronised swimming, possibly for the next Olympics. It is compulsory for both men and women to wear bathing caps and many sport optional goggles to protect their eyes from the chlorine. Ever aware of his tight schedule, Fyodorov changes and Boris drives him to the Institute.

If you hail a cab in Moscow and ask for the Eye Institute on Beskudnikovsky Boulevard, the driver will pause, scratch his head, and ask, 'Where's that?'

'Quite a way out past the TV Centre, I'm not sure exactly where.'

The driver will then call across to a colleague, 'Volodya, d'you know where Beskudnikovsky is?'

'Which house d'you want?'

'An Eye Institute.'

'Oh, that'll be Fyodorov's.'

'Yes, yes,' you nod.

'You should have said Fyodorov's place before. Let's go.'

Fyodorov's place is located in a forlorn modern part of Moscow, it's hard to say exactly where. Moscow has a complicated network of one-way systems and traffic, which drives on the right, is never allowed to turn left, so you will often drive round in many circles in order to arrive at your destination. For this reason, after the first sighting of Beskudnikovsky Boulevard, it is a further ten minutes' drive before you find yourself in front of the Institute. At first glance, the hospital looks like a large block of flats. However, the constant stream of people into and out of the building belies this: many wear patches over one eye, others walk carefully with the aid of white sticks. Their presence and the existence of the Institute bear testimony to what Professor Fyodorov cares about most: eyes and the health thereof.

Fyodorov is a remarkable man and an internationally renowned eye surgeon. He was born in the Ukraine in 1927 into a military family, his father the general of a cavalry division. During the war the family moved to Armenia and their fortunes changed. Where Fyodorov had once been taunted and called bourgeois for owning a bicycle, he now hunted wild pigeons and ducks to feed his family. At the age of sixteen, Fyodorov decided to become a pilot and entered the Flying Academy in Rostov. A year later as he was running for a tram, he got his hand caught in the doors and was thrown under the wheels. He lost half his left leg. Although he was still determined to fly, the Academy would not have him back.

In quest of another career, by process of elimination he chose medicine. Money was scarce and he took up photography to earn a little extra while studying. 'I became a businessman,' he recalls with a laugh. When the time came to choose a specialisation, he opted for ophthalmology as a logical extension of his hobby. 'I have always loved clarity and precision. And, after all, the eye's lens is like a camera lens, and the retina is the film.'

When he graduated from the Medical Institute in Rostov in 1952, he was sent to work as an eye doctor in the European Russian village of Veshenskaya. At the end of his two years there (graduating students are allocated jobs for a period of two years on completion of training), Fyodorov worked as a doctor in a regional hospital before getting a job as the head of the faculty at an eye institute in the provincial town of Cheboksary. 'I wanted to find some sort of revolutionary method that would enable the blind and semi-blind to see properly. I read about the English doctor Ridley. No one believed in his operations using artificial lens implants. And I thought I would take this idea and try and perfect it.' The Institute's deputy director was aghast. 'What, here in Cheboksary? That's impossible! They're not even researching such a difficult problem in Moscow itself and look at the technology they've got there.' Fyodorov was undeterred, 'It's like when people started flying, the first airplanes weren't too good and it was dangerous, but now we fly all the time, the planes don't crash and we're not afraid to fly.' He started to manufacture lenses and implanted them in rabbits . . . they were successful.

A year later a twelve-year-old schoolgirl arrived at the Institute. She was blind in one eye, the result of a congenital cataract. Fyodorov implanted one of his newly developed artificial lenses. 'I didn't even have a proper microscope then and without a microscope it's very difficult to implant the lens, it's so tiny. I had made this lens in the kitchen at home as no one else made them then and you couldn't buy them anywhere. So I implanted the lens with the help of an ordinary everyday microscope and had to put books on the stand to keep it from falling over. Luckily the operation was successful. The girl is grown-up now; this was twenty-five years ago, so she's thirty-seven now. She's a teacher and she's got a son called Svyatoslav, well, after me.'

When it was reported in the press the operation caused an outcry. Many doctors condemned it as an anti-physiological outrage. The Cheboksary authorities who had initially been proud that such an operation had been pioneered in their provincial town and not in the capital withdrew their favour and stopped his work. Fyodorov resigned and went to Moscow to the Ministry of Health, determined to persuade them to permit him to continue. He returned to Cheboksary triumphant, bearing the deputy minister's approval. This had little effect. The people of Cheboksary undertook to set his work in motion – in a year or so . . . Fyodorov moved to Arkhangelsk as head of the eye faculty of a hospital. 'I was now the boss and could do things in my own way.' The first two operations he undertook in Arkhangelsk were not successful, the lens was not perfected. He was now faced with the problem of how to perfect it.

There is a story by the 19th-century Russian writer Nikolai Leskov about the craftsmen of Russia. The story goes that a Russian Tsar on visiting England was presented with a steel flea so tiny that it could barely be seen with the naked eye. The Tsar was overwhelmed by the skill of the English. On his return to Russia, one of his courtiers, determined to prove to the Tsar that his own Russian craftsmen were the best in the world, took the flea to the ancient town of Tula, famous for its craftsmen. There a left-handed, squint-eyed smith shod the flea with shoes so minute that they could only be seen under the finest microscope. This *levsha* – left-handed man – was then sent by the Tsar to England with the newly-shod flea to demonstrate the supremacy of Russian craftsmanship. (Leskov's tale is universally known in the Soviet Union, and the word *levsha*, while meaning left-handed, has entered the vernacular with another meaning and is now shorthand for 'skilled craftsman'.)

So, too, Fyodorov set about the task of finding himself a *levsha* who could perfect his lens. There is only one man who can help you, he was told. And he found him – in Leningrad, a man with golden hands who made the lenses. With these perfected lenses, Fyodorov built up a reputation for himself and people came flocking to him from all over the Soviet Union. In 1967 Fyodorov moved to Moscow and started building up hospital number 81, his Institute.

Today is Wednesday, not only swimming day, but also Fyodorov's operating day. As he strides through the doors of the Institute and up to his office on the first floor, people greet him respectfully and try and have a few quick words with him. 'No, I won't give it to you. You should think of these things earlier,' he says sharply to one woman in response to some problem. Fyodorov at work and Fyodorov at home are two different men. At home, he is relaxed, expansive, humorous and generous with his time; at work, he is aware of every second passing, impatient and exacting of his staff. Rumour has it that if he isn't badgering you for new ideas every minute, he doesn't think much of you. He is equally demanding of himself. 'If a clinic isn't as good as it should be, the people who work there are at fault and in particular the director. I look on every clinic as an orchestra. If the orchestra has a good conductor then it will be wonderful, even if it's in a small town.'

His acolytes hover near him anxiously, ready and eager to do his bidding. Notable among them is Volodya, the bespectacled young assistant who is never far from his side. Not everyone fears him: his wife Irène, formerly a gynaecologist, now works as a nurse and assists him in the operating theatre. 'He's no different at work as far as I'm concerned, he's just my husband.'

In hospitals the world over, surgeons are as gods and Fyodorov is no exception, although he doesn't think this should be the case. 'The opinion that the surgeon is a uniquely skilled craftsman is old. There are those who think he is a magician or wizard, but nowadays it's technology that does the work, not the doctor. An average doctor using fantastic equipment is going to get better results than an exceptionally skilled surgeon using not so good equipment. The personality of the doctor is secondary in modern medicine. I wouldn't want my life to depend on the skill of one doctor. Today, doctors must be engineers, and technicians as well. Everything can be predicted and measured.'

Fyodorov's office is a long, plush and impressive room that houses the latest ophthalmic equipment at one end and a large desk under a portrait of Lenin at the other. If Fyodorov were to worship a god, it would be the god of technology. 'Our Institute is the child of technology. The main thing is to arm doctors. Medics are also an army, an army which does battle in peace-time. Every day we prepare for battle, the battle is that of reconnaissance, diagnosis. The training for battle is the preparation of the operating theatres and, finally, the battle is in the operating theatre.' His office and indeed the entire Institute abound with imported gadgets and instruments, all of which are used to their full capacity. Microscopes are fitted with video cameras that are connected to several monitors; a cordless telephone saves having to cross the room; a pocket computer and dictaphone help the Professor order his life; a music centre provides entertainment in the form of disco music in a rare moment of relaxation. Now and then Fyodorov casually lifts a 32-kg weight and raises it above his shoulder, fitting a work-out into his schedule. Volodya is in and out of the office ensuring that everything goes smoothly.

While for Fyodorov the personality of the doctor should no longer matter, the patients all waiting to be operated on by him today are delighted that he and no other will be performing their surgery. 'Of course, I can't operate on everyone who asks for me.' Clearly everyone would have him if they could. He now performs about ten to fifteen operations a week and since he spends a great deal of time abroad at conferences and international meetings, the number of operations that he himself can perform is limited.

In order to enter the care of the Institute at all, you have first to visit your local polyclinic. Whereas in Britain you have a particular GP assigned to you, in the Soviet Union the polyclinic in your area serves your health-care needs. A polyclinic will have several doctors in attendance and nine times out of ten they will be women. General practice is woman's work in the Soviet Union, and fairly low-prestige and badly paid work – about 130 roubles a month (a bus driver earns 200). Anyone entering a Soviet polyclinic or hospital would be forgiven for thinking they had entered the kitchens of some vast hotel; the doctors, male and female alike, wear white coats and tall white 'chef' hats. In Fyodorov's Institute, the doctors' gowns are slightly different. He had them specially designed by top Soviet dress designer Slava Zaitsev to meet the comfort and needs of his doctors.

If you go to a doctor with a flu virus, she will give you aspirin and mustard plasters to apply to your chest and back. These plasters seem to do little other than leave large red marks on your body. Soviets are great believers in folk-remedies and natural cures; homeopathy has long been a recognised form of medicine there. Vasily, a Moscow driver, swears by it. 'My grandfather lived to be ninety-five, d'you know why? He knew all about berries and herbs and which ones you should eat when and what for. He never had a day's illness in his life. Now, me, I won't live that long, I had an accident and fell out of a tree, I'm all right but I think it's ruined my chances of such a long life.' But Vasily is a chip off the old block and swims in the broken ice in winter. Many Soviets are 'professional' hypochondriacs, and at the first sign of a headache or cough they go off to 'cure themselves' with 'natural' remedies.

Another reason for the common use of 'natural' cures may well be the shortage of medicines. The drugs that the Western doctor would prescribe are in short supply in the Soviet Union. Tamara, a young television representative we met in Georgia, went to see a friend of hers whose husband, aged forty, was very ill. Cancer had just been diagnosed and he had been given the name of a drug he needed. Tamara came away with a piece of paper bearing the name of the drug. 'I'll have to try and get it from Poland, I must find someone there who can get hold of it for me. You can't get this anywhere in the Soviet Union.'

Drugs, when you can get them, are extremely cheap – a few kopecks – and health care is free. However, by all accounts, corruption is widespread, and many doctors are not above accepting gifts or favours in return for preferential treatment. 'I'm lucky being able to knit well,' said one Moscow woman. 'The dentist always does my teeth nicely and I make her a sweater in return.' This sort of mutual back-scratching is so much a feature of everyday Soviet life that no moral censure attends it.

Once your polyclinic has referred you to Fyodorov's Institute, you may have to wait six months to a year for an operation, as you would for an NHS operation in Great Britain. Fyodorov's Institute is first-class by anyone's standards and houses patients from all over the world. The people Fyodorov himself operates on tend to be patients from the West who have come to Moscow specifically to be treated by him; members of the Soviet *nomenklatura*; friends; those whose cases he takes a special interest in because their illnesses are rare and pose new problems and opportunities to try out new techniques; and only, finally, the ordinary man in the street.

On one typical consulting day, Fyodorov saw an Irishman, two Indians, a Russian general, two Uzbeks (the wife and daughter of a hunting companion) and various other Russians. If a patient comes in and Fyodorov cannot help him, he immediately calls his colleagues and explains the problem. They work out what new method or equipment is needed for the particular operation required and the research laboratories annexed to the Institute are instantly put to work on the problem. Fyodorov does not waste time and has a seemingly tireless energy for new projects and ideas.

One of the patients on the operating table this morning is six-year-old Sashenka (short for Aleksandra) from the Ukraine. A year ago she fell on a pair of scissors and blinded herself in one eye. This is her second operation and Fyodorov will be implanting one of his artificial lenses to restore her sight. Her mother is waiting anxiously in the children's ward. 'She had been in hospital in the Ukraine for two weeks and there was no improvement, nothing did any good. So they said to us, get on the plane and go, because the only man who can help you is Svyatoslav Nikolaevich. We thought perhaps here in the Institute someone else would operate on her, but he examined her and said, "The little girl has her whole life ahead of her, I'll do it all myself." It's like a miracle, he says that after this operation she'll be able to run and jump and see properly.'

Mrs Kozubenko (Sashenka's mother) is staying at a nearby hotel. She spends all her time in the hospital and cooks for her daughter in the ward's kitchen. It is quite usual for patients to be fed by their relatives while in hospital. Food is notoriously bad in Soviet hospitals, though Fyodorov says that there will soon be a cafeteria for the patients. The cost of the flight from the Ukraine to Moscow will have been covered by the Kozubenkos themselves. They are an average family, but internal airfares are very low in the Soviet Union and the eighty-minute flight from Kiev to Moscow will have cost only about twenty roubles. It will cost Mrs Kozubenko a mere four roubles a night for a hotel room, as opposed to the forty roubles per night for the Western traveller. (Package tours, however, are cheaper, for the Soviet Union is greedy for foreign currency and tourism is its greatest source.) Thus Sashenka's treatment in Moscow will not break the family bank.

Soviet citizens travel freely and frequently within their own country. Aeroplanes are always full and people think nothing of flying thousands of kilometres for weddings, funerals or simply visits. The news, then, that Sashenka might have to return for a third visit in a couple of months for some final laser treatment is greeted with equanimity. Yet travel to countries outside the Soviet Union is no easy matter. It is expensive, you usually have to travel as part of a group, and you may be refused permission altogether.

In Fyodorov's hospital, the operating wing is a way of life. 'The atmosphere in an operating wing should be comfortable; the patient should enter the theatre as though it's a pleasant outing and not a cavalry charge.' Music, usually Western 'pop hits', plays at all times during the operations. Of the many doctors gathered round Fyodorov while he operates, more than one is incongruously tapping his foot to the rhythm. The operation in progress is clearly visible in magnified form on a video monitor. The atmosphere is relaxed, Fyodorov cracks jokes and discusses the latest technology, '. . . these knives don't cost that much to produce here, about three roubles for three, they're cheaper than half a litre of vodka'.

There are two patients in the theatre at a time. As Fyodorov finishes the first, he leaves a colleague to complete the stitching and goes on to the second. Adult patients have their operations performed under local anaesthetic. Sashenka, like all children, has had a general anaesthetic. All the operations in this theatre are cataract removals and/or artificial lens implantations. At the end of the operation, the patient gets up and is helped into a wheelchair and taken to the ward. Having completed four or five operations in this theatre, Fyodorov sets off for another theatre where he will perform a different kind of surgery.

In about 1973, while on a visit to the United States, Fyodorov saw the Woody Allen film *Sleeper* (a film, incidentally, that is loosely based on a play by the Russian poet Vladimir Mayakovsky, *The Bedbug*). Woody Allen awakens from a frozen sleep in the 22nd century. Gazing through his spectacles, he espies a similarly bespectacled doctor. Everyone is wearing glasses. Fyodorov comments, 'I thought this had to be illogical given all that mankind can do. Surely by then we will have got rid of spectacles. And I realised then that I really must come up with something to correct short-sighted vision.'

The method for such a cure was discovered quite by chance. 'Eleven years ago, a young boy was brought to the clinic. His friend had accidentally hit him in the face and his glasses had broken and a few splinters of glass had got in his eye and wounded his cornea. A couple of days later, it turned out that he could actually see better than before. I decided that if some sixteen-year-old lad could correct short sight with the help of his fist, then surely I ought to be able to do something.'

It is perhaps for this operation that Fyodorov is now best known: radial keratotomy. In the short-sighted person, light is focused in front of the retina instead of on it. Using Fyodorov's method, the cornea is marked with up to sixteen lines radiating outwards from the pupil. Then incisions are made along each line. This alters the shape of the cornea making it flatter so that it now bends the light in such a way that images are focused on or near the retina. This is what spectacles do but, after the operation, the cornea makes the correction itself. The operation lasts fifteen minutes and the results are almost immediate.

Fyodorov has performed the operation for ten years on literally thousands of people. Once again, this operation is performed under local anaesthetic. (General anaesthetic is used much more rarely in the Soviet Union than it is in the West. Even operations like appendectomies are performed under local.) On completion of the operation, the patient gets up, walks out of the operating theatre and goes home, to return the following day as an out-patient for examination. The operation is carried out in two stages, first one eye and then, a week later, the other. For two to three days it feels as though you've got grit in your eye. Marisa, a reporter with Moscow Radio, is having her second eye operated on today; she has recently made a radio programme about the Professor and his work. The operation is soon over.

'Was it painful?'

'Not at all, last time it was a bit, but this time nothing. The eye that was done first is fine now, I can see perfectly. I'd recommend it to everyone. By the way, Svyatoslav Nikolaevich, don't worry about the programme, it's on next week.'

'Good. Marisenka, you'll warn me, won't you?'

The operation is available in the United States and Great Britain. 'We gave American doctors the technology in 1976. For two years they didn't risk it and now they've done over 70,000 operations. But English doctors, even up to two years ago, were saying that it wasn't possible to make incisions into a healthy cornea and get successful results; something bad was bound to happen in the future. But that's just the usual dogmatism of people who are used to old methods. No one wants to alter their habits or their traditions, not even in the medical world.'

Although the operation is available in Britain, it is only offered privately at a cost of £500 for each eye plus surgeon's fees. Many patients have preferred to travel to Moscow on a two-week package tour to be treated by Fyodorov. Soviet medical care is free to foreigners, and he receives letters daily from all over the world from people wishing to enter his care.

Fyodorov's main concern is how to increase the output in his clinic. Medicine is labour, the Institute a factory. 'My dream is to make it a factory of human happiness. People come in ill and leave cured and happy.' Like any other factory, production should be high. While on the one hand the happiness he provides is the personal happiness of the cured patient who can now perceive the world around him in all its beauty, on the other, Fyodorov, as a Soviet citizen and member of the Communist Party, sees it as his duty to provide healthy workers for the State. He invented a 'conveyor belt' to step up production in his 'factory'.

'I realised that I could help millions of people, but not with this crude method of production. I would have to divide the operation up into separate stages. That way you would only need the most highly qualified doctor for the main stage. I came up with the idea of a conveyor.' Fyodorov's conveyor has now been in operation for over a year. It cost more than 850,000 dollars to make and install, payable in foreign currency as the equipment was made in West Germany. 'Of course, we could have made it here, but in any case we had to buy German microscopes because they're the best and so we decided to do everything there in order to save time. Time is more important than any amount of money.'

The operating table complete with patient is clipped onto the belt, a door slides up and the table enters the operating room. Five patients are operated on simultaneously by five doctors who each perform a stage of the operation. Each stage is timed at three minutes for radial keratotomy, six to seven for cataract removals and five for lens implantations, at the end of which the patient's bed moves on automatically to the next doctor. Finally he exits through a sliding door. On the first day of use, sixty operations were performed here. 'I call my conveyor belt my automated road from blindness to sight. The patients like it too. Now that they know exactly how long the operation will last, they feel much calmer.'

Fyodorov has by now proved himself to his country and when he presented his plan for the conveyor to the Ministry of Health and the Council of Ministers, he quickly found enough support to get the go-ahead for it. He is constantly thinking of ways to expand and help more and more people and is supervising the construction of a vast Institute, run on the lines of his own, in the Azerbaidzhanian capital Baku on the Caspian Sea. He is now planning to add a fourth building to his Institute. In the end, the whole thing will have cost the State somewhere in the region of twenty-five million roubles, excluding the many millions of valuable foreign currency the State will have had to pay for apparatus. Fyodorov also has an operating bus that he takes round the country to teach other Soviet clinics how to perform his operations. The bus is fitted with all the latest technology – Fyodorov insists on and gets the best – and video screens show spectators what is happening inside. This year Fyodorov is flying the bus to India to teach his techniques there.

There are two fundamental ways in which Fyodorov differs from his compatriots: he works every available second he has, and he is not afraid to criticise his country and to ask for what he needs for his work. Russians, as a general rule, *are* afraid of hard work. In the words of one Moscow citizen, 'We like to talk about it, but not actually do any. Take last Saturday for example, it was a subbotnik [a day when voluntary unpaid work is performed collectively to mark particular occasions, for example, Lenin's birthday]. We all got together and had a good long discussion about it and then off we went home without actually doing anything at all.'

Where many Soviets are fearful and make their criticisms *sotto voce*, Fyodorov speaks out loud, provocatively, and uses the media to make himself heard. His chief complaint is that the equipment he needs for his work is not manufactured in the Soviet Union and has to be bought from the West. In a recent interview with the Soviet newspaper *Trud* ('Labour'), which has a circulation of seven million, Fyodorov called for the production of high-quality microscopes. In Marisa's Radio Moscow interview with him, he complained that when he does get Soviet equipment it is inferior.

'I find myself forced to repair instruments in primitive conditions. So I try to refuse this equipment. When I visit other clinics I see that the equipment produced by our factories and costing 15–20,000 roubles is left standing in the corner of the operating theatre. Hats and gowns are hanging on it – it has become a coat rack. The problem is that we doctors don't actually have the right to refuse this inferior technology. These rights belong to the Ministry's Union of Medical Technology which, in all my thirty-two years in medicine, has not yet sent a representative to either my operating theatre or our polyclinic. There is a huge wall of misunderstanding between us and so they do what is profitable and easier for them to do and I am powerless. I am forced to use their weapons.'

After the programme has gone out, Fyodorov smiles and says with a mischievous twinkle, 'That ought to get a representative over here soon.'

Another way that Fyodorov has managed to work the system is by having his own laboratories in the Institute to manufacture the instruments he wants. This way he keeps in close contact with production and ensures that he gets what he needs. His laboratories similarly manufacture his artificial lenses and he sells them to the West, thus earning some of the foreign currency he so badly needs for equipment. As the Soviet rouble is non-convertible currency, anything that is bought from the West has to be paid for in Western currency. It is for this reason that the tourist is encouraged to spend his dollars and pounds.

It is now 5 o'clock. Fyodorov has eaten nothing since breakfast with the exception of some 'astronaut food' sucked from a tube as he walked from one theatre to another. He now has time to sit down to lunch which he has daily in a private dining room adjoining his office. He has a cook at his disposal. While luxurious, this is also practical: he is able to keep in touch with his secretary by intercom and to combine the business of eating with meetings. The two men dining with him today are fellow-hunters, both of whom have been operated on and who are combining a post-operative check-up with a friendly lunch. The room is comfortably furnished, hunting trophies in the form of antlers and stags' heads decorate the walls.

'I love guns because I'm a man. Every man should love guns, it's in our blood, this love of guns and of hunting. That's how men are. Women like looking after the children, but we like to hunt and get food. But really, the main point of hunting isn't whether you actually kill or not. It's seeing the sun rising and setting, seeing the mist over the river, hearing the ducks quack, the day awakening, the grass rustling. It's being able to feel nature.' This close affinity with nature is most Russian. Russians are never happier than when gathering mushrooms at dawn or cooking shashlik in the open. Fyodorov is no exception in this respect.

After lunch, Fyodorov does his ward rounds and checks up on the patients he has operated on that morning. There are no more than four patients to a ward and the Professor has all sorts of plans afoot to create murals and comfortable rest areas, 'so that the patient's eye can rest on beautiful things after he has regained his sight.' After meetings and consultations with various doctors, Fyodorov's day is over by about seven.

This evening he plans to take his family to a café in Stoleshnikov Lane off Gorky Street. The café has recently been renovated and the Fyodorovs are keen to try it. So are many others, and when the Volga pulls up outside, a long queue has formed outside the entrance. Boris drives off and may or may not spend his two free hours doing what nearly all other drivers like him do – moonlighting. You can hail any car in Moscow and ask it to take you to your destination. Taxis obviously work for a metered rate (unless they're off-duty and are themselves doing a little 'on the left' as this sort of private enterprise is called). You will pay as much as the driver thinks he can get out of you for a ride in a black Volga, and if you're from the West, you may make your payment in Western cigarettes.

At various times of the day there is always a shortage of taxis, and these official Volgas, turned unofficial taxis, fill the gap. The drivers, who rarely accept less than three roubles for the shortest distance (where a legitimate taxi would cost seventy kopecks), make a substantial amount of extra money this way. Boris earns 300 roubles a month (twice the salary of a GP), and with this moonlighting drivers like him are very well-off indeed by Soviet standards. This practice is illegal, but it is so widespread that a blind eye is turned.

The Fyodorovs go to the front of the queue and enter the café. There is a curious anomaly in Soviet behaviour. Although it is a society committed to classlessness, Soviet citizens recognise power and authority instantly and accept that important people have privileges they themselves do not enjoy. They do not question it, and no one in the queue now objects.

The café is dark and cave-like. Fyodorov, his wife Irène and three of his four daughters order champagne. Service is prompt for them and they are soon drinking and eating. Irène is blonde, plump and pretty. She is always happy, everything delights and interests her. After many years of marriage, she and Fyodorov spend as much time together as possible. 'Don't ask him to tell you about love, he'll start giving you some nonsense about molecules and cells. Men can't talk about these things, ask me instead. We met when I took my aunt to see him, she'd gone blind. I fell in love with him instantly. That was it. We got married. It was all very simple, but completely by chance.' Fyodorov's appreciation of his wife is obvious. 'Irène has Greek blood, that's why she has such a beautiful profile.'

The eldest daughter, Ira, is twenty-nine. She is a surgeon in Fyodorov's Institute and a very talented one, in spite of her father's view that 'women aren't technically minded, they can't grasp technical matters, that's a masculine trait'. The twin daughters are in their early twenties, both newly married. One plans to be an ophthalmologist, the other a linguist. The youngest daughter of sixteen is still at school and planning to follow her father's profession as well. 'Of course it's nice that they are following me but I've never put any pressure on them at all. I just invited them to the Institute to have a look, they made their own choice.' None of the children live with their parents. When they moved to Dostoevsky Street a year ago, the youngest child stayed on in the old apartment with her grandmother as it was near her school. It is common for children to be placed in the care of their grandparents.

The family chatter happily over supper, exchange news, and Irène and Fyodorov show snaps from a recent trip to the West. Then it is home and to bed. The following day will begin early for Fyodorov at 7 a.m. with a ride round a Moscow park on one of his horses. The Dostoevsky Street apartment has three big rooms, kitchen and two bathrooms. The kitchen is fully equipped with microwave oven and Western units. In spite of the marked Western influence, the carved wooden furniture and the bearskins on the walls impart a distinctly Russian flavour. Fyodorov's 'den' is lined with expensive rifles and hunting knives. Life is comfortable. 'My driver lives almost as well as I do. He has a three-roomed flat just near here, his own car, two lovely children. His wife works at the Institute as an anaesthetist and gets 200 roubles a month, he earns 300, not much less than I do. So there's no big difference in the way I live compared with other people. And I like that about my country, the relationships between people are those of equals. I go off hunting with my driver and there may be other people too, hunters, peasants, Ministers of State, and there's no difference between us, we all have an interest in common. We're like kids from the same street. Money doesn't make any difference, old money, new money, more money, less money, who cares? And if I do earn more than others then that's because I work more. Socialism isn't about everyone getting the same, it's about being paid according to your labour. The main thing is that people shouldn't be exploited. A miner earns more than I do. He's got a difficult and dangerous job.'

While it is true that differences based on class are minimal and people of all ranks will sit around a table together, it is, nonetheless, undeniable that Fyodorov has a privileged lifestyle. It is also true to say that he works harder than almost anyone. He is well rewarded for his labour. The Fyodorovs have a dacha some 70 kilometres north of Moscow. 'I went to the Moscow Council and asked for some land in an area where many of my friends have dachas. There was an acre going there and I bought it for 180 roubles. Then we built a small house, a sauna, and stables for the horses.'

Fyodorov's dacha neighbours are similarly well off. Soviet pop star Alla Pugachyova is among them. The house is in an area that is closed to foreigners and we were unable to get permission to see it. Many areas of the Soviet Union are 'closed' for a variety of reasons; they may be near militarily sensitive zones, they may not offer adequate facilities for the foreign tourist. In this instance, the area is probably closed because top Soviet government officials have their dachas nearby.

Raj and Thunder are Fyodorov's two horses. They spend the summer at the dacha and the winter in military stables in Moscow. Raj is an Arab and his nephew was recently sold for a million dollars in the United States. 'Horses aren't so expensive here, about 500 to 1000 roubles. I bought Raj for 150 roubles because he was sick. I cured him and now he's fine.' Fyodorov finds horse-riding rests and relaxes him. He likes to go off hunting on horseback for days at a time. 'You feel like a centaur.'

Life in the Soviet Union for Fyodorov offers everything he could ask for. A successful and innovative eye surgeon, he is widely travelled and a member of the Communist Party. 'There's a direct link between medicine and politics. The Party programme complements my work. The aim of the Party is that everyone should have food, somewhere to live, work, happiness. How can people be happy if they are ill? The sort of medicine that I dream of, my "factories of happiness", will fit organically into such a programme. In addition, I want to ensure that not just I live well, but that others do too. Each and every one of us must help our neighbour, that's the aim of the Party.'

To enter the Party you need the nomination of two people who can vouch for you. As a member, Fyodorov has responsibilities. He gives lectures all over the Soviet Union. The Party collective at the Institute is planning to build a holiday home and to buy yachts so that employees can take time off and relax. 'Members don't have an easier time. In fact, I'd say things were a bit more difficult. You have more responsibility. If someone didn't carry out his duties properly at work and wasn't a Party member, he'd probably just be reproved. But a member would be summoned by some sort of Party secretary and an unpleasant conversation would ensue. So, actually, life for a Party member is probably a bit harder and more responsible. He certainly doesn't have any advantages.'

Others, less skilled at getting what they want, would take a different view. It is not uncommon for people on the possible brink of a breakthrough in their careers to be advised by a friendly official to join the Party and turn such a possibility into an eventuality.

Fyodorov, unlike the majority of Soviet citizens, is a frequent visitor to the West. 'When I was young, our people rarely travelled abroad, but now tourism is growing and many more travel. The problem is that the currency isn't convertible which makes it difficult to travel. Tourism is very expensive for us. It's not because we're afraid that if someone goes abroad they will stay there and not come back. If they want to stay, let them. Everyone has the right to choose where he wants to live.' In practice, it proves rather difficult for people to live where they choose, even within the Soviet Union where fictitious marriages to obtain a coveted Moscow permit are not uncommon.

Fyodorov enjoys travelling, he likes the architecture of London and the galleries of New York. He travels as the guest of numerous ophthalmic organisations. The State pays for his airfare and his host usually covers the bill for his hotel. On a recent visit to London he and Irène stayed in the capital's select Mayfair Hotel. They were further provided with a silver Rolls-Royce and impeccably spoken white-gloved chauffeur. This was paid for by their hosts. Their only complaints were about the Western preoccupation with money and people's alienation from each other. 'Sometimes it's hard for people to make contact with each other. I like the fact that there's a lot of technology in the shops and you can choose what you want, you just have to have the money. There are no shortages and complications in this area.'

For Irène, it was her first visit to London. The doormen of the Mayfair Hotel instantly fell prey to her charms and became her slaves. 'Marlon Brando was staying in the hotel. One day I got back from shopping and saw a big crowd outside the hotel. So I asked the doorman what was going on. "Marlon Brando's expected any minute, but he won't be coming in here, he'll be going round the back, so you should go over there." Well, I've always loved Marlon Brando. In fact when I first met Slava, I thought he was just like him. So my friend and I went round the back and we did manage to see him. Anyhow, later on Slava came back in the Rolls-Royce and as he got out of the car, a photographer took his picture saying, "You're Marlon Brando." Slava said, "No, I'm not." "Oh," said the photographer, "you're that famous Russian eye surgeon, that's all right as well." '

[O.L.]

SEVEN

The Trial of Tamara Russo

Remember Boris who used to live opposite the prison? He's moved – now
he lives opposite his house.
Russian joke

On a Friday morning towards the end of April 1985 a fifty-year-old woman
walks quietly and sadly into Courtroom Number 4 in Beltsy, a small town
in Soviet Moldavia. Her clothes betray her peasant origins – she is wearing
a red and white headscarf, a knitted cardigan, a black skirt with printed
flowers on, and woollen tights. In appearance she could be any one of the
thousands of ageing Soviet women who sweep and scrub and sit on duty in
public buildings, whiling away the time with their thankless chores.
Throughout today's proceedings she will clasp her hands tightly on her lap,
and keep her head bowed to hide her embarrassment and remorse. For
today she is not on duty but on trial. Her name is Tamara Russo. She is
accused of theft.

'Tamara Aleksandrovna Russo, stand up please.' The judge's command
is stern. Lyubov Bubulich is only a couple of years younger than Tamara,
but the similarity between the two women ends there. In court Lyubov's
manner is brisk, her expression grave, and her clothes neat, formal and
judiciously chosen: dark blue suit and light blue blouse buttoned tightly at
the neck. Her shoulder-length hair is worn up. As she reads from her
documents her dark-rimmed spectacles and a thin line of red about her lips
intensify the impression of severity. Only when she smiles, which is not
often in criminal trials, does the gap between her two front teeth hint at
something warmer and more vulnerable in her personality.

Tamara is to be charged under Article 145 of the Criminal Code of the
Soviet Republic of Moldavia, which covers stealing from a fellow citizen
and carries a maximum sentence of five years in prison. Lyubov is one of
seven 'People's Judges' in Beltsy, which has a population of 140,000
people. In the Soviet Union as a whole one judge in three is a woman.
People's Judges try all cases except those crimes the Soviet system
considers most heinous: armed robbery, rape of a minor, smuggling,

organised murders, crimes against the State, and any trials involving the death penalty. These are left to the Supreme Court. Lyubov's court may impose sentences of up to fifteen years in prison for what she calls 'especially serious crimes', though as a judge since 1974 the severest penalty she has imposed is only eight years – on a thief with two previous convictions.

Much of her time is taken up with mundane civil cases: divorce, recovery of debts, claims for damages and disputes between workers and employers. More than one in every three Soviet marriages end in divorce, and if the parting couple have children or cannot agree about who keeps the samovar, they must appear before a judge, who will arbitrate. The only legal ground for divorce is what is loosely called 'the inability to live together', though the most common underlying cause in Lyubov's casebook is the husband's drinking. Divorce can be an expensive business; the judge may extract up to 200 roubles in court fees from the couple, with the guilty partner paying the lion's share. When maintenance payments are added – one quarter of the man's salary for one child (the woman usually gets custody), one third for two children, and one half for three or more – it is not difficult to see why a fair number of Lyubov's criminal cases involve defaulting ex-husbands.

As Tamara answers Lyubov's standard opening questions, the gulf between the two women's backgrounds and circumstances is starkly apparent. Tamara was born in a peasant household in the countryside outside Moscow, and now works as a hospital orderly earning ninety roubles a month, well below the average national wage. By contrast Lyubov is a Moldavian, born and bred in Beltsy, who has made her way up the career ladder from legal adviser to defence lawyer and finally judge. She now earns 240 roubles a month. While Tamara left school at fourteen, Lyubov trained first as a teacher, then took a degree in law at Moldavia's only university, in the capital Kishinyov. Tamara is seven years a widow and is not a member of the Communist Party. Lyubov has both a devoted husband and a Party card. Virtually the only thing they have in common is that neither has a criminal record. If Tamara did have previous convictions, they would be taken into account – indeed, held against her – by the court in today's case.

There is no 'dock' in Soviet courtrooms. If the defendant is in custody a policeman will sit beside him or her on the front row of the public seats. In this case Tamara simply sits on her own facing the bench. In front of her and to the right at a separate desk is Yevgeny Tolpolar, who has been nominated defence lawyer in this trial.

One of Lyubov's first duties is to explain to Tamara her rights. She may see all the materials and written evidence relating to her case, she may ask questions or submit new evidence at any time, and she will be given the last word before the court retires to make its decision. Here, at the outset, she may object to the composition of the court, to which she is now introduced.

Apart from Lyubov herself there are two people's assessors on the bench, ordinary citizens with no formal legal training who have been elected for a term of two and a half years. There is no trial by jury in the Soviet Union. The people's assessors sit for twelve days a year, usually in several stints of two or three days, and they have the same rights as the judge, whom they may in theory outvote in the final verdict. In reality they tend to be solid and dependable citizens, who can be relied on to accept the judge's interpretation of socialist legality. Today's assessors are certainly smartly dressed and have the approved air of gravity about them. According to Soviet statistics just under half are Communist Party members, and slightly over half are women. Not surprisingly Tamara has no objections to them, nor to her defence lawyer, nor the court secretary scribing away diligently in one corner. She simply wants to get her ordeal over with.

Lyubov deals quickly with the trial's opening formalities. The witnesses are asked to leave the room until they are called. 'But don't go away, you will be needed,' she stresses, in a tone of voice that suggests a history of disappearing witnesses. Outside, in the main lobby of the four-storey courthouse, knots of people sit patiently. They might be witnesses in one of the several cases being heard in other courtrooms, or waiting to deliver a petition to one of the judges or to seek advice from today's duty lawyer. Among them is a wife suing for divorce, whose case cannot proceed because her husband has not shown up. One of Lyubov's fellow judges has ruled that the husband may not have received the summons, so the case is held over until next week. Non-appearances of witnesses and postponements are not unusual here, though, unlike in Western courts, delays tend to be mercifully short.

All Soviet trials start with the 'judicial examination' to establish who is present and what their rights are. Today there is a problem. One of the witnesses in Tamara's case is ill in hospital. Methodically, Lyubov consults the assessors beside her, the defence lawyer and Tamara herself: can the trial proceed without the missing witness? They agree it can, though Tamara would be within her rights to request a postponement. Lyubov turns last to the plaintiff who is sitting across the aisle from Tamara and has been visibly bristling with indignation since he came in. 'We can do it with him or without him, whatever you like,' he says.

'No,' replies Lyubov firmly. 'Your opinion is important to us. That's why we ask you – can we begin the case? It's your right to say.' Now the plaintiff readily agrees, like a child who has been given a good telling-off by a bossy schoolteacher.

At this point the defence may raise objections to the way the police have gathered the evidence. The previous day we watched as a defence lawyer successfully argued for a case to be sent back for reinvestigation on the grounds that his client's rights had been abused by the police. The defendant had been interrogated without legal representation, which was illegal in his case, as he had a history of psychiatric disturbance. Today, however, Lyubov is able to move on quickly to the consideration of evidence, which starts with a long police report on the case. She reads it out at breakneck speed, pausing only to decipher the handwritten script (typewriters, still less photocopiers, do not yet seem to have reached provincial Soviet police stations).

According to the report, the police had been asked by Timofei Podurets, today's plaintiff, to investigate the theft of his luggage from Beltsy Railway Station on 7 February, about ten weeks ago. He had been waiting for a train and went out onto the platform to smoke, leaving his possessions on a window-sill in his *avoska* (a string bag beloved of all Soviets – from the word *avos* meaning 'just in case' – in case something decent is suddenly on sale and you need a handy bag to put it in). When he returned his *avoska* had gone, snatched and taken home, it is alleged, by Tamara Russo.

In her statement to the police Tamara explained that she had drunk a bottle of fortified wine with a friend, then struck up a conversation with a man at the station. When the man left the waiting-room she saw his bundle on the window-sill and took it home. Then she came to her senses, realised that she had stolen the old man's bits and pieces, and returned to the station to give them back. She was too late – Timofei had already stopped a policeman, and a bystander remembered her green coat and red headscarf. Although she had time to dump the bag on a bench, she was spotted and arrested. At first she denied everything but later took the police to the bag, which was still lying where she had left it. Worse still, she had omitted to replace a pair of glasses and a pair of sandals when she packed up the bundle at home.

As Lyubov reads out the other statements made to the police, which all confirm the same story, the evidence looks grim for Tamara. She stares fixedly at the floor, recalling perhaps not only the original crime, but the gruelling investigation which followed.

In Soviet law this pre-trial investigation is the crucial stage of criminal proceedings. It is then that the evidence is collected and a decision taken whether to bring the accused to trial. As in many continental European countries, the investigators – called Procurators in the Soviet Union – interrogate the accused and draw up the charges. They not only conduct the prosecution but supervise the legality of court procedure, a dual function which makes the Procuracy the most prestigious and powerful part of Soviet law. Eighty-three per cent of them are Party members, 98% are men. The defence lawyer is not allowed to participate in any way until the Procurator issues the decree to prosecute. As a result of the thorough investigation, only those cases in which the Prosecutor is confident of getting a conviction go to trial, so the prosecution's success rate is very high. A Western observer could be forgiven for thinking that Soviet criminal trials merely verify the evidence collected during the investigation and rubber-stamp the guilty verdict already arrived at by the Procurator.

Certainly, by the time Lyubov reaches the formal charges, there is little doubt that Tamara will plead guilty. Her only chance of being acquitted is on a legal technicality. Lyubov tells us afterwards that she 'very rarely' hears not guilty pleas. 'It's usually when someone wants to protest out of principle. Once we had someone who insisted on his innocence – it turned out he thought it wasn't manly to confess!'

On the other hand, a confession or a guilty plea alone will not be enough for a conviction. Perhaps the Soviets have learned from experience. In Stalin's show trials of the 1930s, thousands of so-called enemies of the state were executed after confessing under extreme duress to the most far-fetched offences. Nowadays all the independent evidence has to be fully considered whatever the plea. Lyubov suggests another more practical reason too. 'An accused man might plead guilty and then change his evidence later. His confession isn't reliable. Proof is essential.'

Soviet trials are more loosely organised than ours. There is no separate case for the prosecution and case for the defence, and no formal cross-examination of each other's witnesses. Indeed, in relatively minor cases like Tamara's, the Procurator does not attend at all. Instead the judge acts as inquisitor, questioning everyone in turn. The defendant is usually first.

In a faltering voice Tamara explains how she had picked up the *avoska* at the station and forgotten to put back the sandals and the glasses when she decided to return it. 'I confess everything, it's the first time anything has ever happened like this. I was so frightened I didn't notice I hadn't put everything back in the bag.' As the rest of the court looks on in silence she sobs, 'It won't happen again. I don't know how I could've done it.'

Lyubov waits for Tamara's tears to subside, then continues her questioning gently but firmly. 'Why didn't you put all the things back?'

'They must have fallen out. I was frightened I had done something wrong, so I was in a rush to go back to the station.'

'Why didn't you confess to the police straight away?'

'I was scared. I've never committed a crime before. It would have been better for me, I see that now, much better. When I realised what I'd done, I saw the man might need his things, I didn't throw them away, I took them back.'

Lyubov is quite accustomed to people breaking down in court, even a little hardened to it. In another of her cases we saw a wife who was suing her ex-husband for maintenance payments explode with anger when the court failed to reach a ruling in her favour. 'We can't be heartless,' Lyubov says later, 'but we've got to be objective. Tamara Russo was upset because of her own crime.' Sentimentality is not one of the qualities Lyubov admires. 'A judge must be warm-hearted, not emotional. Honest. Good-natured.' She pauses between words, pondering carefully as if the question has never been asked her before. 'Sensitive. And conscientious.'

According to Lyubov, it was these positive characteristics that people recognised in her when she was first elected as a People's Judge in 1974. She was proposed as a candidate by the workers at the Locomotive Depot, where Lyubov once worked as a legal adviser. As in all Soviet elections, she was the only candidate in her constituency, and was elected unopposed. She has twice been re-elected for five-year terms. In theory, anyone over twenty-five with a higher legal education can be nominated, but although only half of the candidates are Party members, the whole process is carefully supervised by Party organisers. Lyubov herself was not a Party member when she was first elected, but she was asked to join soon afterwards. 'Before then I was not mature enough. I was afraid I wouldn't be able to live up to the responsibilities entrusted to me. Now I have to be an example to other people everywhere, in everything I do.' Her duties include what she calls legal 'propaganda', which includes giving lectures and leading question-and-answer sessions to educate the masses about their rights and responsibilities under the law.

Lyubov sits in court only two or three days a week. One day is set aside for reading up on cases, and another for receiving inquiries from the general public in her office. Sometimes civil cases can be resolved at this stage, before they come to court. Her main task is to guide ordinary people through the labyrinthine procedures involved in preparing legal documents. On one typical day we saw a divorcing couple seeking advice on how to dispose of their jointly-owned apartment, a sad old lady wanting information about her husband who was in custody charged with perjury, a young man seeking damages from a driver who had injured him in a road accident, and another man trying to arrange for a divorce summons to be served on his wife.

'Do you often drink?' This time the question comes from one of the people's assessors, a man aged about forty in a dark suit.

'We drank one bottle between the two of us,' Tamara replies, and for the first time there is a hint of indignation in her voice. 'I hardly ever drink, I have responsible work.'

But the question is relevant, for a large proportion of petty crime in the Soviet Union is due to drink. No official statistics are available on such a delicate subject, but our observations of a typical couple of weeks in a provincial court show alcohol to be the common factor right across the board, whether the case be divorce, theft, brawling or illegally distilling spirits at home.

In the spring of 1985 the Soviet authorities announced tough new measures against alcoholism, including shorter licensing hours and stiffer penalties, though they stopped short of increasing vodka prices. Mikhail Gorbachev is the first Party leader to see the folly of earning huge revenue from taxes on drink, since that income is lost several times over in the absenteeism, crime and disease which alcoholism causes. It is an age-old problem in Russia, where vodka is drunk neat, quickly and often, usually accompanied by sentimental toasts. Outside off-licences you are often approached by someone wanting to go halves on a bottle or by a desperate pair of boozers looking, as they say plaintively, 'for a third'. Even here in Moldavia, where wines are made locally and cheaply (every country household has its modest vineyard), the host's table is not considered complete without a bottle or two of 'Russkaya' vodka.

The defence lawyer is next to question Tamara. Yevgeny Tolpolar is a Second World War invalid who now rises unsteadily to his feet and peers at the court through thick glasses. Yevgeny and Tamara only met the previous day. He was assigned to her case, as she had not arranged for representation herself. Defendants may conduct their own defence, but few do, especially if they are as bewildered by the legal process as Tamara. Straightforward advice from a lawyer is available free of charge at any of the legal consultation offices, which are similar to citizens' advice bureaus in Britain. To have a lawyer defend you in court costs about thirty roubles a day, though most people pay less as cases only last three or four hours. The fee can be paid in weekly instalments, and it is waived altogether on the rare occasions when a defendant is acquitted.

Remarkably, defence lawyers are not state employees, but belong to 'colleges of barristers' – independent associations which run their own finances and recruitment. They are one of the few Tsarist institutions not abolished by the Soviets, partly perhaps because Lenin himself was a barrister by profession. There are fifteen lawyers in the Beltsy college. Before her elevation to judge, Lyubov was one herself.

Like barristers everywhere, Yevgeny is a skilled manipulator of words and witnesses. At first you wonder whose side he is on as he questions Tamara. 'How could it happen that you stole someone else's possessions? Didn't you think you were breaking the law? Why didn't you return the bag to the man immediately?'

In fact he is trying to extract from Tamara's increasing distress some voluntary expressions of remorse to elicit the court's sympathy. His tactic seems to be working, as mitigating circumstances emerge from his probing.

'What is your opinion of your crime?'

'I behaved badly.'

'Do you live alone?'

'Yes – my husband died seven years ago.'

'How is your health?'

'I have high blood pressure.'

'Don't you know you shouldn't drink with that complaint?'

'I know, but I did have a drink, and look what happened.'

'Did you apologise to the plaintiff?'

'Yes. That night I told him I was sorry and asked him to forgive me.'

'What do you ask from the court?' By this time Tamara has once again been reduced to tears.

'I ask you not to punish me severely. I have two sons, I'm so ashamed, they don't know I'm here. This has never happened before, never. I'm afraid they'll find out. I don't want them to know at my sons' place of work.'

Lyubov intercedes to ask where Tamara's sons work. She seems genuinely moved now, as if the mention of sons has reminded her of her own Valera, who is twenty, her only child and the apple of her eye. For she too is worried. Valera has been expected home from university in Leningrad for days, but is missing and has not phoned. Her anxiety has been mounting, belying the image of hard-headedness she displays in court. She values family loyalty and affection highly, as is abundantly clear on those occasions when she succeeds in persuading a divorcing couple to reconsider (we once saw her beam across the courtroom and wish the reconciled pair 'a large and secure family'), or when she reflects in her moralising way on broken families. 'People approach marriage in such a light-hearted way. Family life is like a tiny egg – it must be allowed to grow. You should learn to appreciate each other's personality, and find ways of dealing with differences.'

Before Tamara is allowed to sit down Lyubov has one last question. 'Do they know what you have done at your work?'

'Yes, I told them. They asked me, "Tamara, how could this happen?" I said, "I had a drink, that's how!" ' Again, Lyubov's question is relevant, for an important part of crime and punishment in the USSR is the public parading of a miscreant's sins in front of his workmates. In the Soviet Union you are responsible not just to your own conscience, but to the collective to which you belong, so your private shame will always be compounded by public humiliation. Earlier in the week we heard how a man, who had been given a suspended sentence by Lyubov for stealing £100 worth of flour, had been forced to denounce himself in meetings at the fertiliser plant where he worked. Reports to the court on the sincerity of his remorse at these meetings helped to persuade Lyubov to lift his sentence.

When Timofei Podurets, the plaintiff, is giving evidence, Lyubov cannot suppress a smile at his melodramatic performance from the witness stand. In rich colloquial Russian and with sweeping gestures and lively facial gymnastics, this fifty-eight-year-old machine-operator at Beltsy's sugar factory gives his account of the fateful evening in February. His tale is a long one, embroidered by irrelevant diversions about train timetables and sanatorium holidays. After he discovered his bag was gone, he says, 'the main worry was my shaving things – I wouldn't feel right without those'. Unlike the defendant he is required to sign a statement acknowledging that he understands his legal responsibility to tell the truth. There is no oath, but he can be charged with perjury if he knowingly deceives the court.

'Why did you leave your bag on the window-sill?' asks one of the people's assessors.

'I didn't think it would come to any harm. It's the first time anything like this has happened to me.' Timofei's faith in his fellow citizens' honesty is on the whole well-founded. The Soviet Union does not publish crime statistics, so exact comparisons are impossible, but it would appear that crimes against the person are far less common there than they are in the West.

In his questions Yevgeny tries to find out from Timofei what he thinks about Tamara, and what he thinks the court should do.

'I look at it this way,' Timofei replies, never short of an opinion and eager to share it. 'The court should show her that she shouldn't behave like she did. A small fine – it's her first offence – a fine will do. If it happens again, that's when you should put her away.' Yevgeny says he has no more questions and sits down with a contented nod to Tamara.

As each of the two witnesses tell their story they confirm the events already described several times to the court. Giorgi Chebatar actually saw Tamara take the bag from the window-sill, but took no notice, assuming that she was Timofei's wife, as they had been talking together a few minutes earlier. Yelena Milinchan saw Tamara replace the stolen bag on a bench. She watched the police question Tamara and heard her deny taking the bag.

Yelena is from the countryside outside Beltsy, and like many rural Moldavians speaks Russian poorly. In all the Soviet Republics the normal language of the courts is Russian, but non-Russians have the right to speak through an interpreter. Although Lyubov and her two people's assessors are fluent in both Russian and Moldavian, Yelena's testimony in court has to be laboriously translated from Moldavian. Moldavia has been a full Republic only since 1940, when the Red Army expelled the Rumanian royalist regime. But the Moldavian language is closely related to Rumanian, and the four million Moldavians' culture and lifestyle is much more Rumanian than it is Russian. In the countryside most schools teach Russian only as a foreign language. All the other lessons are in Moldavian.

After the witnesses have testified Lyubov reads out the remaining evidence submitted by the Procurator. This includes photographs of the *avoska*, an official valuation of the items stolen (man's shirt 9 roubles, avoska 70 kopecks, family size toothpaste 1 rouble 78 kopecks, glasses 3 roubles, sandals 8 roubles), and a character reference about Tamara from the hospital where she works. It describes her as a conscientious worker whose behaviour is above criticism.

There is also a letter from Beltsy's psychiatric clinic saying that Tamara has never been a patient there. 'If we have any doubts about a defendant's state of mind,' Lyubov explained, 'we ask for a psychiatrist's report. We cannot prosecute someone who is disturbed.' This sounds humane and just, though Lyubov fails to say that similar reports have been used by other Soviet courts to lock up critics of the system in mental hospitals. Political dissent has often been viewed by the authorities as evidence of psychiatric illness.

Lyubov never deals with dissidents. They are tried by special courts which cover so-called 'crimes against the state', such as anti-Soviet propaganda and parasitism – both used as convenient catch-alls against political opponents. The Soviet constitution specifically says that the law must protect the individual's rights, but only so long as he in turn respects what is called 'socialist legality'. If you suggest to Lyubov that human rights are therefore not adequately defended, she is incensed. 'That is a slanderous view of our system of justice. We defend everyone's rights in an identical way. We are not allowed by law to favour the state over the individual. If the state breaks the law, the law protects the individual.'

All the evidence has now been presented, so Lyubov invites the defence lawyer to sum up on Tamara's behalf. Yevgeny starts by complimenting the court on its rigorous investigation of the facts, and then points out that Tamara has fully confessed her crime. She has behaved well in court, he says, her crime was not premeditated, she has no previous convictions and a good reference from work. And, although she is charged with stealing thirty-eight roubles' worth of Timofei's possessions, the court should bear in mind that she returned most of it, leaving a mere eleven roubles' worth at home, and then only by accident. All these mitigating factors, he suggests, might lead the court to consider an alternative to a prison sentence, which would give Tamara a chance to pay back her debt to society.

As laid down in Soviet law, the last word must go to the defendant. 'I realise I have committed a bad crime. Please don't punish me severely, I'll make up for what I've done.' Tamara's voice trails off, the tears return, and she hardly notices Lyubov and the people's assessors retire to a small room at the back of the court to consider their decision.

They are out for two hours, and their deliberations are secret. Tamara sits and fidgets nervously; she looks lonely and humiliated. Yevgeny ignores her; he uses the time to write his May Day cards (Soviets send each other congratulations on all the main public holidays). Timofei inspects the ceiling. Two floors above, workmen are repairing the roof, which was damaged during the winter and is now leaking water into the office belonging to the Chairman of the Judges. Spring is late this year after an unusually cold winter. Lyubov has had to plant her cucumbers and tomatoes late, and she is worried that the weather will spoil the May Day parade next week. Revolution Day on 7 November, and 1 May, are the main dates on the Soviet political calendar. In Beltsy the central square is ablaze with red banners. Fences are being repainted, streets are being swept; marching bands and decorated floats go through their paces for the big day. Meanwhile workmen are building temporary stalls for all the extra goods – clothes, food and especially drink – which will go on special sale at the end of April to ensure that the political celebrations will be followed, as always, by exuberant private festivities.

From the moment when the Procurator decided to commit Tamara to trial there has been little doubt that she would be found guilty. The question which occupies so much time in the court's mind is the sentence. Should she be imprisoned or not? In Soviet law there is no principle of legal precedent, each case must be decided on its own merits. Lyubov and the people's assessors would need to discuss more than the incident of theft. They would be judging Tamara's overall conduct as a citizen, taking into account all they have learned about her during the trial. Lyubov says the most rewarding part of her job is the chance it gives her to be a moral teacher to people, to nurture good citizens. 'When I was a child I used to play with dolls, but not like other girls do. I would tell them off about their behaviour and criticise them. My mother was amazed and couldn't imagine what would become of me!' As a Judge she favours giving suspended sentences which, she says, allow a criminal time to atone for his guilt and justify the court's trust in him.

When the court returns, everyone stands while Lyubov solemnly reads out the verdict from a handwritten paper inside her stiff-backed red file. She says the court has established Tamara's guilt and summarises yet again the evidence against her.

'The court considers that defendant Russo was aware of committing a criminal act. Only if she had immediately returned the bag to the place from where she stole it would there be grounds for excusing the crime. Moreover, Russo categorically denied stealing the bag at the time of her arrest. On the other hand, the court takes into account that Russo was in a drunken condition, that this is her first offence, that she has shown genuine remorse, and that she is of good character.'

Tamara is sentenced to one year's corrective labour at her place of work, that is to say, 20% of her wages will be deducted for a year. For someone who earns as little as ninety roubles a month this represents considerable hardship. In practice, she will have to work 20% extra hours for the same pay. In addition defence costs of twenty-five roubles are awarded against her. If she wishes to appeal she must apply to the Moldavian Supreme Court within seven days.

Lyubov turns to face Tamara. 'If you behave well at work and justify the trust put in you, you will have a chance to go before an inspector of correctional labour and have the sentence revoked before the end of one year. Do you understand?'

Tamara nods but looks dazed. In the lobby outside she shakes her head in disbelief – not at the sentence, which she says is 'the correct decision', but at her own behaviour. 'It was a stupid thing to do. Just see what a glass of wine can do to you.'

By contrast Lyubov is delighted that Tamara agrees with the court's verdict. 'When we feel we've chosen the right degree of punishment, we feel we've achieved our aim. Our intention is not to punish people, but to educate them.'

Two days later there is good news for both women. First Lyubov's son Valera finally arrives home after she has endured nearly a week of intense anxiety. Her relief is mingled with disapproval when it turns out that he had simply decided to take a few days' break with his friends in Kiev and 'didn't have time' to ring home. There is more than a hint of reproach in Lyubov's voice when she tells Valera that his girlfriend in Leningrad has been ringing the house wanting to know where he was.

Then the Supreme Soviet in Moscow announces unexpectedly that in honour of the 40th anniversary of victory over fascism, men over sixty and women of any age who have been given a sentence of up to five years in prison will be amnestied. Together with thousands of other petty criminals across the country, Tamara has her conviction quashed overnight. Amnesties, it seems, are a regular feature of important Soviet anniversaries, as well as an effective way of preventing prison overcrowding. According to Lyubov they are 'yet another example of the humanity of our system of justice'. Whatever the truth, Tamara will not easily forget her ordeal in Lyubov's court, but both of them will have extra cause to celebrate May Day this year.

[A.B.]

EIGHT

Baltic Chic

> A Frenchman is visiting a woman, who waits for him in bed. Overcome by
> passion, the Frenchman starts to tear off his clothes. He takes off his hat
> and flings it out of the window, his coat and throws that out too, his tie . . .
> 'What are you doing?' cries the woman. 'Don't worry,' the Frenchman
> replies, 'by the time I've finished all these clothes will be out of fashion.'
> Soviet joke told by Krista Kajandu

The moment you get on the Tallinn-bound train, things feel different. The
compartment guard gives you a warm welcoming smile, the beds in your
compartment are neatly made, biscuits stand ready to be eaten with your
tea, which is served in cups and saucers instead of the customary glasses,
and a little vase with the inscription 'Estonia' holds a sprig. You have
entered another Soviet republic and its national flavour immediately
asserts itself.

Estonia is one of the three Baltic states and one of the fifteen republics
that make up the Soviet Union. It is a small republic on the Baltic Sea, 320
kilometres west of Leningrad, with a population of one and a half million.
Tallinn, the capital, has had a chequered history. It was founded by the
Danes in 1219, although there is mention of a town as early as 1154. After
the Danes, the Teutonic Knights and the Swedes controlled it, until in 1721
it came under Russian rule when Peter the Great established a Russian
naval base there. After almost two centuries of Russian domination, the
Germans occupied the town in 1918. Then followed a brief period of
independence until Estonia was annexed by the Soviet State in 1940.
(Many Estonians, unwilling to live in the Soviet Union, used the confusion
of the war years as an opportunity to flee to the West.)

These Scandinavian, German and Russian influences all combine to give
this small republic an identity of its own. Tallinn is a charming medieval
fortress town, the old region consisting of two parts: the upper town which
dates from the 13th century and the lower that evolved from the 14th to
16th centuries. The small narrow streets and cobbled paving stones are
familiarly European, as indeed is the look of the people themselves. By
contrast, the new part of town, built after the war, could be anywhere in the
Soviet Union.

One of the first things that strikes you when you get off the train is how much better-dressed people are here. The Soviet Union is notorious for ill-fitting, poor-quality clothing. These well-groomed Estonians are a notable exception. 'Maybe it's because we're a border republic. We have more contact with the outside world,' said one fashion-conscious Tallinn citizen. Tallinn lies on the Gulf of Finland eighty kilometres from Helsinki, and Estonians thus have far greater access to Western trends and fashions than most other Soviet republics: Finnish television can be picked up clearly – although only in black and white – and most Tallinn citizens are faithful followers of *Dallas* and *Dynasty* and avid fans of *The Benny Hill Show*. The fact that these programmes are transmitted in Finnish presents no particular problem for Estonians, for their own mother tongue is from the same family. Estonians also speak Russian, albeit poorly and with a strong accent.

Krista Kajandu is an attractive and elegant woman in her mid-forties. She is chief designer at the Tallinn Fashion House. April and October are particularly busy months both for her and for the ten designers who work under her. This is when the biannual Tallinn Fashion Show takes place. October sees the presentation of the autumn/winter collection and April that of spring/summer. The visitor who comes to bury Estonian fashion and not to praise it is in for a rude shock: the clothes in this 'Paris of the north', while not attaining the excellence of their Western counterpart, are, in the context of the Soviet Union, very chic indeed.

Only a few days remain before the fashion show and there is still a great deal to do. For Krista, the next few days will be very busy. The Tallinn Fashion House has two buildings within easy walking distance of each other in the old part of town. 'We've outgrown ourselves. They've been promising us a new building for years, but fashion gets low priority. Please ignore the mess.' In fact, all the designers like the location of the buildings although they realise that they will have to sacrifice beauty to utility and move to the more spacious new part of town to get the extra room they so badly need.

The Fashion House falls within the jurisdiction of the Ministry for Light Industry, which possibly possesses the lowest budget of all. Priority is given to heavy industry and defence. 'The Ministry dictates the plans that we have to fulfil. You know, financial plans, this plan, that plan, I don't even know what they all are. They give us an idea of how many designs we must create, how many we must sell, how much we must earn.'

The first item on Krista's agenda this morning is a meeting with representatives from other Soviet fashion houses. She leaves her office and runs over to the other building on Virus Street where Tiina, the surprisingly young director of the Fashion House, is waiting for her. Krista and Tiina, both in their appearance and their work, far surpass their guests in elegance. They sit talking over coffee and biscuits. (In Estonia coffee is drunk at every possible opportunity.) The Russian guests ask questions eagerly, full of admiration for their Estonian countrymen. Mary-Ann, one of the House's four full-time mannequins, models designs from the last collection. 'Do you manage to fulfil your plan?' asks one visitor.

'Yes,' Tiina and Krista laugh, 'only just.'

The implication is clear; how is it possible to fulfil the plan and produce goods worth having? The Plan has become the enemy of every industry. In the rush to produce the quantity stipulated, the quality is entirely overlooked. This is one reason for the almost universally shoddy workmanship. The plan dictates production targets and deadlines, and failure to fulfil it carries fines and loss of benefits. Quality control appears not to be so rigidly enforced.

The chief problem facing designers in the fashion industry all over the Soviet Union is fabric. 'If we could buy all our fabric from the factory that made the best, everything would be fine. But we're obliged to buy fabric from several factories and some of them work rather badly. If we were able to insist on only buying from the factory that worked well, then the other factories would have to start working well too; they'd have to compete. Otherwise no one would buy what they made and then they wouldn't be able to fulfil their plan. So, in the end, everyone would work well.'

Krista is unwittingly espousing the need for a free market economy. However, this is contrary to all the laws of Soviet socialism. Private enterprise is not as long dead in Estonia as it is in other parts of the Soviet Union. The knowledge that they are falling behind their European neighbours rankles. 'Before the war, we were far ahead of Finland in everything. And now they've overtaken us simply because we can't always get hold of the things we need. It makes me absolutely furious.'

One of the ways that Krista tries to overcome the problem of low-quality fabric is to have it made, as much as possible, in the Estonian factories. This way she and her designers are able to keep an eye on the quality of what's being produced. Finland, in return for its political freedom, has all sorts of trade obligations to the Soviet Union. It is required to buy 10% of the cotton it needs from the USSR. 'We get 90% from Egypt and 10% from the Soviet Union,' said a Finnish designer. 'The 10% is such bad quality, we can hardly do anything with it. At least, 90% of what *we* use is first-rate stuff. I cannot imagine how the Soviet designers manage. What constitutes only 10% of our cotton, constitutes 100% of theirs.'

For the Tallinn designers this is an embarrassment and, at present, an insuperable problem. Yet today's Russian guests are impressed by the textiles used in the designs that Mary-Ann is modelling, thus revealing that the materials they are themselves forced to work with are worse still. 'Was this coat shown at an international exhibition?' one woman asks.

'No, no, here at our own last October . . . but we'd have been happy to agree to go abroad to an international exhibition. We're not against travelling.'

Everyone laughs in agreement. A trip abroad is a much-desired perk. Krista has been to Czechoslovakia, Poland, Hungary and Finland. 'The Finns weren't ahead of us in ideas, their fabrics were better, but in the actual designs we can stand next to them.'

As well as being of poor quality, fabric is extremely expensive. Fourteen to fifteen roubles a metre is considered cheap. This is one reason why clothes in the Soviet Union are so expensive.

A great imponderable of Soviet life is how anyone can afford clothes at all. The average wage is somewhere in the region of 150–180 roubles a month. A thin acrylic sweater that you might find in Britain in a clearance sale for £3.99 costs sixty roubles in a Soviet shop. A pair of Western jeans (Levis and Wranglers are the most sought after) cost 120 roubles on the black market. Jeans are now manufactured in the Soviet Union in an attempt to curb speculation. However, here too the fabric is inferior. While rent and living costs may be minimal, food is not. Food prices are comparable to prices in the West with the exception of staples like bread and milk which are cheaper. It is inconceivable to most of us to spend a month's salary on an item of clothing. But money has little value in the Soviet Union, perhaps because there is not a great deal for the consumer to spend his wages on. Since the essentials are assured, housing and employment being provided by the State, comparatively large sums can be spent on the limited consumer items available.

You have to buy as you see since nothing is in plentiful enough supply for the customer to assume it will still be in the shop the following day. If you don't have the cash, then your friend Sasha/Seriozha/Masha probably has some extra that he/she is perfectly willing to let you have until next month. This nonchalant attitude is refreshing in comparison with the money-orientation of the West. Because clothes are so expensive, the average Soviet citizen has very few. He will have one pair of jeans to the Westerner's three and they will have to last him for years until they are a mass of careful darns and patches. Needless to say, the acquisition of clothes on the black market is illegal, but by now is so widespread as to be tacitly tolerated. Anyone going to the West for a visit will have an endless shopping list filled with requests from friends and from people whose needs it may be wise to accommodate, as they may prove necessary or useful in the future. People will go to extraordinary lengths to get what they want and need. At a Moscow dinner party, it transpired that one of the guests was a designer in a small fashion house. 'I've got some material,' said Igor, another guest. 'How about if I bring it to you? Could you make me a pair of trousers? These ones have nearly had it.'

Krista is saddened by how badly most people dress. 'Sometimes you see a mother with her child. She is dressed beautifully, but the child looks terrible. You have to educate people, show them that it is possible to look nice and that you don't have to spend a lot of money. Of course I think clothes are important, or I wouldn't have chosen this profession. They can show your inner world, they can reflect your mood and feelings. That's not to say they're the most important thing, though. Honesty and a sense of humour are much more important. And the worst thing of all is to be stupid.'

The Tallinn Fashion House caters for all areas of the fashion industry. For two months of the year, the designers work on their designs for the fashion show. Each of them has to come up with eleven designs in a particular category. The categories are dictated by the time of year: in winter, outdoor wear is largely featured; in spring, lighter clothes. 'I let the designers choose their own themes for the most part. Although they should do a different one each time, they must know how to do everything.'

The show is for the public to see, but they cannot buy the clothes or even order them. The principal aim of the show is actually to sell the designs to factories. Once a factory has bought a design, it will put it into production. There is no guarantee that it will make up the design in the fabric used by the designer, and the factory-produced item may not, therefore, be as elegant as the original. The same design can be bought by any number of factories. Since the Tallinn House designs are better-styled than usual, they will be more complicated to make, so it is unlikely that they will go into mass production. They will probably be produced in relatively small quantities and be snapped up as soon as they get into shops.

'Our clothes are supposed to be better than average. That's what we're here for, to show what's possible. But we are restricted by the fact that we work for industry. If we come up with anything too intricate, the factories simply won't buy it and then we'll have problems. We have to sell our designs in order to stay in business.' Out of an annual total of 1000 designs, the Tallinn House sells 900. About half are purchased by Estonian factories. The other half are bought by factories all over the Soviet Union.

When not working on models for the show, Krista's designers are creating clothes for mass production and limited production. A factory in Tallinn is one of their many outlets for mass production. The factory is a bus ride away in the new part of the town. If the stylishness of the Fashion House was a surprise, the drabness of the factory clothes is just what you would expect. Krista is shown a range of clothes. Different standards operate here and what would clearly be unacceptable for the Fashion Show gets the vote of approval for mass production.

An enormous shop-floor is a mass of whirring machinery one minute and imposing silence the next, as the women who work there are sent off for their midday gymnastics. In a large hall a few floors below, these women are taken through a keep-fit routine to relieve the discomfort of their sedentary job, to the strains of 'Michael, Row the Boat Ashore'. Then it is back upstairs to the sewing and the ironing, as garment after identical garment is turned out.

'I like some of the designs here,' says Krista. 'That one over there is one of ours. It's very nice, but you see it depends entirely on the material it's sewn in. It always comes back to this same problem.'

The factory clothes are much cheaper than the ones that are made in limited quantity. They are a polyester nightmare, but they are what you see women all over the Soviet Union wearing. The Fashion House has a small workshop responsible for the production of a limited number of high-quality designs in high-quality fabrics. These clothes should be fresher and more fashionable. If a factory model sells well, the factory can produce more. We don't ever produce more than 300 of any one design. The people who buy our limited edition clothes are paying more and should have less of a chance of meeting other people wearing the same garments.'

The Fashion House is a pace-setter. It aims to develop everyone's sense of fashion. It is the most sought-after place of work. Factory designers never get the opportunity to have fashion shows and are confined to creating clothes for mass production. Most designers on completion of training start off working in a factory. Krista was no exception and spent two years in the very factory whose designs she now assesses. But for a year of those two, she was lucky enough to work on a film as costume designer. Her talent was recognised and she went to work at the Fashion House. She does little designing herself these days. 'I do miss it. It's just a question of time, and I hope to do some more.'

Those who work under her are the cream of Estonian designing talent. There is only one male designer. When Krista was training there were only four male students in the institute. The fashion world is a predominantly female one. Leonid may be the only man at the Fashion House, but he is also the only Russian and the best designer. His father was Armenian and his mother Russian. As his father was an army man, they travelled widely and finally settled in Estonia some fifteen years ago. Leonid is in his early thirties and lives with his mother in Tallinn. His Estonian isn't bad but, as Krista points out, 'sometimes Leonid pretends he has understood and he hasn't really. So now I usually speak to him in Estonian first and then repeat myself in Russian.'

Leonid is the most flamboyant of all the designers: he sports knee-high boots over his trousers, necklaces, bracelets and a single long earring. His sexuality is ambiguous. This is not something that is tolerated in the Soviet Union, where homosexuality is illegal and a criminal offence, but it does exist. The average Soviet man is a macho creature who finds his masculinity threatened by the suggestion that homosexuality is a fairly common phenomenon. At the merest mention of the word, he will snigger and shuffle nervously. One Leningrader developed an uncontrollable rage at the idea of men being homosexual. 'I think they should all be lined up and shot. No, I mean it, I'd be happy to shoot them myself.'

This rage at any deviation from the accepted norm is not unusual. Soviet citizens are, generally speaking, fearful and unaccepting of the unfamiliar. As a result of such an intolerant attitude, Soviet homosexuals (known in Russian as 'blue men' for some reason no one can explain) are forced underground and lead a secretive life. Many of them are married with families. They gather in places where they are likely to meet potential gay partners and have quick affairs. In Moscow, the small park outside the Bolshoi Theatre is rumoured to be such a meeting place as are the public baths in a street nearby.

All relationships have to be conducted with the utmost discretion and secrecy. Elsewhere in the Soviet Union, life for the homosexual is even more difficult than in the relatively sophisticated capital. The current modishly androgynous Western man with his pierced ear is a sight so unusual in Soviet Uzbekistan, for example, that Tofya, the local television representative there, refused to believe that one such young man was male at all. 'It's absolutely impossible, look, it's got breasts. Oh, my God, you're right, it is a boy. Oh, my God.' Estonia, however, is more tolerant than Samarkand, and Leonid with his conspicuous style appears to attract little attention. In any case he is working in an industry that, by its very nature, allows him to be preoccupied with appearance, both his own and others'.

Leonid's theme for this show is spring coats. The coats are made of beige mock-camel hair – 'the material's actually not very good' – edged with convincing synthetic beige leather. They are beautifully sculpted with wide shoulders and swirling skirts. 'I think my last collection was my swansong. I designed black evening dresses. They were inspired by Italian opera, by the dramatic heroines of Puccini and Verdi. The dresses were really designed to be worn for a night out at La Scala.' Leonid's one worry about the April show is the models. 'They must be more professional and their movements should be more synchronised. The coats are very firmly constructed, their movements should be too.'

Leonid is easily the most imaginative of the designers and finds the demands of working for industry constraining. He is a friend of Moscow's number one fashion designer, Slava Zaitsev, who effectively has his own business. Zaitsev, himself a former fashion house designer, is now the couturier of the Soviet élite. He is the head of the only independent house in the Soviet Union. Each garment is an original and prices are high, 250–300 roubles for a day dress and 850 for an evening outfit. It would not be surprising if Leonid were to follow in his footsteps. Fashion appears to be one area where a certain degree of private enterprise is tolerated.

There is an outlet for the unusual one-off garment in Tallinn. With four days to go until the show, Krista is in and out of her office, on the phone, having last-minute consultations with her designers, overseeing fittings. Suddenly, she grabs her coat from the hook in her office, 'Come on, you must come with me to a cultural happening.'

The 'cultural happening' is a drive away along the coast. Ice floes stretch out to sea and ships stand immobilised. The panorama is spectacular. The happening is an exhibition of one-offs by Estonian designers and features the work of several of Krista's colleagues. Housed in a modern Scandinavian-style building, the exhibition is crowded. The clothes bearing prices are for sale, but they are expensive, 150–200 roubles for a dress. Leather bangles with sparkling chips of glass styled by Leonid are the only items being snapped up and even they sell at twenty-five roubles each. The visitors look at everything admiringly. Here and there, people take out notebooks and rapidly copy down the designs. No one objects to this plagiarism. 'That's part of the reason for the exhibition, to give people ideas.' When items are bought, the designers receive 75% of the sale price, the other 25% goes to the State. Such additional income is most welcome. Leonid and his colleagues earn a mere 130 roubles a month – low even by Soviet standards. Krista takes home 200 roubles.

Another source of income is the Fashion House's magazine, *Silhouette*. Designers get extra for contributing to the magazine which has a print run of 325,000 in Russian and 26,000 in Estonian. The magazine actually has patterns for the clothes illustrated and the competent seamstress can make her own clothes. If you cannot sew yourself, you can go to a fashion atelier and have clothes made to your specification. One such place in Leningrad is popularly known as 'husband's death' – this can be an expensive business and getting something worthwhile can involve a long wait.

Most Soviets are used to having to make things themselves. This extends far beyond clothing, to pickling mushrooms, tomatoes and apples for the long winters, making jam and even, illegally, brewing your own vodka. Krista is keen to teach people to make things for themselves and every Wednesday she goes to a State farm to teach women how to knit. Unlike a collective farm, where the worker is a shareholder, the State farm worker is an employee and is paid wages. Krista calls the women her 'birds' as this is a poultry farm. Perched on children's chairs in the farm's nursery school, the women are grateful for a chance to give their families the slip, have a drink with the girls (they all bring food and drink) and knit intricate sweaters for themselves, their husbands and their children. Krista is not paid for this, yet even in this busy show week she finds time to make the forty-minute journey to the farm and help her 'birds'. There are about fifteen women in her class and she gives them each a ticket for the show.

After the exhibition, there is just enough time to call in at the shop that stocks the Fashion House's limited-edition clothes before Krista has to meet her husband for a lift home. The shop has some jackets in and Krista is anxious to see how they are selling. It is an ordinary shop in the new part of Tallinn and the wares are displayed badly. Most of the clothes are depressingly drab. At the far end of the shop a queue starts to form.

The Soviet queue is an extraordinary phenomenon: it starts when one person sees a yet-to-be-unpacked delivery of goods. Within moments, a mass of people will be lined up throughout the shop and along the pavement outside. People smell a queue from afar and join it instantly. 'What are they selling?' a new arrival will ask of the person in front.

'No idea, let's wait and see.'

In order to be equipped for every eventuality, for who knows what might be available, the Soviet shopper carries plenty of ready cash and the familiar *avoska* bag. Most men carry briefcases, which rarely contain the papers one would imagine they do, but usually hold a good piece of fish that was on offer at the canteen at work, or some foreign (better-quality) soap. Today's queue is due to the sudden arrival of T-shirts. Notwithstanding the ice floes, spring is intermittently in the air. Krista's jackets are not in as great demand as the T-shirts, but sales are good.

Juhan, her husband, is waiting for her with their car, an old Moskvich pickup. 'We keep it because we can put Sargon [their St Bernard dog] in the back.' They kiss and exchange news of their respective day's work as they set off on their twenty-minute drive home. Juhan graduated from the Polytechnic Institute as an economic engineer. He is now vice-president of the Association of Estonian Handicraftsmen, 'Uku'. The Association employs 2500 people. 'We give them all the materials and tools they need and they work at home. When their goods are sold they get 60% of the price. We must preserve our national creativity, skills and knowledge and pass them on to the young.'

This cottage industry is most effective and the goods for sale in the shop on Tallinn's Pikk Street, the Association's outlet, are worth buying. Blankets, shawls, aprons, national costumes, jewellery are all on sale here. Again, prices are high. Upstairs there is a 'museum' which houses intricate national costumes and jewellery, and Krista often borrows accessories for her fashion shows. Livia, Krista's deputy and one of her designers, has national costume as her theme for spring. This is a subject that is approached with a great deal of respect and care; it is close to the heart of every Estonian. Krista and Livia have already spent a morning in the Pikk Street shop choosing appropriate brooches, necklaces and shoes. 'We have good and lovely customs,' says Krista, 'they must be preserved.'

In the basement of the shop on Pikk Street, what used to be a cellar is now a recreation area for staff and their guests. Ancient, winding stairs lead you down to several grottoed rooms, a kitchen and a sauna. Juhan often uses it when he and Krista want to have a party or a night out with several friends.

'We play music and dance in here. Those who want to can have a sauna and the other room is used by those who want to talk. It's much nicer than going to a restaurant where the bands play so loudly that you have to shout at each other.'

To have a place like this at your disposal is a rare luxury. Most Soviet citizens, when not entertaining at home, are forced to rely on restaurants. Restaurants in the Soviet Union are less places for eating and more venues for dancing and meeting new people. You go for the entire evening, arriving as early as 6 p.m. and leaving at 11 p.m., when all restaurants close. Anyone can come up to your table and ask you to dance. You may be mid-mouthful, but you will be expected to throw down your knife and fork, leave your half-finished meal and dance to the band who will be invariably playing covers of Western pop songs. Songs such as 'Feelings' and 'It Never Rains in Southern California' enjoy great popularity as do Italian romantic love songs.

In inviting someone to dance, strict protocol is observed. If there is a table of both men and women, and a man from another table wishes to dance with one of the women, he will first ask the permission of the men at the table. If they grant it and the woman herself refuses, the suitor will be most put out. How can the woman refuse when the men with her have agreed? After your dance, you will return to continue your now-cold meal, which was never more than warm in the first place. The band plays at a deafening pitch and renders conversation almost impossible.

Krista and Juhan prefer to go to one of Tallinn's quieter restaurants. One such place consists of several small dining rooms, in a beautiful building in the old lower town. It is more like a club and tables have to be reserved in advance. Food is served to you in rooms of classical elegance with views of old cobbled streets. Classical music plays quietly in the background. 'This way we can enjoy our food and our conversation. Afterwards we go to the cellar and make coffee, drink some more and dance.'

Krista and Juhan met through friends in 1963. They married five years later in 1968. 'We have a good marriage. You have to have respect for each other. I know my recent work would have been impossible for me if I didn't have Juhan. You have to feel that someone's shoulder is there for you.' They are an attractive couple and live their lives with gusto. Juhan is tall and good-looking, and like many Estonian men he wears a moustache. Both he and Krista have faces full of humour. Although they protest that Estonians, like Scandinavians, are shy and take time to get to know other people, Krista and Juhan are warm and friendly.

Home is just outside Tallinn in an area with a distinct feeling of the country. Many Estonians live in houses and do not have to suffer the cramped living conditions of their city-dwelling Russian neighbours. Krista and Juhan have a bungalow, situated in a large garden. They are childless, their family consisting of Sargon, an enormous animal with a distinguished pedigree, and two cats who are so deeply in love that they lie curled around each other at all times.

When Krista and Juhan met, Krista had a one-roomed flat in town. An elderly relative was living in the house. They swopped; the most common way of changing accommodation in the Soviet Union. Krista and Juhan have worked on the place themselves and what used to be a one-room house now has three rooms plus kitchen and bathroom. Their home serves further to reinforce their European nature. It is open and airy and the bigger of the two reception rooms doubles up as a bedroom. What is an ample sofa by day becomes their bed at night. There is a large fire-place immediately opposite it. 'We like to sit on the floor and watch the fire and drink "tiger's milk" – a delicious drink of cream mixed with spirit that Juhan's mother makes for us. It is deceptively smooth with a kick to it, just the sort of thing a tiger might produce.'

An evening spent at Juhan and Krista's is a relaxing, sensual affair. Coffee and sandwiches (the mainstay of Estonian life) are followed by a sauna. Estonians are firm believers in the cleansing, recuperative powers of the sauna. Early in the evening, Juhan stokes the small furnace with wood. 'We must wait until the temperature is right. It should be about 110°C, then you'll start feeling good.'

The fuel comes from the woodpile in the garden and there is no shortage. The small pine-covered sauna takes four comfortably and the whole process lasts some time with breaks for beer and dashes into the shower. Warm and glowing, it is now time to lie in front of the fire, sip tiger's milk and look through the large picture window at the still-blue sky. The den next door is a refuge of red walls and red velvet seating, a place to curl up and watch television with the cats who have appropriated it. The accent is on peace and comfort.

This is very different from Russia where people's homes are rarely comfortable. Sofas and chairs are hard and unyielding. This Estonian well-being is a welcome change. 'We don't have a dacha, but living here we don't need one. The garden's big enough to relax in and the sea's only fifteen minutes' drive away.' Juhan and Krista's contentment with each other and with their home is palpable and contagious. Apart from a visit to some close friends, they plan a cosy weekend at home before the rigours of the week ahead and the fashion show.

Their friends, Peter and Marya, live in a high-rise block of flats in an area of Tallinn that could just as easily be in Minsk or Tashkent with their depersonalised acres of concrete expanse. Krista and Juhan may not envy them their flat, but they do covet the view from their roof which looks far out to sea and over the old town, affording remarkable views at night. Tallinn is very far north and like Leningrad enjoys 'white nights' when the sun barely sets at all. Although it is only April, the sun is still high in the sky and doesn't set until 10 p.m. They have come by taxi in order that they may drink safely. It is against the law to drink at all if you are driving in the Soviet Union. If you are found to have had any alcohol at all, your licence will be confiscated immediately.

Estonians, in common with people all over the Soviet Union, are not averse to a glass or two. However, they are beginners in comparison with their Finnish neighbours. Every Friday, a ferry-load of Finns arrive from Helsinki for the weekend. They come for one reason; to drink Estonian vodka until they can no longer stand up. This has earned them the title of 'our four-legged friends' from their hosts. Vodka is much cheaper in Soviet Estonia than in Finland. While this may encourage drunken, undesirable visitors it is, nonetheless, a valuable source of foreign currency. For the tourist, picturesque Tallinn with its subterranean bars and atmospheric restaurants is far more hospitable than Moscow or Leningrad.

Party banners and slogans are conspicuous by their absence and the normally ubiquitous face of Lenin is rarely sighted. Last year, a prominent member of the Estonian Communist Party defected to Sweden with his wife, a well-known singer, leaving their year-old baby behind. This event was preceded by a demand from the Kremlin that greater attention should be paid to communist indoctrination and to the job of inculcating a spirit of Soviet patriotism among Estonians.

Estonia's strong national identity and reluctance to conform to the accepted Soviet norms of behaviour present Russia, the dominant republic, with a problem. People in positions of power and authority must be ideologically sound and dependable. Out and about in Tallinn, the visitor is treated with greater courtesy if he speaks a language other than Russian. This is an eloquent expression of the attitude towards the ruling culture. When Estonians go to Moscow, they stay in the Estonian hotel. 'It's all much more familiar for us there, we feel at home, the food is better.' Moscow itself is found to be culturally interesting, 'but far too big. We couldn't bear all those crowds, all that noise and bustle. Life is so much more peaceful here in our own little republic.'

Krista often has occasion to speak Russian, 'especially recently as everyone's getting interested in fashion, journalists, newspapers, radio. And not just when we're putting a show on.' She travels often to other parts of the Soviet Union. After the show in Tallinn, she and Tiina will take the models and the clothes to Moscow to an All-Union show. This is an annual event; only eight fashion houses are selected to show their collections. The Tallinn Fashion House has been a member of this select few for some years now. 'Once, Juhan was also there on his own business trip. We were booked into different hotels. I had to smuggle him into my hotel room. Can you imagine smuggling your own husband into your room? Then he managed to persuade his floor-lady to let me in.' Each hotel corridor is ruled by a woman who ensures that order prevails and gives you your key. 'But she would only let me stay for seven hours, then I had to leave. It was wonderful, just like having a secret affair.'

Booking into hotels is no easy matter for the individual. Reservations usually have to be made through an organisation by your place of work.

The idea of walking unannounced into a hotel lobby and requesting a room is anathema to Soviet hotel procedure.

There is a joke told in the Soviet Union: on his death, a Soviet citizen was asked whether he'd prefer to go to communist heaven or capitalist hell. The Soviet citizen, delighted to have free choice, opted for capitalist hell. A year later he asked God if he could transfer to communist heaven. God agreed. In communist heaven everyone gathered around him eagerly. 'Well, what's it like in capitalist hell?' 'Exactly the same as here. The work's identical, they're pumping water too.' 'How many hours do they work?' 'The same.' 'So what did you come here for if there's no difference?' 'Well,' said the Soviet citizen, 'there's a very big difference. There you have to work from eight in the morning to eight at night. But here, first there's a party meeting, then a conference, then another meeting, then there's time for a smoke and by then the pump could have broken down . . .'

In a sauna, one Estonian confided, 'The trouble with Russians is that they don't like working. Now we do, we like it.' And indeed, most Russians will do anything to avoid actually having to do any work. Two assistants in a shop will eye you with distaste as you enter, carry on their conversation and only on its leisurely conclusion stroll over to you with obvious reluctance. Not so in Estonia. There, meals are served quickly and efficiently, sales staff serve you as soon as they can. Krista and Juhan enjoy their jobs and devote their energies to them. Estonians are irritated at being held up by Russian laziness.

The weekend over, the next day or two are a whirl of activity for Krista. Last-minute problems, fittings, dress rehearsals fill every moment. Finally the clothes are packed in metal containers and taken off to the Sports' Hall which is to be the venue for the show. Things are still far from ready there: the catwalk is not yet built and chairs must be put out. The hall will hold 1500 people and the first show is already sold out. The show is held twice a day for three consecutive days. Posters around town have been advertising the event for the past two weeks. Tickets are two roubles each. The money goes on the hire of the hall, the models' wages, the music, the lights and the clothes themselves. With luck the Fashion House should break even.

Factory representatives have been sent complimentary tickets by Krista and Tiina. The day of the show has finally dawned. Krista feels as she always does before a show, a little nervous. 'I've been so busy I haven't eaten. Look at my skirt, it's falling off me.' Hundreds of women and the occasional man mill around outside waiting for the doors to open. Inside the models are still applying their make-up, and beginning to change modestly into their first outfits. They are wary of anyone with a camera in the changing area. A few years ago, Soviet TV made a programme about the show and filmed them changing. Photographs were taken and the snaps of bare breasts were then passed around, so the models are understandably afraid that any photographs of them will be peddled as pornography.

The Fashion House employs only four full-time models. For the show, many more are needed and non-professional models are hired. This show will see six male models, more than ever before. Some are students, one a taxi driver and one a lift mechanic. The work is not very well paid – one rouble for each fitting and larger sums for the shows themselves. But the amateurs really take part for the fun of it.

The atmosphere behind the scenes is building up and Leonid admits to feeling 'nervous, as usual'. The designers run around flattening a lapel here, tweaking a collar there. Krista, with a list of notes made during the rehearsal, gives final advice and, at the last minute, withdraws one dress from a collection. 'I actually don't like this collection at all. It really hasn't worked out, but what can I do? The designer is a lovely woman and I couldn't bear to upset her.'

At last, the music starts and the show is on. Leonid's designs lead to the beat of Santana. The show is much more impressive than one would have imagined possible. The models are, for the most part, well co-ordinated and stylish and they strike just the right balance between sullen boredom and pouting self-assurance that is the hallmark of all mannequins. The audience, made up of women of all ages, is enthralled. There is a section of children's wear and when the children come out, applause echoes throughout the hall. There is no quicker way to the Soviet heart than through a child. What was pleasure before turns now to rapture and the 'oohs' and 'aahs' are clearly audible as smiles wreathe the face of every spectator. As before, notebooks are out and designs hastily copied. The designers hold a secret ballot to see whose designs are best: Leonid comes first, Livia, with her national costume, is second. Juhan and Krista sit hand in hand in the first row. The show has gone well, designs are being bought by the factories. Next month's plan must now be fulfilled . . .

[O.L.]

NINE

The October Harvest

Our best hope is that the half-savage, stupid and dull people of the
Russian villages and countryside will die off.
Maksim Gorky, 1922

Mariya Kulinich is seventy-eight. She is an illiterate peasant woman who
has lived all her life in Starovelichkovskaya, a small village in the
farmlands of southern Russia's Kuban Valley. She was a child of ten when
the Russian Revolution took place, and a young woman of twenty-four
when her village and others around it were turned into a collective farm.
Her husband died in 1967, and out of the nine children she has borne, only
three sons have survived. They all work on the collective farm – Viktor, the
oldest, is a cinema projectionist; Aleksei drives one of the farmworkers'
buses; and Slava is a combine-harvester operator. They are a close family.
The three sons live with their wives and families (Mariya is five times a
grandmother) in neighbouring houses which they built themselves on the
site of their father's old cottage.

The families' homes belong to them, and they rent the land for about
twenty roubles a year. 'All land really belongs to the state,' says Viktor,
'but when it's next to my house it's really considered mine.' Mariya, known
to everyone as 'babushka' or Granny, lives with Slava in the middle house.
It is the only one with indoor plumbing and a real bath. Most of the time
the others make do with stand-pipes and improvised shower sheds in the
yard. There is a constant flow of family traffic between the three houses, for
although Slava has the bath, Viktor has the best television set, and
Aleksei's yard can fit the biggest dining table for family celebrations.

This summer Slava is anticipating two possible reasons to celebrate. He
is in the running for the collective farm's annual award for the most
productive combine-harvester operator. The prize is a cash bonus and
great public acclaim. If he wins, figures showing his winning yield will be
posted outside the main administration building; his photograph might
even be displayed together with the community's other leading workers.
The competition has been running since the beginning of the grain harvest
which now, in early July, is at its peak. Work in the fields lasts up to twelve
hours a day, seven days a week, until all the grain is in. It is a lucrative

period for Slava. He will be earning over 500 roubles a month, nearly three times the average national wage. Even during the rest of the year, when they drive tractors and ploughs and overhaul their machines, the combine-harvester operators are among the best-paid workers on the farm.

Slava's other cause for celebration should be the arrival of his first car. Like most Soviet motorists he paid for it in advance and has had to wait a year for delivery. He is lucky – if he lived in one of the northern cities the wait might be much longer. Here in the south the process is relatively quick. Owning a car is still a luxury in the Soviet Union. Even the cheapest model, the much-maligned Zaporozhets, costs around 4000 roubles. The more reliable Zhiguli, made in Russia under licence from Fiat, is 6000 roubles for the most basic model. And so few of them are produced that they are often more expensive second-hand than new!

With his savings over several years and a low-interest loan of 5000 roubles from the farm, Slava has chosen to buy the most expensive family car on the market – the Volga, at 15,000 roubles. It is the size of a Cortina, and exceptionally resilient to Russian winters. The other brothers share Slava's sense of excitement about the car. 'In the olden days,' says Viktor, 'peasants couldn't even dream of owning a car. Now most of us have our own transport – if not a car, then a motorcycle or bicycle.'

Mariya is less impressed with the trappings of modernity. Her memories go back to times of famine, civil war and German occupation, when even the most basic necessities were scarce. The suffering she has endured is written on her wrinkled, weather-beaten face. Her teeth are capped in silver. The veins in her arms and legs are swollen blue, but although she moves slowly and uncomfortably, her mind is still alert. 'I used to have a large family, nine children, but many of them died. Six of the poor souls passed away. Only three of them survived. When they were young they worked in the fields tending the cattle. Their father looked after the herd and they went with him.'

During the war her husband fought at the front while she eked out a living for herself and her children. 'We had to mill the grain ourselves to get flour. There was no fuel so we had to walk everywhere, seven miles every day to the fields and back. I'd leave home early in the morning and get back late, and find the children at home by themselves. We had a cow which I milked so they could have milk to drink. When our soldiers came through the village, they ate what little we had, they were so hungry. But there was no meat for them.'

Photographs taken just after the war show Mariya to have been a severe and formidable-looking woman. Since then, as material pressures have eased, she appears to have mellowed. Her experience of hardship has certainly not blunted her sense of humour. She speaks quietly and gravely, then laughs at her own gravity and shrugs off the sufferings of the past with a reminder that things are much better now.

Much of Mariya's daily life is occupied with old customs and skills that modern life on the farm have all but made redundant. While her sons and their wives are at work, she spends her days teasing wool by hand for spinning, or feeding the family's few animals. Even her language is old-fashioned, rich in peasant colloquialisms and proverbs which defy translation. In winter it is she who looks after the large stove which, in the time-honoured way, has pride of place in the middle of the house and provides heat for the whole building. She hardly ventures out before spring, when she paints the wooden window frames and shutters in bright blues and greens.

As a child Mariya was part of the vast rural population who took over ownership of the land after the Revolution. Her family were among the peasants in southern Russia who succeeded in cultivating their own land and feeding themselves adequately. But as the state paid such low prices for their produce, there was little incentive for the peasants to sell. When his great campaign to industrialise Russia gained momentum in the 1930s, Stalin desperately needed to procure grain from the countryside to feed the cities. He could not force millions of small and scattered peasant households to sell their grain, so he reorganised them into huge collective farms, often the size of whole villages. Only then could he control and requisition their output.

The process of collectivisation was fast and violent. In a series of convulsions across the countryside, huge quantities of land and livestock were brought into the new farms' ownership. Confused or defiant, the peasants slaughtered nearly half the nation's animals and burned large areas of cultivable land rather than hand them over. With the methods and language of a military campaign Stalin declared war on an enemy he called the 'kulaks'. Before 1930 the term had applied to village money-lenders, but Stalin used it to identify a class of richer peasants who, he claimed, had seized property illegally and were bent on sabotaging the revolution. Many poorer peasants took advantage of the mayhem to wreak brutal revenge on their more prosperous fellows. Thousands of kulaks were dispossessed, exiled, or worse. Stalin's hammer, it seems, was mightier than his sickle.

Nowadays families like the Kuliniches do not refer to the terror that accompanied collectivisation. Viktor and his brothers were born just too late to remember the upheavals of the early 1930s, and they do not question the benefits and durability of the system Stalin introduced. As on all of the Soviet Union's 26,000 collective farms, the land and the machines belong jointly to the whole community of peasants, who elect a chairman and board of directors to manage their affairs. They are obliged to sell the farm's crops and livestock to the State, which fixes quotas, prices and delivery dates. The collective farms account for roughly 60% of the country's agricultural output. The Kuliniches say they are relieved not to have to think about important decisions on the farm. Viktor finds the collective identity reassuring; it gives them all a stable and secure environment in which to work and raise their families.

'Our generation can't imagine what life would be like without the collective farm,' Viktor says. 'What would private farming be like? If all the land suddenly belonged to me, how would I cultivate it? It's a good thing to work collectively. The better the farm does, the more comfortably everyone in the village will live.'

The official history of the 1930s skates over the most disruptive aspects of collectivisation. On the ground floor of the farm's administrative building, a large room has been set aside for the Museum of Military and Labour Glory, which records the village's history in a series of faded photographs. Inside the museum the atmosphere is hushed and reverential. The displays show the founders of the farm, robust and resolute-looking, standing proudly in front of the first tractors. It shows how dismal the drudge of harvesting by hand had been before the new collective farm brought in modern machines. The 1930s are depicted as a time of heroic sacrifice and hard-earned progress.

The October Farm, named after the month of the Revolution in 1917, covers 65 square kilometres and has a population of 11,000 people. Its main crops are grain, beetroot, cucumbers and sunflowers for oil: all essential elements in the Russian diet. The centre of the farm – the administrative buildings, machine depots and most of the farmers' houses – is in Starovelichkovskaya, an old Cossack village dating from Peter the Great's time. Two hundred years ago the Cossacks were daring horsemen who resisted the Russian invaders in the nearby Caucasian mountains. Now the only trace of them is in the songs and costumes of the farm's folk choir who perform in the Soviet-built House of Culture. Descendants of proud Cossack steeds are now old and docile and employed as workhorses.

Aleksei drives his busfuls of workers to all the outlying areas of the farm. He shares the roads with horses and haycarts and the occasional truck. Private cars are rarer still. Fathers transport their families in motorcycles and sidecars; mothers balance toddlers on the crossbars of their bicycles.

Geese, ducks and the odd turkey wander across back streets rutted with dried mud. They must be awash in winter, when summer's greens and golds are replaced by muddy browns and greys. Here and there an old woman on a low stool keeps watch over the family cow grazing on a grass verge. In one direction a horse and cart passes. The driver wears a peasant tunic and a cloth cap. Ducks meander across their duckponds. From high in the trees rooks caw into the midday stillness. It is the kind of timeless, idyllic scene that Tolstoy and Turgenev described so fondly a century ago. Only the electricity pylons stretching into the distance and the occasional supersonic boom from the Soviet Air Force flying far overhead remind you that Russia is no longer a land of wooden ploughs and threshing flails.

The basic shape of the village has changed little since Tsarist times. The main street is straight and tree-lined. To each side of it houses and vegetable plots stretch back from the road. Beyond these the collective fields are widely spaced around the village perimeter. But now lamp-posts as well as trees line the avenues, and on the lamp-posts decorative posters have been nailed like Western billboards. They depict muscular tractor-drivers and heroic harvesters, idealised images of everyday life on the farm. Outside the main administration the posters quote selected statistics from the Five-Year Plan, and give the latest news about the farm's productivity competition with its neighbours. 'Bread for the motherland', a campaign against wasting bread, and another to help prevent bush fires by discouraging smoking in the fields, are waged through colourful roadside slogans. The cornfield is a battlefield in the onward march towards communism. Everywhere the responsible citizen is exhorted to fulfil his socialist obligations – to be a diligent worker and a vigilant patriot.

In the summer, one of Aleksei's routes takes him from the centre of the village, past the lake where the children swim and the horses are watered, and along three kilometres of shady avenues to the densely planted orchards. His busloads of women fruit-pickers in their cotton dresses and cheerful headscarves exchange a steady banter with Aleksei. He remembers one occasion when his bus broke down on the way to collect his passengers from the orchards. The women were temporarily left stranded and Aleksei has not been allowed to forget it. Of all the brothers Aleksei is the most reserved. Grey-haired Viktor does most of the talking when they are together, though when it comes to decisions and action Slava is the most energetic. He is certainly enthusiastic about the harvest. 'Our grain crops are the crown of everything,' he says. 'We work so hard we don't really think of the time passing.'

At its height the harvesting is an impressive sight. Rows of combine-

Doctor Svyatoslav Fyodorov riding Thunder while a groom rides his other horse

Above Winter at Fyodorov's dacha *Below left* Fyodorov relaxes in his dacha with a friend *Below right* Sashenka presents Fyodorov with flowers *Opposite above* Red Square in Moscow: St Basil's Cathedral and the Kremlin *Opposite below* Red Square: changing of the guard

Clearing the ice before the thaw

People's Judge Lyubov Bubulich opens the trial

Above left Timofei Podurets, the plaintiff *Above right* Tamara Russo, the defendant
Below People's Judge Lyubov Bubulich and one of her lay assessors

Above Moldavia: family celebration in the countryside
Below Traditional Moldavian dish made from maize flour: *Malalyga*

Moldavia: Beltsy children at May Day parade

harvesters, which we would call threshing-machines as they do not cut the corn themselves, crawl across the farm's enormous flat fields. In the distance these orange-painted contraptions look like giant mechanical insects gobbling up the corn, disgorging unwanted hay into piles behind them, and funnelling the grain into the trucks which trundle alongside. They move slowly and deliberately, throwing up clouds of fine corn dust between the gold of the fields and the blue of the sky. Slava and the other drivers are perched high in their cabins; from time to time their mates jump down to clear excess hay from the front blades. Otherwise, the process looks after itself. In the West such scenes would be the stuff of cornflakes' commercials. For Slava, they are further evidence of the modern miracle of mechanisation.

In addition to his wages Slava earns a share of the farm's produce – grain to feed the animals the family rears privately, and sunflower oil for cooking. Viktor's wife Shura is a general helper at the farm's granary yard, where the grain is taken after threshing, for sifting, drying and grading. Shura's and Slava's work earns them what Viktor calls 'a bonus, a perk for being a farmworker', in the form of food for the household. Partly because of such bonuses, Soviet farmers' earnings are for the first time growing at a faster rate than those of industrial and office workers.

Here in the south they are lucky. In the valley of the Kuban river the sun shines and the rain falls in the right proportions to guarantee high yields of good-quality wheat. The region where the October Farm is located is the nearest equivalent the Soviet Union has to the American wheat-belt. The land is rich and fertile, with some of Russia's finest orchards and vineyards. Since 1970 even rice has been cultivated, and with dramatic success. But the October Farm is by no means a showpiece. Neighbouring collectives have shinier machines, plusher buildings and boardrooms full of state medals. But as the October's director told us, with a hint of regret, 'We've got no Orders of Lenin, and too little topsoil.'

Elsewhere in the country much of Russian agriculture is bedevilled by drought, poor soil or inadequate sunshine. The grain harvest regularly falls below planned targets and forces the Soviet Union to import the shortfall from North America. While Soviet industry produces twenty-two times what it did in 1940, agricultural output is only two and a half times greater. The last Five-Year Plan called for improvements in food storage, transport and processing. Mikhail Gorbachev himself has complained that investment in collective farms is too low, while interference from above is too great.

Part of the reason for agriculture's low overall productivity can be found in the Kuliniches' back garden. Like collective farmers all over the country they grow fruit and vegetables and raise animals to earn extra money. Often this private enterprise is given higher priority than the collective fields. The family's plot backs onto their houses – lush and green, and bordered by fruit trees.

'We grow things we need from day to day,' says Viktor. 'Tomatoes, carrots, onion, garlic. We also breed pigs, chickens and ducks. When the animals are fattened we take them to the collecting-point on the farm where we can sell them, and exchange them for animal feed.'

During the day Mariya looks after the animals, chopping marrow for the pigs and shooing the dogs away from the chickens in the yard. An old tyre sliced in half serves as the chickens' water trough. In the summer huge flat fish caught in local streams hang on lines to dry like washing. Viktor, whose work at the cinema is usually in the afternoons and evenings, digs the garden.

Soon after collectivisation, despite Stalin's fears that the peasants would make illegal profits from them, the private plots were returned to individual households. Each family was allowed half a hectare per person for private use, and the rest of the farm's land remained collective property. On the October Farm small loans are available for buying seedlings and fertilisers. Over the whole country homegrown produce now provides, quite legally, about a third of all vegetables, fruit, milk, eggs and meat on sale. All this food does not, however, make its way into State shops, where prices are fixed by law. It is sold at markets, where the farmers themselves decide how much to charge. Prices are high, but the collective farm markets are often the only place to find fresh fruit, meat and vegetables.

Mariya is too old and frail to take the Kuliniches' surplus food to the small market in the village. That task is left to Slava's wife Valya, who goes perhaps ten times a year. Compared to town markets Starovelichkov-skaya's is small. Busiest at weekends, its few dozen stalls stand on open land to one side of the village's main square. The customers are mainly locals with no allotments of their own. Oversize tomatoes are the main attraction, but trade is slow. Shoppers on bicycles come and go. Old women gather to gossip. From a small cart a *kvas* seller dispenses glasses of his copper-coloured drink, which is fermented from stale bread. Across the road is a small cluster of state-run shops: a chemist, a kiosk selling magazines, a clothes' shop and the hardware store.

During the long summer days Mariya is at home alone. The grandchildren may be away at summer camp, where most Soviet children spend at least part of the summer; or the older grandsons may be doing temporary work in the fields. At home the radio is permanently switched on, a constant background noise to everyday life, though Mariya hardly seems to be aware of it. Twice a day, at 6 a.m. and 1 p.m., the local station manager interrupts Radio Moscow with a selection of local news and announcements. Paint is peeling off the walls in his tiny studio, though new premises and equipment are promised soon. For the moment the building and the broadcasts are rough and ready, with a shabby but sturdy practicality which seems typically Soviet. Above the electronic buzz of his transmitter the station manager reads from a single handwritten sheet details of meetings, entertainments and changes in the farm's work schedule. Virtually every home in the community has a set switched on all day, so the station's service reaches everyone. The Kuliniches still recall the day when a child got lost on the outskirts of the farm, and was reunited with his family following an urgent appeal on the radio. One of the station's more mundane tasks is to announce the programme at the farm cinema, where Viktor is the projectionist. Now in his late forties and prematurely grey, Viktor is a lifelong film enthusiast. 'My father took me to see my first film. It was soon after the war. They used to show films outdoors then. It was called *A Country Schoolteacher*. I remember it like it was yesterday.'

The open-air cinema is now abandoned and overgrown with weeds. Instead, the farm has built a new cinema where Soviet and selected foreign feature films are shown twice a night. The programme changes every couple of days, and Viktor says he has lost count of the number of films he has watched from his projectionist's booth.

Once a week children from the village kindergartens come to the cinema to see a programme of cartoons. 'They're popular with all ages,' says Viktor. 'I think it's the right kind of entertainment for kids.' The little girls wear bright blue and yellow ribbons; the boys have pointed red caps, showing they belong to the Pioneers. They march along the street towards the cinema in pairs, a regimented, colourful crocodile, babbling with enthusiasm.

Both Slava's and Aleksei's wives are also involved in the village's public services. Valya is a seamstress at the Farm's 'Centre for Everyday Services', which includes a laundry, a repair workshop for electrical goods and a production house making dresses. Clothes are expensive in ordinary shops, so the Centre offers simple dresses at specially reduced prices to farmworkers and their families. The most popular line is party dresses in flowery printed patterns. There is a touch of style in the frilly sleeves, but the designs are modestly cut – well below the knee and well above the cleavage. Much of the work is done by machine, but Valya herself sews the more intricate sections by hand.

Aleksei's wife Alla is the village's book purchaser. She orders books from Krasnodar, the nearest big town, and distributes them to the bookshop, the school libraries and individual subscribers. She is the only one of the adults in the Kulinich family to have completed her full ten years' schooling. For her children's generation, those ten years are now compulsory, and her son Seryozha is the first of the grandchildren in the family to finish school. He will not be continuing to higher education, so like most Soviet young men his first step into adulthood will be two years in the army. He has three months' grace before his eighteenth birthday in the autumn.

Apart from National Service there would be no need or incentive for the Kulinich grandchildren to leave the village permanently. In many other parts of Russia young people are abandoning the countryside for the material pleasures and skilled jobs of the towns. Some collective farms have been left with a shortage of trained specialists and physically strong labourers. But the southern steppes are a relatively attractive place to live. The older Kuliniches are certainly hoping that their children will stay. 'It's up to them,' says Viktor, who has two teenage sons. 'I can't guarantee they'll stay here; no one's forcing them. Of course, all parents would like to live with their kids. We're not as young as we were, and I hope they'll help us out.'

Since the war the shortage of labour in the Soviet Union has meant that both parents in a family have tended to work full-time, often leaving elderly grandmothers to look after the children. Mariya Kulinich is no exception. 'I've got one granddaughter and four grandsons – it was me who brought them all up. My sons were working and building their houses, so I looked after the children. They were always under my feet, the little terrors! They're growing up now, the older ones'll be starting work soon, so what's left for babushka to do? It's time for her to rest.' She chuckles to herself and for a few moments her thoughts seem to wander. Just as quickly she picks up the thread again. 'When we were youngsters we didn't live like they do now. People live well now. If only I could live now, but I'm too old and ill.' Once more she laughs at herself. 'Death can't be far away.'

Her only regret is that her children and grandchildren have not retained her own faith in God. In pre-revolutionary Russia the peasants used to keep one corner of the hut reserved for religious devotion. Mariya still has an icon hanging over the bed where she sleeps in Slava's house. But over the neighbouring bed a metre away her fourteen-year-old granddaughter Larisa has pinned photographs of her favourite film stars and pop singers.

'Young people don't go to church any more,' Mariya says. 'They don't believe any more. It's the women who go, the old women. I believe in God and go to church. I've had those icons since I was a little girl. I keep them because my father and mother kept them. We got our faith from our forefathers, who passed it on to us.'

Though Mariya is adamant about her faith, she knows that the family is only humouring her old-fashioned beliefs. She looks askance at Larisa's new idols, but the icons passed down through generations of uneducated peasants will have no place in the lives of her grandchildren, who have been schooled in Soviet atheism. 'I can't prove my faith to anyone. I'm illiterate. I can't read. Those who can read understand everything, but I never learned to read so I can't tell you what it all really means.'

A small church still operates on the farm, but the Soviet authorities no longer recognise church weddings. Instead they have provided a secular equivalent in the Palace of Weddings, where couples may get married with all the traditional trappings except God. The tradition of grand, expensive peasant weddings has endured into the 1980s. For the bride's father it is a matter of pride to offer his guests the most lavish hospitality possible. Champagne, vodka, enormous quantities of food, dancing and revelry will continue until the small hours, and restart with renewed intensity the following day, long after the bride and groom have discreetly disappeared.

Slava Kulinich expects his daughter Larisa, now fourteen, to stay on the farm until she too gets married. 'Then we'll see; maybe her husband will take her away somewhere.' Slava says Soviet education gives Larisa the same opportunity as boys her age to obtain qualifications and find work. But it is still customary for a young wife to join her husband's household, just as Slava's own wife, and his brothers' wives, did twenty years ago.

The Soviet Union's much-vaunted equality of the sexes was born of pragmatism. The post-war generation was so short of able-bodied men that women were obliged to work as tractor-drivers and road-builders. But the 1980s are seeing a gradual return to the traditional division of labour. On the October Farm men only drive the combine-harvesters; women tend to do labour-intensive work, such as fruit-picking. The roadgangs resurfacing the route from Krasnodar to the farm use men to operate the steam-rollers and women to shovel the tar. Men drive cars or motorcycles; women ride bicycles. While the Kulinich grandsons tinker with their mopeds, Larisa does the washing-up.

The most senior woman official on the farm is the Director of Fruit Production. She is a large, red-faced lady with imposing presence, who has spent her whole life in the village. She has just returned from a trade-union sponsored trip to England, one of the lucky few in the Soviet Union allowed to travel abroad. She was evidently impressed by the range and quality of goods in English shops. 'But no one could afford to buy all those beautiful things. Your people must be poor, I hardly saw anyone in your shops.' To a woman brought up in a society where demand by shoppers always exceeds supply from manufacturers, the only interpretation of the absence of long queues in London's high streets was that the English simply could not afford the expensive items on sale. No amount of arguing could persuade her otherwise.

As the harvest period nears its end Slava is told that he has narrowly failed to win the combine-harvester of the year award. The folk choir, the accordion-player and the dancing-girls from the high school will not be coming to the Kuliniches' house this year to fête the winner. A worker from a rival section to Slava's will carry off the prize instead. Slava is quietly proud of the work he does, but he does not seem overly disappointed to have missed out on such a public honour.

Far more exciting is the news from Krasnodar that his Volga is finally ready for delivery. All he has to do is arrange to take a couple of hours off work to go and collect it from the depot 65 kilometres away. But there is a problem. Although he has been a combine-harvester operator for fifteen years, Slava has not yet passed his driving-test. 'It can wait,' he says. 'The main thing is to get the car. Then I'll go to classes, learn the traffic regulations and take the test.'

So it is Aleksei who drives the car back to the village, with Slava in the passenger seat. It arrives without licence plates and windscreen wipers, and is covered in grease from the factory, but the whole family is delighted with it. Slava's normal self-restraint evaporates as he sits behind the wheel experimenting with the controls. Viktor examines the car radio, while Mariya is persuaded to climb in the back seat. 'Try it out for size,' Viktor jokes. To her own surprise and everyone else's she likes it so much she has to be coaxed out to join the rest of the family in a celebratory meal.

A duck has been roasted, pies have been baked, and the obligatory vodka is on the table. 'You've got to drink to a moment like this,' says Viktor earnestly, as if the new arrival will not be properly theirs without the appropriate toasts. It is a kind of baptism by fire-water.

'Congratulations Slava! Here's to you learning to drive and taking us all out!' Viktor raises the first toast, and many others follow.

'Let's take babushka out for a ride, too!'

'Here's to the car not breaking down!'

'To a successful end to the harvest!'

For the Kuliniches the car is a shared prize and a shared triumph. Slava says how pleased he is that they will no longer have to rely on public transport when they go away. Trips to the Black Sea resorts and the Caucasian mountains are already being planned. Their enthusiasm suggests that despite the ethos of social ownership cultivated by the collective farm, personal property and individual initiative are still enduring values.

After the party Slava will return to the fields to complete his day's work. The routine of the collective farm is central to the lives of families like the Kuliniches. But with their flourishing private gardens, their backyards full of privately reared animals, and a brand-new car in the drive, they seem, like many Russian peasants, to have discovered their own version of the communist way of life – Leninism with loopholes.

[A.B.]

TEN

Sumgait Strikers

Sport not only strengthens the body. It develops the mind, teaches attentiveness, punctuality and precision of movement. It cultivates will-power, strength and skill – the virtues that should distinguish Soviet people.
N. A. Semashko, Commissar for Health, 1918–30

On Thursday evenings the footballers from the Lenin Pipe-Rolling Mill in the Caspian Sea town of Sumgait arrive early for training. This is partly a sign of their enthusiasm – the season is reaching its climax and the team has qualified for the finals of Sumgait's town championship. But it is also because the women's aerobics class uses the gym before them. Leotards, rock music, rows of gyrating bodies in shapes to suit every taste beats a kickaround outside or a quick cigarette round the corner before the trainer turns up.

Trainer Ragin Magerramov arrives right on time. He bounces a ball impatiently at the side of the gym as if to remind the aerobics teacher that her time is up, and more serious sportsmen are waiting to take the floor. Ragin is a small, dark, wiry man. With his slight frame he looks more like a jockey than a footballer. But at forty-two he has been the factory football trainer for eleven years, and played inside forward in the team before that. Like all his players he has a full-time job at the factory – he is a machine-tools specialist. Football is his voluntary 'social work'. He helps keep the workers fit and organises matches with neighbouring factories. Friendly rivalry, a bit of fun at weekends.

That's the theory. The town championship may be of little importance compared to the national leagues fought for by teams such as Dinamo Kiev and Moscow Spartak, but the emotions it arouses are just as intense. Ragin has never heard Bill Shankly's famous dictum that 'football should not be treated as a matter of life and death – it's much more important than that', but he laughs at it and nods. 'That's how we play, too. Azerbaidzhanis are a passionate people, we play to win.' As he races round the gym in his distinctive blue tracksuit, chasing the ball like a sixteen-year-old, barking instructions to his players, blowing the whistle jammed between his lips, there is no doubting his commitment.

According to Ragin, the factory's 9000 workforce is equally enthusiastic. 'The workers here are real fans. Every year there's terrific competition in the factory for places in the squad.' This is plausible enough, but when we met the deputy director of the factory he expressed surprise that the factory even had a football team. 'Ice hockey's my game,' he told us apologetically.

The factory sports club, which owns the gym and finances the team out of trade-union funds, is called *Polad* – 'Steel' – the Pipe-Rolling Mill's main product. As well as aerobics and football, the club runs athletics, basketball, wrestling and judo teams, and climbing expeditions into the Azerbaidzhani mountains. There is also a section called 'radio-sport' for CB radio hams. Only in the Soviet Union, it seems, can a hobby meant for individuals alone in trucks and attics be organised collectively. Aerobics has spread rapidly across the country, even to remote towns like this one. Its popularity is in combining the Soviets' love of taking exercise *en masse* with their fascination for modern Western music. Tass has recently even announced that a new aid agreement with Ethiopia will provide for two Ethiopian sportsmen to visit Moscow to learn how to teach aerobics! It makes a change from arms shipments, but what use starving Ethiopians will have for the Russian version of Jane Fonda's routines is hard to imagine.

The sports club chairman is a former football star for the Azerbaidzhani Republic side. In his heyday he was made a 'master of sport', the most prestigious of many decorations awarded to Soviet sportsmen by the State. In middle age he has grown plump, chain-smokes, and fills his office with sporting trophies and pretty secretaries. But he follows the players' progress closely and hammers out team selection with Ragin.

Polad have qualified for the annual finals with teams from five other factories, transport depots and construction sites. That Polad have never won the competition is mainly thanks to their arch-rivals Kaspii, the team from the Synthetic Rubber Factory, who regularly beat them into second place. Polad and Kaspii are generally acknowledged to be the best teams in town. Ragin remembers last season's match with them bitterly. 'We were winning 2–1 with a minute to go, and they scored. 2–2! We lost on penalties. Games between us have always been very competitive. They usually beat us very narrowly, 1–0 or 2–1. I don't deny they're a stronger team, with a lot of experience, and good team play.'

Earlier in the season Polad lost 5–0 to Kaspii, though Ragin is quick to point out that his first choice goalie was not playing that day. Revenge is overdue. Kaspii, quite simply, are the team to beat. 'It'll be a needle match, always is.'

The big match with Kaspii is still a week away. Before that, Polad have two games to play, which they expect to win. The first is on a Saturday morning against the Aluminium Works. For a nominal fee the clubs hire Sumgait's sports stadium, which stands impressively on the shore of the Caspian Sea. It has seats for 6000 spectators (though no more than a couple of hundred will turn up for this match), floodlights and a press box, also empty.

As the teams come on, it is striking how unlike Russian sportsmen they look. Ethnically, the Azerbaidzhanis are a Turkic people. About half of their total population live between the Caspian Sea and the Iranian border, in the Soviet Republic of Azerbaidzhan. The rest are in Iran itself or Iraq. The players look too frail for football. Their faces are slim and swarthy and, like practically all young Azerbaidzhani men, they sport thick black moustaches. Although they all learned Russian at school, when they yell at each other for the ball, or question the referee's eyesight, they speak their native Azerbaidzhani, a language closer to Turkish than Russian. Under Bolshevik rule since 1920, Azerbaidzhan's Muslim culture has slowly been absorbed into the Soviet way of life. Indeed, imported sports like football were one vehicle for integrating far-flung ethnic groups into Russian majority culture.

The Aluminium Works present no problems to Polad who run out 3–0 winners. But Ragin is not satisfied with his players' performance. 'We should be scoring more goals, we had plenty of chances. I've got no complaints about the defence, but our strikers are not alert enough. We need someone really tenacious.' In the dressing-room after the game most complaints are directed at the two forwards, Mekhraddin and Willi. Mekhraddin scored a goal but is accused of being selfish on the ball. Willi is eighteen, a relative newcomer to the team, talented and fast. But he has had difficulty settling in and today he had a quiet game. Some of the older players are beginning to grumble. 'We need someone who is really going to push forward . . . You had the ball about eighty times and only passed it twice!'

Ragin has other problems, too. The Kaspii trainer Aziz Alishanov was at today's match, spying. Ragin and Aziz are old sparring partners. They joke about the big match next weekend, but beneath the jocularity there is tension, for Aziz is a good friend and admirer of Ragin's goalkeeper Seryozha, who by common consent is the best in town. Polad rely on Seryozha's good form to hold their defence together. Could Ragin be worried that the rival trainer is trying to poach Seryozha, by getting him a job at the Synthetic Rubber Factory and making him eligible for Kaspii?

'As a trainer it bothers me. Seryozha has been approached several times. But no trainer would agree to let his protégé go. And I have faith in my lads. Seryozha won't go, whatever factory makes him an offer.'

One man who would not be sorry to see the back of young, clean-cut Seryozha is the veteran reserve goalie Valera. He used to be Ragin's first choice until the twenty-one-year-old trainee machinist joined the factory. Valera is thirty-three, a welder by trade, and he knows his days between the posts are numbered. With ten minutes to go against the Aluminium Works Ragin sends Valera on as substitute. A less optimistic soul than Valera might see that Seryozha has been taken off to save him for later, more important contests, but Valera thinks he is being given a chance to regain his place. Within a minute he dives dramatically to take the ball off the toes of an opposing forward. For his trouble he gets a boot in the face, but despite the pain he is determined to go on.

Off the field Valera will tell you proudly about his physical resemblance to the great Italian World Cup goalkeeper Dino Zoff, and he has photos to prove it, but the likeness fades fast when you watch him play. Ragin is blunt. 'Valera has no self-confidence. When he comes out for the ball he loses his nerve and gets out of position. And he's no good at running the defence. He should be telling defenders who to mark, when to tackle. He should call for the ball.'

At Polad's next training session Valera and Seryozha take turns in goal as the other fires in shots. Valera's enthusiasm is unabated. He tells Seryozha to shoot as hard and fast as he can. Seryozha obliges. In the opposite goalmouth Ragin has his forwards practising shots from outside the penalty area. It is Sunday morning, and the rest of the stadium is full of athletes of all ages, jogging, jumping, throwing, sprinting. Tracksuited coaches monitor their efforts with stopwatches and tape-measures; music blares out from giant loudspeakers.

The scene will be the same at stadiums and sports grounds across the Soviet Union. For sport in the USSR is more than fun and games. Russians often ask if you play sport. If you do, they nod with approval. If you don't, you sense their disappointment not only in your physical fitness but in your mental discipline too. Participation in sport is regarded as part of a good citizen's duty. It contributes to a healthy social order, and it combats drunkenness and boredom. It is a way of rallying the people to government and Party organisations.

Many of the athletes in the Sumgait stadium are trying to pass their 'GTO badge' – a sign of merit awarded by the State to those *Gotov k Trudu i Oborone* – 'Ready for Work and Defence'. To qualify you have to pass a series of tests – from running and swimming to rifle-shooting and throwing hand-grenades (putting the shot tends to stand in for the real thing) – and learn the rudiments of first aid and civil defence. The aim is a national fitness programme which cultivates physical well-being, productivity and patriotism on a mass scale.

Sporting achievements have also given the Russians much-sought-after recognition on the world stage. The Soviet government and people cherish their Olympic champions and ice hockey heroes. Disappointment at missing the Los Angeles Olympics in 1984 was deep and widespread. For sportsmen and women, success brings prestige at home and travel abroad, which is for many the biggest prize of all. Intriguingly, while musicians and ballet-dancers regularly take advantage of foreign tours to defect to the West, Soviet athletes never do. The Soviet Union seems to be better at satisfying its sportsmen than its artists.

Ragin is close to his players but strict too. Smoking and drinking are forbidden altogether (a typically Soviet rule, absolute and unenforceable), even though Ragin smokes heavily himself. As a trainer he favours the psychological approach. 'I used to be a player once and I know how to deal with the lads. Footballers have different characters. If someone makes a mistake, you have to find a way of talking to him. It's no use yelling, his morale and spirits will fall.'

Half his job, he says, is to reassure the players and calm their nerves. But when his team is playing Ragin paces nervously along the touch-line smoking, worrying, wishing he could be out there. 'First of all, a trainer must have self-control. He must have strong nerves. Imagine it – ninety minutes of tense play. The players run around, pass, take chances, and there's the trainer suffering for a whole hour and a half!'

Ragin's competitiveness spills over into the backgammon he plays at home with his brother. They hurl their dice noisily against the side of the board and slam their pieces down. They play with bewildering speed, only exchanging grunts and exclamations as the throw of the dice dictates the course of the game. Ragin lives with his wife and four children in a three-room apartment in one of the many five-storey blocks outside the town centre. His oldest son is fourteen, another budding footballer who trains with the Spartak Car Depot team.

Football is never far from Ragin's mind. He has been writing a novel for five years, 6oo pages of it so far. Its subject – life, love . . . and football. His characters are taken from his observation of the everyday life of footballers. 'Some writers are famous, some footballers are famous. But to be introduced as a trainer-writer, that would be something,' he laughs. His novel is not yet published, but Ragin is hopeful. 'I'll submit it, then I'll wait.'

But what does his wife think about all the football fanaticism? If she wanted to object, she is not given the opportunity. In this male-dominated Azerbaidzhani society Ragin answers for her. 'A wife understands these things. A sportsman is a sportsman. If he has to go to training, or travel away from home for an important match, she understands. You go home and she asks how the game went. If you lost she's in a bad mood and so are you. If you won everyone celebrates. A footballer's wife is also a fan.'

But when centre-forward Willi goes home, criticisms of his play still ringing in his ears, his family are not greatly interested. For a start his brother and sister-in-law, who share the flat with Willi and his parents, have just had a baby son, who is the centre of attention. Willi is not married, he and babies do not seem to get on, so he escapes to the living-room to watch television. There on the wall is a small plaster bust of Stalin, relatively common here in the Caucasus. Stalin himself came from Georgia, the next-door Republic to Azerbaidzhan. To many people in these parts his name still evokes healthy virtues of discipline and a resolute approach. Taxidrivers often keep cigarette card-size portraits of him on their dashboards.

On Monday morning Ragin and the players make their way into work at the factory. Some live a short bus ride away, others travel up to half an hour by trolleybus from the outlying suburbs. Valera lives in a village well outside Sumgait, a far cry from the Italian luxury which his hero Dino Zoff no doubt enjoys.

Sumgait is only thirty-five years old, one of thousands of new Soviet towns built since the war. A population of 200,000 has grown up around the industrial park of chemical and metallurgical plants. The smoke-stacks, the pylons, the bleak apartment blocks and the endless convoys of khaki-coloured trucks all make for a desolate landscape. After the war construction was an urgent priority all over the country. There was no time for the niceties of town planning – and it shows. In the middle of town there are vast empty spaces where new buildings are planned. By the sea a wrecked coaster has been tugged to within reach of the forlorn-looking beach where one day it will be converted into a restaurant. In spite of its new market centre and its ivy-covered Party headquarters, Sumgait still gives the impression of an overgrown settlement that has not had time to mature into a city.

Azerbaidzhan owes its rapid industrial development to one source – oil. Before the Revolution primitive wells and sludge pumps extracted oil from just below the surface. In recent years, as most accessible reserves have declined, deep underwater drilling in the Caspian Sea has taken over. The steel pipes for this are produced at the Lenin Pipe-Rolling Mill.

In many ways the factory is typical of big Soviet plants: security checks at the gate (to stop outsiders entering and State property leaving); slow-moving trains shunting to and fro; workers in hard hats and scruffy jackets waiting for something to do; steam rising from mysterious vents; the whole atmosphere thick with lethargy and pollution.

The players from Polad work in almost every part of the factory, though they seem to be spared the heaviest and noisiest work – the foundry, with its fountains of molten steel and sparks exploding twenty metres in the air, and the deafening rolling-mill, where red-hot steel rods a metre thick are hollowed out into pipes. Alik, the team captain, is a maintenance supervisor in the electronics shop. Willi is a lathe operator, Valera a welder. Gosayan, a forward, runs the factory canteens and food stores. Midfield player Aiden is the driver's mate on the locomotive that carries the steel from the foundry to the Mill. His fellow half-back Farkhad is one of two artists employed by the factory to design political posters. He has stencilled the English word 'painter' on the back of his overalls. While the others have pictures of international soccer stars on their walls, Farkhad's office pin-ups are photo-kits of 'new Soviet man' and 'new Soviet woman', models for the figures he draws. On the wall beneath them is a poster of Mick Jagger. The remaining players are an assortment of metal-cutters, loaders and general labourers.

There are two places in the factory which none of the players recall going to. One is the orchard, where retired and invalid workers supply the factory canteens and kindergartens with figs, pomegranates and other fruit. The other is the so-called 'relaxation rooms'. Here, a factory manager told us, the workers may go at any time to unwind. The first of the two rooms has all the aids to relaxation of a Western dentist's waiting-room: colour magazines, ornamental rock pool, a full wall-size picture of a forest in spring, and goldfish. The second room offers a slide-show of soft-focus scenes from nature – summer flowers, silver birch trees, shady avenues – accompanied by soothing music and bird-songs. Apparently, the management has decided that the workers need a rest from the foggy, barren landscape outside. But no one takes up their thoughtful offer, and the doors seem to be permanently locked. To their credit the workers seem to have rejected this bizarre therapy.

This week half-back Aiden is on second shift, and so he is at home during the day with his wife, who is pregnant, and her parents. They have been married nearly two years, since Aiden finished his military service. He still wears his hair army-style, cropped close to his skull. 'I got used to having it that way,' he says. Apart from football, his passion is collecting records, especially modern Western music. This is no easy task. If he lived in Moscow he might have acquaintances who travel abroad and bring back records. He might be able to buy them from tourists or get hold of pirated tapes. But in Azerbaidzhan he has to rely on official channels.

The Soviet recording company 'Melodiya' remakes some of the more respectable Western albums under licence, but as with all foreign products, they are in short supply. Aiden knows some of the tricks of finding 'deficit' goods, as they are called. 'The best thing is if you know someone at the shop. They can tell you when new records are in.' Or, though Aiden does not say as much, they might put records aside for you in return for some other deficit product you can obtain. Ordinary, over-the-counter shopping is a pretty forlorn business. 'Sometimes at the end of the month the shops put things on sale they've been keeping back. On the last day of their sales plan there might suddenly be something new.'

By the time Polad's next match comes round, the last before Saturday's big game against Kaspii, Ragin has again had to tell his reserve goalie Valera that he is not in the team. His heroics as substitute in the previous match were in vain. Today the opposition is 'Sintez', the organic synthesis plant. 'We need two points from this game so we can face Kaspii in a calmer frame of mind,' says Ragin. In the dressing-room before the game his tactics are straightforward.

'It's slippery out there. Lots of water on the pitch. Shoot when you can. Try to shoot from distance, and leave the rest to Allah. And stop them getting their shots in.'

As they are about to go out, Ragin suddenly realises that they are wearing the same colour shirts as their opponents. It is a bad omen. The second strip is hurriedly found – yellow shirts instead of red – and Ragin has a last word with his captain Alik about marking the opposing forwards tightly. The first half is a disaster. Ironically, it is Alik's poor backpass in the pouring rain that allows Sintez to score. Ragin sends on a substitute to bolster his midfield which has been losing out to the muscular organic synthesists. To compound Polad's misery a knot of supporters under umbrellas are chanting 'Sin-tez, Sin-tez' from the stands.

At half-time the dressing-room is bedlam. Ragin has been agitated and impatient watching from the touch-line. Now he is furious. The team's normal camaraderie evaporates. Accusations and counter-accusations are hurled across the room.

'Willi should have shot – he was only three metres from goal!'

'Mekhraddin, you stand like a nail fixed in one place!'

'Why is no one on the right wing?'

'There's no coordination . . . You're not trying hard enough.'

In the second half the rain gets heavier and the sky darker. The stadium's floodlights are not working because of damage done by an earlier storm, so the match ends in virtual darkness. Despite sustained pressure on the Sintez goal, Polad's equaliser does not come. They lose 1–0, and the championship is thrown wide open.

The precise implications of the result are hard to discover. Ragin knows it's bad news, but given the arcane points system operating in the tournament, only the chief referee can clarify the situation. Amazingly, he appears to be the only man in town with a complete set of match results and an understanding of the subtleties of goal average and goal difference. And he has gone home. As happens so often in Soviet life, the simplest piece of information is a nightmare to find.

By evening tempers have cooled. A group of players, and Ragin, meet at Gosayan's house to watch European football on television. Gosayan is a popular host – not only does he have a colour TV, but as catering manager at the factory he can be relied on to put on a good spread after the match. Indeed, the generous paunch that he has developed since he took on the catering job worries Ragin, for the trainer's nippiest striker has lost some of his speed.

The players are well informed about foreign football, and endlessly curious. Are there factory teams in England? Are their facilities better or worse than ours? How come Liverpool have started the season so badly? Why do so many English stars go to play in Italy? That could never happen here, they say. Russian footballers would stick with their Spartaks and Dinamos out of pride and patriotism.

Indeed, many of the problems besetting British football are a mystery to Soviet spectators. Violence on the terraces is virtually unknown. There are no lucrative contracts, no large transfer fees, and no football pools. To us a Soviet match would probably seem a tame affair, with discipline on the pitch and sobriety off it. But on rare occasions football games have been the scene of political protests. In 1977 a match in Vilnius, the capital of Lithuania, between a local side and a Russian team erupted into a Lithuanian nationalist demonstration. Anti-Russian chants during the game were followed by rioting outside the ground, as the crowd tore down banners celebrating the 60th anniversary of the Revolution.

To the authorities the trouble with sport is its spontaneity. Unexpected

Above Krista Kajandu (left) gives last-minute advice to one of the models
Below Leonid Girin's collection: spring coats

Leonid Girin – Krista's best designer

Above Two of the models find time for a chat and a cigarette

Below Tallinn: view of the old city

Mariya Kulinich at home in Starovelichkovskaya

Above Ragin Magerramov presides over a training session of Polad, the Lenin Pipe-Rolling Mill's football team in Sumgait

Below Willi, Polad's centre-forward, is a lathe operator at the Pipe-Rolling Mill

Above Tatyana Naumova with a Hero of Socialist Labour
Below Tatyana Naumova congratulates newly-weds in Nakhodka's town hall

Above Kindergarten children perform under Lenin's watchful eye
Below Nakhodka town hall

Above Sergei in rehearsal
Below Sergei Kuryokhin and Boris Grebenshchikov

incidents can flare up without warning, a particularly sticky problem when a match is being covered live on television. On one famous occasion in the late 1970s, a fight broke out during an ice hockey game between the Soviet Union and Czechoslovakia. As the Russians and Czechs wielded their hockey sticks and wrestled each other to the ice, the camera pulled out to give the widest possible shot of the arena, until the brawling players looked like tiny flies mating on the ice. Meanwhile the commentator covered the lull in play with a few well-chosen banalities.

This particular evening four Soviet teams – two from Moscow, one each from Minsk and Dnepropetrovsk – are playing in Europe's three club tournaments. To be successful in Europe, alongside teams such as Liverpool and Juventus, would be a big boost to Soviet pride. For all the popularity of football in the country, both the national side and the club teams are relative failures in the international game. The policy of catching talent early and cultivating it in special sports schools with high-class coaching and equipment has not yet produced a star-studded Russian team. The Soviet Union has never won the World Cup, and in twenty years of trying, Soviet clubs have won just one European competition. It is a curious paradox that a society so geared to collective performance achieves better results in individualist events like gymnastics, field athletics, weight-lifting and chess, than it does in team games like football.

At the players' final training session before Saturday's game Ragin's post-mortem on the 1–0 defeat is frank. He identifies the lack of team cohesion as Polad's biggest problem. 'The team doesn't play together. Everyone plays his own game. You hold on to the ball too long. Too much individualism!' Technique and good shooting are all very well, he tells them, but a footballer must also have vision. He must be able to read the game, to know where his colleagues are instinctively. Ragin singles out individual failures. Aiden was lazy, Vaghiz made mistakes in defence, Nadir should have left his personal problems in the dressing-room. Briefly, tempers flare up again. 'Who are you to criticise me?' someone asks.

'If you don't want to play, go and join another team,' Ragin responds. 'What a friend says to you shouldn't hurt.'

On the morning of the big match Ragin discards his blue tracksuit in favour of a suit and tie. Win or lose, this is a special occasion. Alik gives his boots an extra polish and checks the studs, perhaps to help prevent another slip like Wednesday's. The pitch is still wet, which should help Polad by hampering Kaspii's more sophisticated skills. A respectable crowd for a Saturday morning has turned up. In the dressing-room Ragin announces his final selection – Willi retains his place, Aiden has been dropped, again there is still no place for Valera in goal. Music greets the teams as they emerge on to the pitch. The two trainers shake hands and exchange the traditional Russian pre-match greeting. 'The field is flat, the ball is round, let battle commence!'

The match starts quietly, no one wants to make an early mistake. Kaspii build up their attacking moves slowly from midfield. Their play lacks urgency, there is even a hint of complacency as they taunt Polad with their one-touch passes. The first clear chance falls to Willi, but he shoots over the bar. Kaspii's tall central defenders are thwarting Polad's forwards, but the pressure begins to tell with a series of niggling fouls in the Kaspii half. After thirty minutes the big electronic scoreboard shows 0–0.

The most animated part of the ground is the Polad bench where Ragin and his substitutes cannot sit still in their agitation. Ragin yells at his forwards to attack down the left wing where the defence looks weaker. Another effort goes wide, and Ragin paces along the touch-line, smoking and fretting. You can't afford to miss chances against Kaspii. Suddenly, a free kick on the edge of the penalty area, the shot rebounds off the wall and breaks for Polad to score. The substitutes leap off the bench as one man. For a moment Ragin is ecstatic, then his anxiety increases again. How can he defend his lead? Within minutes he has sent on his tallest substitute to strengthen the defence. Both goalkeepers make good saves. Ragin is visibly glad to have reliable Seryozha in goal.

Polad's narrow lead does not prevent more recriminations in the dressing-room at half-time. This time Willi should have shot instead of passing, the marking is poor, Alyosha must be blind. One player is in tears, inconsolable. He is substituted early in the second half.

Evidently Kaspii have also had a talking-to at half-time. They restart the game with greater urgency, putting Polad's defence under real pressure. For a few minutes it looks like their class may yet tell. But midway into the second half Polad break away and Mekhraddin scores a marvellous goal from 25 metres. Kaspii are broken. Before the end Mekhraddin scores two more goals in a minute, first running on to a long centre from the right, then shooting through a crowd of players in the penalty area for the fourth goal. When the final whistle goes, the scoreboard shows the final score: Polad 4, Kaspii 0. The result exaggerates the difference between the two teams, but Ragin will not let that detract from his triumph. 'If we beat a stronger team, it's the trainer takes the credit. It means I've got something out of the team I've been striving for.'

By his own admission Ragin is a romantic. In his novel the guy gets the girl. 'When people love each other,' he says, 'I hate it when one of them leaves. I like to write about people who are really in love.' And in his dreams, which today have come true, he finally beats Kaspii. But his joy is short-lived. Three days later in the last match of the tournament, Kaspii lose again, this time to Sintez, the Organic Synthesis team who beat Polad earlier in the week. Their two surprise wins put Sintez ahead of Polad by one point to clinch the championship. What's the Azerbaidzhani for 'sick as a parrot'?

[A.B.]

ELEVEN

An Office on the Pacific

> The Communist Party is the vanguard of the proletariat.
> V. I. Lenin

Everyone in Nakhodka admires Tatyana Naumova's energy. At work she is a paragon of Soviet virtues – diligent, dedicated and genuinely enthusiastic about the tasks she has been elected to perform. Her job as secretary of the town council makes her the fifth most important person in local government after the mayor and his three deputies. At home she struggles to conform to the other Soviet ideal of devoted wife and selfless mother. Still only thirty-three, Tatyana has risen steadily through all the right Komsomol and Communist Party channels, and as a Party member is well versed in the canons of Soviet orthodoxy. But faceless bureaucrat she is not – her story shows her to be more than just another career-minded *apparatchik*.

Nakhodka in Russian means 'a lucky find'. The place was given that name in 1859 by sailors in trouble in rough seas off the Russian Pacific coast who happened upon the sheltered bay by accident. The name stuck, and the ice-free bay became a port for fishermen and merchant ships – and for thousands of political prisoners bound for the Far Eastern camps. Since 1950 a fast developing city has grown up in the shape of a horseshoe around the sixteen-kilometre shore.

When the sun rises over the Pacific Ocean in Nakhodka, it is only midnight in Moscow. Muscovites are fond of reminding foreigners that the Far Easterners see in the New Year up to ten hours before they do. Nine thousand kilometres of Trans-Siberian Railway separate Moscow from the terminals in Vladivostok and Nakhodka. The Soviet Far East itself covers a vast area, stretching 5000 kilometres from Alaska to the Chinese border. In the wintry north it boasts reindeer and walruses, while in the balmy south grapes and wild pears grow. The foreign tourists in Nakhodka come from Japan and Korea; visitors from Europe are an exotic rarity. When Tatyana talks of 'going to the West' she means Moscow.

But despite the distance from the capital Nakhodka is very much a

Soviet city. Eighty per cent of the population are Russians, as the indigenous peoples of the Far East tend to live further north, away from the large settlements. The political system, too, is the same as in the rest of the country. The town council of which Tatyana is secretary is chosen by elected representatives, while the town hall where she works is dominated, geographically and politically, by the local headquarters of the only political party in the Soviet Union, the Communist Party.

'Go and see Naumova' is a phrase commonly heard in the town hall corridors. Those who do will find a courteous and composed woman behind a desk piled high with papers. She is likely to be wearing a dark blue suit and a light blue blouse, or a black sweater and a sensible skirt; her long fair hair is always tied back. She was once very attractive, and is still quite elegant, but the pressure of work is beginning to tell in her harassed expression, and her considerable charm is hidden beneath a brisk manner. She takes her work so seriously it is a relief to see her smile about her experiences from time to time. 'An old man came in here once,' she says. 'He took one look at me and said, "How old are you, young girl?" He couldn't believe I was old enough to deal with him!'

As secretary, Tatyana holds a key position in the administration, with immediate access to senior officials and wide-ranging responsibilities for organisational work. She is the first person to whom the elected deputies can take questions or complaints from their constituents. Her days are a frenzy of meetings, phone-calls and hurried staff conferences. In her office she receives anyone from the manager of the port to ordinary citizens befuddled by bureaucracy or simply desperate for help.

Two examples illustrate a typical morning. A young man puts his head shyly round her door. Tatyana sits him down and he explains that he has only recently been released from prison. He has got a job in a factory working the night-shift, but the police keep calling at his apartment in the evenings to check he is behaving himself. He is obviously never there, and the people who share the communal apartment are worried about the late-night visits from the police. Can she help him?

Tatyana asks if he has told the management at his factory about it. It is their responsibility to let the police know he is working properly. He has tried, he replies, but the message is not getting through. She tells him whom he should see in the town hall, and promises to have a word in the right ear herself. When he has gone Tatyana explains that the police regularly check up on people convicted of drunkenness or hooliganism, especially in the first few weeks after their release.

Minutes later, another visitor, this time a tearful young woman from out of town, is relating her sad story. She came to Nakhodka on leave, met a sailor and fell in love with him. He said he loved her and seduced her with promises of marriage. But only today she has found out he is due to sail and will be away for months. He does not want to see her again. Distraught, with no family or friends in Nakhodka, she has no one to turn to but the Soviet authorities. Patiently but firmly Tatyana tells the sobbing girl that sailors are an untrustworthy bunch, she should not be so gullible, and she advises her to return home and try to forget the whole thing. But later on she keeps her promise to the girl to telephone the captain of the sailor's ship to ask him to reprimand the treacherous fellow. 'They say the way to a man's heart is through his stomach,' she reflects bitterly. 'But the way to a woman's heart is through her ears.' And the next day, retelling the lamentable story at home, she complains with a reproachful look at her husband Volodya, 'All men are bachelors at heart.'

As the official in charge of the registry office, Tatyana frequently has to arbitrate in matters of the heart. Normally the waiting period for a couple who want to get married is one month from the day they fill in the application forms. It is the secretary of the town council who gives permission for that rule to be waived in special circumstances. 'It's usually if the woman is very pregnant or the man is about to set sail. Sometimes both.' For another couple she arranges for the bridegroom to be transferred to a later cruise so that the wedding can take place before he sails.

Nakhodka has more women than men of marriageable age, an imbalance which causes further problems for Tatyana. Women are anxious to be married, and if they reach the advanced age of twenty-three or twenty-four without a husband (most Soviets marry for the first time in their late teens or early twenties), they sometimes resort to desperate measures. Tatyana explains. 'Women drag sixteen and seventeen-year-old boys in here with their application forms. Our laws say a marriage involving someone under eighteen has to be approved by the local authorities. So I have to judge whether it's a love match, or just an older woman trying to trap a man!' The marriage certificate will entitle the couple to a flat, so material as well as emotional rewards depend on Tatyana's decision.

Nakhodka does not yet have a Palace of Weddings, the secular equivalent of a church found in most Soviet cities, though plans have been made for one and funds allocated. In the meantime wedding ceremonies take place in a room set aside for the purpose on the top floor of the town hall. At peak times a couple are joined together every ten minutes, a continuous performance featuring brides in white, grooms in suits, rings on fingers and Mendelssohn on tape. The wedding director is a solemn lady whose formidable presence and flowing gown lend gravity to each new pairing. She lectures parents as well as newly-weds on their new responsibilities. Then the Register is duly signed, followed by photographs against a background of flowers in the corner.

An elected deputy attends each wedding to congratulate the couple and hand over their documents. By chance, when Tatyana's turn to officiate comes round on a Saturday in March, her first bride is a bulging beauty who staggers in under the weight of her condition. Tatyana delivers her token speech of congratulation amid embarrassed glances and suppressed smiles from the witnesses.

The word 'Soviet' in Russian means 'council', so the Soviet Union, literally, means a union of councils. The first anti-Tsarist Soviet was formed during the abortive Russian Revolution of 1905, when a group of weavers elected a council of representatives to lead an uprising. Lenin wanted workers' councils to take over state power from the old regime, and his slogan 'All Power to the Soviets' was one of the keynotes of the 1917 Revolution. Now there are governing Soviets at each level of the administration, from the Supreme Soviet of the Soviet Union – the nearest thing the Soviet Union has to a national parliament – through to the republics, regions, cities and districts, right down to neighbourhood Soviets dealing with day-to-day problems among apartment-dwellers. In Nakhodka the population of 160,000 elects 345 deputies to the town's Soviet every two and a half years. At their first plenary session the deputies elect from among their number a chairman (the mayor), three deputies, a secretary, and ten additional members to the fifteen-strong executive committee, which then runs the town's affairs.

The mayor of Nakhodka is Aleksei Tkachyov. In his mid-forties and alert, articulate and businesslike, he belies the image harboured in the West of the grey, inert Soviet official. He is frank about the town's problems – its housing shortage, the water-rationing and poor heating system in apartment blocks. He says he prefers to permit outsiders to see how his administration is tackling its difficulties than to pretend that everything is going smoothly. His openness seems typical of a certain breed of people in the Far East. These are the pioneers who have chosen to work at the furthest outposts of their huge country. The very remoteness of the place seems to give them greater motivation and self-confidence, for the wilderness is no place for faint-hearts.

Although Moscow is politically the heart of the Soviet Union – the place where plans are made and budgets set – the Far East retains some limited areas of autonomy. For example, a local state trading company called

Dalintorg negotiates contracts with Japan and China completely independently from the Ministry of Foreign Trade in Moscow. As a result you can buy Chinese tea and Japanese umbrellas and writing paper in the town's supermarkets. And while the rest of Russia mourned the passing of President Chernenko in March 1985, it was business as usual in Nakhodka town hall, save for a few perfunctory black ribbons. Gennady Zhebelev, general manager of the town's enormous port complex, is outspoken even for a Far Easterner. 'Whether I'm with Russians or foreigners, it's just the same, I speak my mind. I didn't like Chernenko, why should I pretend I did?'

The three deputy mayors have responsibility for separate sections of the town's administration – housing, construction and utilities. With a smile the housing manager describes himself as 'the most popular man in Nakhodka', because it is he who allocates new housing to citizens on the waiting-list. Just as much in demand, but only as the target of complaints and criticism, is the utilities manager, who is wrestling with the vexed problem of the city's water supply – the purifying plant has been unable to cope with recent increases in population. The construction manager is Nina Tyutyumorova, a stern-looking woman in her late forties. She has a penetrating stare and a reputation for toughness. Behind her back everyone in the town hall calls her 'Thatcher'. 'Our own Iron Lady,' as Tatyana puts it. Less daunting a character is Lyudmila Vasilyevna, in charge of delegations from abroad. For her they have another English nickname – 'Foreign Office', pronounced in heavy Russian accents. Blonde, well-dressed, briskly polite, she has the air of a top-notch American secretary. She deals mainly with Japanese traders and Chinese engineers. Nakhodka is also twinned with a Japanese city which sends over groups of kindergarten children in the summer, and with Oakland in California.

The executive committee meets every two weeks. Its responsibilities are for planning and providing the town's public facilities. The committee decides how land is to be used and supervises the work of local industries. On 15 March 1985, the main item on the agenda is the poor performance of Nakhodka's bakeries. The production manager has been summoned to the meeting to account for the bakeries' problems. Under the watchful eye of Lenin, ever-present in portrait form, he is questioned closely by the committee's Finance Director about a 200,000-rouble grant voted the previous year. How was it spent? It was intended to boost macaroni production, why had that not happened? Why are the bakeries still making a loss? Does he expect the town to carry on throwing money at them?

The accused man mentions difficulties with the ovens and poor discipline in the workforce; both problems are being dealt with, naturally, but meanwhile he must respectfully request a further 5400 roubles to make up the bakeries' deficit. In the end a resolution is adopted allocating the necessary funds, but not before critical remarks are made about sloppy accounting procedures. The production manager leaves, ashen-faced from his ordeal.

The most important part of Tatyana's work on the executive committee is drawing up the agenda with the mayor and his three deputies. At these preparatory meetings they draft resolutions based on material prepared by town hall officials. It is here that the real decisions are made, as the full committee tends only to rubber-stamp the resolutions put before it. This makes the final meeting little more than a formal ratification of the leadership's policy.

Those leaders, including Tatyana herself, are all long-standing members of the Communist Party. The mayor is a leading member of the Nakhodka Party committee, and the Party secretary has a seat on the executive committee. Indeed, all over the Soviet Union the overlap between Party and government functions is considerable. Officially, the Party is not part of the State administration, it merely assists and encourages the work of elected representatives. Its so-called 'leading role' in society consists of giving guidance in matters of policy.

But with virtually all key government posts and half the deputies' jobs held by Party members, the Party dominates Soviet public affairs. In Nakhodka the Party group of deputies meets before the plenary session to decide their preferences for the top town hall jobs. Tatyana sees nothing wrong with this. 'The town council executes the Party's will because the Party represents the interests of the people.' She is echoing Lenin's claim that 'the Party is the vanguard of the proletariat'.

Tatyana has been groomed to take her place in this vanguard since childhood. She was active in pioneer and Komsomol groups at school in Nakhodka, excelled in her studies, and in her twenties worked full-time in the Komsomol bureaucracy. Until her election as a deputy and her elevation to secretary two and a half years ago, she had an administrative job at Party headquarters. And when she considers her future career path she says full-time Party work interests her most.

It is not difficult to see why she finds her present job so demanding. One of her main duties is to encourage the deputies to take a more active role in the process of government. Although they keep their full-time jobs, deputies are obliged to check up on the work of state bodies and, by law, 'put a stop to violations of socialist legality'. Tatyana follows up their official questions, advises them on their duties towards their constituents and teaches them how to use the government machinery. For example, she might be required to investigate a dispute between a deputy and the management at his or her place of work.

In another instance, we watched her lecture a group of deputies at Nakhodka's east port. She was asking for their help. 'We have some productivity problems,' she tells them. 'As workers you are in a better position than the managers to tackle the problem.' Apparently, punctuality was the issue. In earlier times the dockworkers were excused being late because of the poor bus service to the new port. Now the buses run more frequently and the deputies have to explain to their mates that they are expected in on time.

Tatyana's patronising approach to the reticent deputies is revealing. 'We understand it's difficult for you. You're representatives of the working class, and we know it isn't easy for you to make decisions.'

At the marine fishery base Tatyana visits Tamara Bredova, a deputy on the Supreme Soviet of the Russian Republic, who is about to travel to Moscow for a plenary session. She wants Tamara to use her deputy's right of access to government officials and call on the Minister of Education to remind him about the new school that has long been promised to one of Nakhodka's residential districts.

Next there is a certificate of honour to award to a worker at the ship repair plant with an outstanding productivity record. As the person responsible for official documents and archival materials, Tatyana often visits factories to hand out such prizes. Even this duty has its comic moments. 'A man once came into my office, saying he had fought in the war and been a model worker for thirty years. He wanted me to make him a Hero of Socialist Labour.' This is one of the most prestigious awards in the Soviet Union. 'At first I thought he was joking. But no, he insisted. I had to explain that the Soviet authorities don't give an honour like that to someone who comes and asks for it!'

Of all her official functions, Tatyana readily admits, election work is the most onerous. In Nakhodka she is the administrator with the unenviable task of achieving the staggering 99% turn-out at Soviet elections. In mid-March she had only just recovered from the local elections of 24 February, when a new town council was elected. 'We did have nine people who refused to vote. Most of them had some grievance, one wanted a bigger apartment. So not voting was a protest.'

But electors in the Soviet Union can only vote for one candidate in their constituency, who always belongs to the 'Party and non-Party bloc'. Their only alternative is to cross out the name of the candidate and write in another one. Only the Party, the trade unions, and youth and cultural organisations may nominate candidates, whose suitability is discussed at pre-election meetings. Tatyana defends this Soviet version of democracy vigorously. 'Under your system different candidates fight for the class interests of their Party. Here the Party and the people are united. We get good candidates because they are approved by their colleagues who best know their abilities.'

In theory the electorate can recall elected deputies who fail to carry out their mandate at any time. In practice the deputies seem to feel more accountable to their superiors in Party and government than to the general public.

The next elections are for four new judges. Tatyana's desk is covered with electoral lists and her phone is constantly ringing with last-minute questions from the polling-stations. At a meeting with electoral officers from the constituencies she talks about cooperation with the police in case of disturbances, and reminds the officers to give flowers to first-time voters. Who pays for the flowers? someone asks. Tatyana consults her assistant. 'They should be paid for out of each polling-station's funds,' she says, to groans from the audience.

The secretary also oversees the work of Nakhodka's 330 comradely courts – the small neighbourhood committees all over town which adjudicate in disputes between residents. Tatyana attends regular meetings of a legal committee monitoring these courts. Her feeling is that they are not doing badly, but their efficiency could be improved. To this end the committee approves a resolution introducing competition between the courts – prizes for the quality of their procedures not the severity of their punishments!

The Soviet system depends on people like Tatyana with the drive and commitment to keep the state machine ticking over. Above all her role is to mobilise the people, to encourage them to participate in the political process. Whatever one thinks of the system, its growth from tiny conspiratorial groups of Bolsheviks in 1917 to the massive and monolithic state of today represents a formidable achievement. It is true that terror and repression have played their part, but the Soviet Union could not survive politically without the voluntary contribution at grass-roots level of tens of thousands of ordinary foot-soldiers like Tatyana. If Communism is a Church, they are its pastoral workers, spreading the gospel among the populace.

The strain of long hours and heavy responsibilities tells on Tatyana's family life. Her husband Volodya, though remarkably supportive for a Soviet man, complains that she pays too little attention to their two daughters. He thinks her nerves are suffering, too, and wants her to delegate more. Other men are even more critical. Gennady Zhebelev, for example, the outspoken port manager, who knows the family well, is convinced that the secretary's job is not for a woman. 'I respect her as a person, you understand. But a woman's first duty is to her family. And with her work-load she doesn't have time to look after herself – a woman needs to think about her clothes, her face.'

Even Tatyana herself has doubts about a woman's suitability for political work. 'I would never want to be mayor, I don't have a man's firmness. The trouble with a woman is that people can always play on her emotions.'

Tatyana and Volodya married young; she was eighteen, he was twenty-one. While she was at university he had a job and studied by correspondence. They both started careers in administration, he on the sport and recreation committee, she in the Komsomol. But when Tatyana became secretary of the town council, she found herself further up the hierarchy than Volodya. Deciding that it was inappropriate for members of the same family to be in this position he left the town hall and became a physical training instructor in Nakhodka's Institute.

Tatyana now works much longer hours than Volodya does, and he is left with the unusual problem for a Soviet man of having to do his share of the housework. As a result, his genuine pride in her achievements is tempered with some misgivings. 'I used to arrive home at 8 or 9 in the evening and think, what on earth can I cook for them all?' Now, under the guidance of his thirteen-year-old daughter Sveta, Volodya is learning to find his way around the kitchen.

Another drawback of his wife's success is that they frequently have to take separate holidays, as her leave rarely coincides with the Institute's summer break. Their photo album shows her relaxing with a tour group on the Baltic, and him enjoying the Olympic Games in Moscow. After the elections for new judges she will take a trip to the Black Sea without him. Many Soviet couples gladly holiday apart, but in Tatyana's and Volodya's case, it is a cause of real disappointment.

As if to compensate for this, Volodya has a rule that Sunday is 'their day', when work commitments are not allowed to interrupt family pursuits. And the relative comfort in which they live, thanks to Tatyana's status, must be some consolation. They have their own car, a smart blue Zhiguli 7, and an ample apartment in one of Nakhodka's newest multi-storey blocks. Volodya's new job has brought him unexpected rewards too. He says his students appreciate him in a way his fellow bureaucrats never did, and they send him letters from their ships all over the world. So good is Volodya's reputation that Gennady Zhebelev has been trying to entice him to work at his sports complex. Zhebelev approached Tatyana first and asked her to lobby her husband on his behalf. But Volodya is staying put.

For all the apparent disruption of family life, the two daughters seem to have fared well enough. At high school and at music school, where she has piano lessons twice a week, Sveta invariably gets high marks. 'It's especially surprising, with such busy parents,' says her piano teacher, with a hint of disapproval in her voice. After classes Sveta collects four-year-old Anya from the kindergarten and takes her home, a chore that Tatyana herself is unable to do. 'At first we were worried about the difference in age between them, but it's worked out very well.'

Come rain or shine, Sundays are spent at the yacht club run by the town's ship repair yard. Summers in Nakhodka are hot and humid, so messing about on boats in a neighbouring bay is ideal recreation. But even in winter, with the temperature below zero, snow on the sand and the boats in hibernation, the family dons tracksuits, woolly hats and wellies, and joins friends on the beach. Only Russians could grill shashliks and boil herring outdoors on blustery winter days in March. On such occasions Volodya is under strict instructions not to have more than a single glass of vodka to warm him, otherwise Tatyana threatens to walk home with the kids rather than be driven home by a drunken husband. No such inhibitions mar Volodya's weekly visits (by public transport) to the *banya*, the Russian steam-baths. 'Going to the banya once a week is as healthy as running every day,' claims Volodya, though the benefits of steaming yourself fit may be outweighed by the vodka intake which the *banya's* male conviviality demands. If nothing else, the combination of steam and spirits is a devastating cure for insomnia.

Despite unmistakable signs of tension at home, Tatyana continues to take on more responsibilities at work. She is one of that rare breed, a Soviet workaholic. Her energy and commitment – some would call it fanaticism – are based on wholesale acceptance of Marxist-Leninist doctrine and Soviet political practice. But beyond her defence of the system she serves, there is a driven, unquestioning quality to her personality. It is as if she is so immersed in the endless minutiae of her job that she never has time to pause for reflection. Lenin predicted that when Communism reached its highest stage the State would no longer be necessary and its machinery would simply wither away. With men and women like Tatyana Naumova in the vanguard, there seems little prospect of that.

[A.B.]

TWELVE

All That Jazz

From the saxophone to the knife is just one step.
Today he'll play jazz, and tomorrow he'll betray his country.
Slogans from a Soviet propaganda poster of the 1920s

The Soviet intelligentsia is divided into two groups: the official artists, writers and musicians, and the unofficial. Those who have official status are members of unions and work regularly. For example, official painters will belong to the Artists' Union and paintings will be commissioned from them. The second group, the unofficial intelligentsia, do not produce work that the Soviet State finds acceptable – they can find no employment in their artistic capacity and are forced to find other ways of making their living. For some reason, Leningrad abounds with such 'unofficial' practitioners of the arts. There is some rivalry between Moscow and Leningrad. Leningraders maintain that they are more cultured and intellectual than Muscovites who, in turn, assert their superiority.

The most sought-after profession amongst Leningrad's unofficial artists is that of heating mechanic. It was once explained by an émigré Russian living in London, 'You sit all day with your books and every now and then you take a look at the temperature gauge, make an adjustment and then carry on reading. No one bothers you.' Before this particular job gained in popularity, contemporary young artists, writers and musicians were all trying to get work as yard keepers. The principal attraction of such jobs is that they leave you free to read, write, think and dream. It is illegal to be unemployed in the Soviet Union. You must be registered as having some place of work. For the unofficial artists, since they cannot work as they wish, a job that requires a minimum of effort is desirable as it leaves them fresh for their own pursuits. Some of them even risk being unemployed.

Soviet life is fraught with rules and regulations and it is much more difficult to live your life unnoticed than it is in the West. The Soviet citizen is frequently required to show his documents and it is therefore important for these documents to be in order. Most people carry their passport with them at all times. At the age of sixteen, you are required by law to obtain a passport. If both parents are Russian, the applicant will put Russian under 'nationality'; if one parent is Russian and the other Georgian, for example, applicants can choose their nationality. Jews are required to put down 'Jewish' as their nationality. And here again, if one parent is Jewish and one Russian they can choose. A Jewish Muscovite with a son by a Russian wife hopes his son will opt for Jewish nationality when he applies for his passport. 'It may make his life more difficult, but who says life should be easy? It'll make him stronger if he is challenged by difficulties.'

Such a passport is for internal use and has the function of identification paper rather than that of entrée to other countries. All citizens must be registered by the police in the town in which they live. It is illegal to live in a town unless your passport bears such a permit, and moving residence from city to city is no easy matter. Many people wish to live in the big cities of Moscow, Leningrad and Kiev, but in order to prevent people from flooding these cities, the State has made it difficult to obtain permits for them. This has led to the practice of 'fictitious' marriages. If you marry someone with a Moscow permit you will be able to obtain one yourself. You will have to give the same address as your husband or wife, but the authorities do not check up to ensure that you are actually living together. 'I've come to Moscow for two weeks,' confided a young woman from Minsk. 'I've brought 1000 roubles with me [five–six months' salary] to "buy" a husband. I think life will be more interesting in Moscow, it's a more cosmopolitan city. I want to live here.'

This has repercussions on 'real' marriages. Sometimes Muscovites and Leningraders are wary of marrying 'outsiders' as they fear being used to acquire a permit. One woman who had married a Muscovite for love never applied for a permanent permit in order to convince him she had had no ulterior motive. (It is possible to get temporary permits through your place of work.) This particular couple are now divorced and she is in the invidious position of having to apply for a temporary permit every six months, a time-consuming bureaucratic task.

Fictitious marriages to foreigners are not uncommon and provide the easiest way of emigrating at present. It takes up to a year to receive permission to leave and you are free to come back and visit. The bureaucratic obstacles lying in the path of every Soviet citizen are not as insurmountable as they seem to the uninitiated.

'Have you noticed the amount of rules we have in our country?' asked a Leningrad artist. 'The answer to any request is always "no", then you have to find a way round it and in the end you can win. It's like a game, I even quite enjoy it.' Although the sense of achievement experienced in 'winning' is profound, the energy required is substantial.

It is evening. In a typical high-rise Soviet apartment building on the outskirts of Leningrad, Sasha and Tanya prepare tea for the guests they are expecting. Sasha is a heating mechanic; he is also a poet and a founder member of Leningrad's revolutionary Club '81, a group founded in 1981 for Leningrad's unofficial creative artists. 'We decided we really had to find a way of existing and working in our own country. We don't want to emigrate. We went along to the Ministry of Culture. They said, "Why do you publish work abroad?" We answered, "Because you won't publish it here. If we could publish here we wouldn't need to in the West." They thought about it and gave us permission to start Club '81.'

The club has its headquarters in the Dostoevsky museum, a small picturesque building that used to be the writer's home. It organises poetry readings and other cultural activities. The members hope that they will be able to extend the boundaries of Soviet art which they find confining. 'We're hoping to publish a collection of members' works,' says Sasha. 'Who knows whether it'll actually happen?' The very existence of such a club augurs well: it is a leap of faith on the part of the authorities, but still only a very small step along the path to artistic freedom.

Sasha and Tanya's flat is like a million others: two rooms plus kitchen and bathroom. The sitting room is their bedroom by night and the second room is their ten-year-old son's. It is easy to guess that this is the home of intellectuals: there are rather more books here than in the average home, the walls are covered with paintings which are clearly given to them by the artists and there are many records. As you enter, a book is pressed eagerly into your hands, or a new record is put on the record player. The intelligentsia are eager to share any new experience with their friends and guests.

There is a ring at the door and Pavel enters. He is in his early thirties. His passion is music and he was one of the founders of the Leningrad Contemporary Music Club in 1980. With the recent growth in popularity of Soviet Jazz, the authorities have been forced to allow for some sort of forum for it, even though they consider jazz to be a symbol of Western decadence. In various towns in the Soviet Union so-called 'contemporary music clubs' sprang up at the beginning of the eighties. They usually come under the auspices of the local philharmonic society and organise concerts and festivals which are visited by jazz and rock enthusiasts from all over the Soviet Union. Not many of these clubs have managed to survive. The Leningrad Music Club staged its first and last week of music in the spring of 1982. The hall was overflowing, but the authorities were alarmed by the excitement the event generated. The club was closed down and the officials who had granted permission for such an occurrence reprimanded.

Many musicians are forced to earn their living by playing in the 'popular music ensembles' to be found in almost every Soviet restaurant. These bands usually play middle-of-the-road Western and Soviet pop and look indescribably bored as they strum abjectly on their guitars or beat listlessly on their drums. Others may end up playing in variety acts in hotels, providing the musical accompaniment to a juggler or dancer. 'Virtually no jazz musicians are doing what they would like to be doing,' Pavel argues. 'They would never willingly work in restaurant bands, or variety groups. Obviously they want to make a living playing their own kind of music.'

Sergei Kuryokhin arrives to discuss the possibility of putting on an unofficial concert. Sergei is one of the Soviet Union's most famous unofficial jazz/rock musicians. His parents sent him to a music school when he was four because he had perfect pitch. He studied the piano and went on to study at the music school attached to the Leningrad Conservatory and subsequently in the Institute of Culture. He was expelled from both establishments. 'I am totally incapable of attending classes regularly. The atmosphere at those places was deadly, it was impossible to be creative.' Sergei finds it hard to play the game and feels that 'a real artist is always a nonconformist'.

Nonconformists are not encouraged in the Soviet Union. In a country where the desirability of the working and the social collective are constantly stressed, unconventional behaviour smacks of individualism. As Sergei says, 'You have to have strong enough will-power, conscience and determination to do your own thing. If you know what you want you will accomplish it. But people with that sort of will-power are rare. Ordinary people get crushed by the system.' It is evident that he has the necessary will-power, but despite his determination and outspokenness, he is disarmingly shy.

Sergei is a strikingly handsome man with a dimpled smile. Like many Russian men, he has an old-world gallantry – he kisses women's hands and helps them as they step from cars and buses. At thirty, he is on his second marriage. His wife Nastya has recently had their first child. She is dark and pretty but says little, letting Sergei do the talking. They live some way out of town in a one-roomed apartment which is so small and cramped that they rarely invite friends to visit. To support his family, Sergei works as a pianist in a sports school, but it absorbs little of his time and energies. He frequently wears a distracted air. This is because he is listening to the music that is ceaselessly playing inside his head, forever drumming out rhythms on table tops and humming quietly.

Sergei is currently trying to gain official status of some kind and has recently received freelance membership of Lenkontsert. Goskontsert (State concert) is the organisation that supplies employment to all official musicians in the Soviet Union. It organises concerts throughout the country and the rest of the world through its branches in every major town. In Leningrad this is Lenkontsert, in Moscow, Moskontsert. Now that Sergei is on Lenkontsert's books, he may be offered occasional work as a pianist. In all probability it won't help him much, but he feels that it may in some way contribute to official recognition in the future.

Another organisation that holds sway over Soviet music is the Composers' Union. While Goskontsert is answerable to the Ministry of Culture, the Composers' Union is an independent trade union for composers and music critics. However, it is generally recognised as being accountable to the Party. It is a powerful union and can make or break a composer, deciding who may be permitted to write music and what kind of music it should be.

The same man has been its president since the Stalinist war years. He is Tikhon Khrennikov, who is generally recognised to have had a stranglehold on Soviet music for the past forty-odd years. It is said that he has personally been responsible for purges in the music world and Prokofiev and Shostakovich suffered at his hands. Current rumours reveal that his successor would be more lenient and that the face of Soviet music could change considerably. However, Khrennikov looks fit and healthy and much younger than his seventy-two years. He is himself a composer and attends the Bolshoi Theatre when his ballet music is performed. He sits in a private box and rises for the audience's somewhat insincere applause. Tikhon Khrennikov is not popular with the intelligentsia and is irreverently called Khren Tikhonov – *khren* literally means 'horseradish' and is slang for 'rubbish'.

There is only one record label in the Soviet Union: Melodiya. It is state-run and only records officially sanctioned music. For Sergei and other jazz/rock musicians, improvisation is the essence of their music. The State can neither censor nor control improvised music. Not surprisingly, it is wary of the musicians' unpredictable live performances and reluctant to permit Melodiya to record them. To date, the only improvised free-form music to have been recorded by Melodiya is that of the Ganelin Trio. 'Do we really have to be in advance of the West even with avant-garde music?' said Shabanov, the director-general of Melodiya. 'Our people don't need this kind of music.' Finally in 1981, after much deliberation and procrastination, Melodiya released an album of the trio's music. Three more have since been released, and all four records were sold out within the first few hours.

The members of the Ganelin Trio, Vyacheslav Ganelin, Vladimir Chekasin and Vladimir Tarasov, are in their late thirties and early forties. All three are Russian but live in the Lithuanian capital of Vilnius, Lithuania being one of the three Baltic States. They all have full-time 'serious' music jobs. Ganelin composes operas and film scores, Chekasin teaches at the Conservatory and Tarasov plays in the State Symphony Orchestra. The jazz trio, which started as a hobby for the players, now enjoys a unique position. The musicians play concerts in the Soviet Union and also perform in the West for they are, after all, a valuable way of earning foreign currency for the State, and Goskontsert charges high rates for their performances. They are also a way of publicising the Soviet Union and showing the West that such music is allowed to exist. The trio themselves see little of this money, but they do get the chance to travel.

In addition to these organised concerts, the Ganelin Trio, like Kuryokhin and other Soviet jazz musicians, organise unofficial gigs. Some time ago in Moscow, word suddenly went round that the trio would be playing, but the venue was not yet known. Another rumour went round – it was to be in the House of the Blind. Most organisations have a building for recreation purposes. Factories have palaces of culture where concerts are staged and meetings held. The blind have their house in a Moscow suburb.

In order to stage such an unofficial concert, you have first to befriend a sympathetic official who will be prepared to pull a few strings. In this instance the administrator of the House of the Blind was probably persuaded to permit the trio to use the premises. No official advertising takes place and everything is arranged at short notice. All information is given by word of mouth and yet the building is full, with the tickets sold out in advance. Several people stroll up and down in front of the building, rushing up to every new arrival in the hope that he or she will have a spare ticket. This practice is common and is known as 'taking tickets off people's hands'. It is notoriously difficult to obtain tickets for worthwhile ballets, plays and concerts. If you arrive early, however, you can often buy a ticket from someone who has a spare or who is unable to attend. You pay only the purchase price of the ticket and it is possible to see entire repertoires of theatre and ballet companies by buying your tickets in this way. Tickets are also for sale at the kiosks situated all over towns and cities, but there is a condition: to buy a ticket for the Bolshoi, for example, you may also have to purchase a ticket for a poor concert on the outskirts of town. This is called buying 'with a load'. Ticket sellers have quotas to fill and this is an easy way for them to rid themselves of unpopular tickets. None of the tickets are expensive however, and you simply discard the ones you don't need.

The House of the Blind is crowded with people aged from between thirty to forty. Here and there you see some who could pass for hippies with their long hair, flared trousers, Indian shirts and headbands. Everyone takes their seats shouting hellos and shaking hands. It is clear that you are in the midst of a close-knit group of jazz enthusiasts; it is like being at a large, well-behaved party. The trio take the stage and start tuning up. Ten minutes pass and only then do you realise that they have not been tuning up at all, they have started to play! Their music might be perceived as free-form, but, in fact, it is rigidly structured. They improvise around this structure and digress from themes to which they later return.

The musicians play about fifteen instruments between them, often simultaneously, and the sight of Chekasin playing two saxophones at once is a showstopper. The audience is delighted, their faces are wreathed in smiles. Chekasin is an eccentric performer, lifting and shaking his leg as he plays and deliberately making discordant sounds. The audience laughs with him. To the Westerner none of this sounds particularly unusual or original, but within the context of the Soviet Union such musical anarchy provides a welcome release after the strictures of daily life.

The Ganelin Trio visited England in 1984 and played several concerts. They were extremely well-received by jazz enthusiasts. The trio themselves feel that their music is remote from West European avant-garde jazz. 'We borrow some elements from jazz,' explains Chekasin, 'but we also borrow from chamber music, folk music and other genres.'

Like Chekasin, Sergei Kuryokhin too rejects the notion that what Soviet avant-garde musicians are doing today is imitative of Western musicians. Sergei admires Chekasin enormously and they often play together. 'I think he's one of the greatest saxophone players in the world.' Sergei has never released a record in the Soviet Union. In 1981 an album of his music entitled 'The Ways of Freedom' was released in the West by Leo Records. The record sleeve states, 'Sergei Kuryokhin does not bear any responsibility for publishing this tape.'

Leo Records was started as an independent company and Leo Feigin is the producer of the label. He left Leningrad and the Soviet Union in 1973 and works for the BBC external services broadcasting their jazz programme to the Soviet Union. Leo is tirelessly committed to acquainting both the West and the Soviet Union itself with Soviet jazz. 'It is absolutely essential that this music be heard. It is fantastic, it is the most extraordinary thing that has ever happened.' Leo is not alone in his enthusiasm. The records that he produces here find their way back to the Soviet Union and are the chief means by which musicians there hear about their fellow musicians' existence and work. The response is unprecedented.

Leo receives many letters from grateful listeners from all parts of the Soviet Union who were not aware that such music existed in their own country. The walls of his office are covered with their drawings and sketches.

Leo Records was established in 1980 and is run on a shoe-string. To date the company has produced twenty Soviet jazz records and Leo Feigin is wholly responsible for the Ganelin Trio's Western exposure. As soon as the company can afford to they turn the tapes they receive into records. Unfortunately distribution of the records is not as widespread as Leo would wish. 'I am confronted by an iron curtain of ignorance in the West.' Leo does not do this for the money, but out of a genuine desire to make Soviet music known in the West and so make the lives of the musicians easier. If they become well-known in the West, others too, like the Ganelin Trio, may be allowed to visit and play at international music festivals.

Leo's idea of jazz programming differs greatly from that of Western disc jockeys. 'I do not see my programmes as entertainment. They are music news programmes for musicians and fans. My task is to tell my listeners what's happening in the West *now*, to keep them up to date with all the latest developments and trends. If I play old tunes I get disappointed letters saying, we don't want entertainment, we want news. I broadcast long interviews, I translate articles and play long pieces of uninterrupted music.'

Leo is one of the few Russians without nostalgia for the motherland. Many who emigrate suffer a painful sense of loss and find it very difficult to make the transition. Leo is an exception. 'As soon as I got off the plane in London I felt at home. I have some nostalgia for the musical life of New York where I spent some time, but none at all for Leningrad.' It is evident, however, from Leo's work and preoccupations that he has not forgotten his roots. He sees his activity as a contribution to Russian culture. 'I personally think that this development of new music in the Soviet Union is a continuation of the tradition of great Russian culture that was arrested by the October Revolution. The Revolution turned culture upside down and introduced socialist culture. But, in spite of nearly seventy years in power, the Soviet authorities haven't managed to break this great Russian tradition.' Slowly the West is now waking up to this new Soviet music and some records are getting very good reviews.

The World Service, Voice of America and Radio Free Europe are constantly being jammed by the authorities. Notwithstanding, many people listen to them and, if you have a powerful enough receiver or are prepared to tune in very late at night, you can usually pick up the signals. These radio stations are an important source of information particularly for the intelligentsia, who tend to be more sceptical of what they receive through the Soviet media. Western radio stations provide them with information about their own country as well as about the outside world.

The Soviet media are highly selective in their news coverage and rarely dwell on the negative aspects of Soviet life. However, this is gradually changing and it is now possible to read of crimes committed, the problems of alcoholism and 'speculation' in the Soviet press. Speculation is a common Soviet crime and widespread both at street level and among those in positions of authority. In his short period of power, Yuri Andropov was committed to expunging Soviet society of corruption. He decreed that the director of a well-known Moscow food shop be shot for speculation and corruption. The director had become a millionaire by selling the caviare intended for his shop elsewhere and pocketing the profits. He had thought he was unassailable as he had a valuable protector in the Moscow police force. Unfortunately for him, this particular police chief was already himself in custody for corruption.

One of the best ways of finding out what is really going on in the Soviet Union is to go for a long walk with a member of the intelligentsia. Walking is a favourite Soviet pastime, less for the exercise it affords than for the opportunity it provides of airing your views freely and with no fear of being overheard. There are two schools of thought amongst the Soviet intelligentsia: the first states that your every movement, meeting and conversation is overheard and recorded by the KGB and you must be watchful at all times. The second refuses to worry about it for, even if the KGB may or may not be listening, they are doing no wrong as far as they can see and there is no sense in thinking about it. Nonetheless, everyone behaves with discretion and saves their best political jokes for out of doors. People are careful not to say too much on the telephone. 'Meet me by the Mayakovsky statue in fifteen minutes,' they will say. You meet and spend the next few hours strolling about the city exchanging news and views. There are benches everywhere in Soviet towns and, whatever the weather, they are always full of people sitting closely together and chatting quietly and intimately.

Although many artists find Soviet society repressive, few actually want to leave forever. For many, the very fact of their 'Russian-ness' is integral to their artistic make-up. Sergei Kuryokhin is very conscious of his national identity and even calls himself a 'nationalist-chauvinist'. In spite of the fact that he is well acquainted with current trends in Western jazz, rock and folk music, Sergei feels more influenced by his own cultural traditions. His music contains elements of the Russian gypsy song and ideas from classical

Russian composers. Improvising on a wide variety of themes and ideas, his music is apparently formless and not always easy to listen to. 'I often play Rachmaninov at home. The thing is that I haven't heard any very interesting classical piano music recently. Actually, I think the piano may be dying out.' Sergei does not play as often as he used to and is composing and conducting more and more.

At Sasha and Tanya's apartment in Leningrad, the talk is about the extraordinary possibility of an official music festival in Leningrad. The doorbell rings once again and Boris Grebenshchikov comes in. He is the same age as Sergei and they have a group called 'Aquarium' that plays more conventional rock music. Dinara Asanova commissioned Boris to write some songs for one of her films. She was intending to use more of them in the film she started making before her death. Dinara was also planning to include Sergei in a projected film about Soviet jazz. If she had lived, she might well have helped Sergei and his associates to gain official sanction.

One of Sergei and Boris's many problems is finding somewhere to rehearse. As they have no official status, nothing is provided for them. For the official artist, life is relatively simple: painters, for example, are given a studio by the State and provided with materials. Unofficial painters have to waste time and energy looking for the paints and brushes they need and use a corner of their indubitably cramped homes as their studio. Much of Sergei and Boris's time is taken up with running around trying to persuade friends and colleagues to help them out.

A date for the festival has been confirmed and the venue is to be a Leningrad Palace of Culture. Clearly the authorities feel that since they cannot stop the musicians playing, it is better that they should know about it and control the event. There is some talk of a jazz festival in the Latvian capital of Riga in June. It is being organised by the Riga Jazz Club and this is to be the third such festival. In previous years, this has been a successful event with musicians travelling from as far as Siberia and Arkhangelsk to play. Until now, the Riga Jazz Club has had official status through its connection with the Riga Philharmonic Society. The connection no longer exists and this may cause problems. Soviet life is an elaborate game of reading signs, assessing moods and trying, through well-placed contacts, to determine whether there may be some relaxation or further clamp-downs.

Sergei and Boris are excited about the Leningrad festival. For Sergei an audience is absolutely essential. 'My present-day compositions can be called social art. People should be stirred up and shocked.' The look of the thing is as important to him as the sound of it.

The day of the festival dawns. As usual, the only advertising has been by word of mouth. Even though the event is official, the authorities do not want to generate too much interest and excitement by advertising it. The Palace of Culture is on a side street near the centre of town and a substantial crowd already mills around in the road. There are hippies and punks among them, an incongruous sight next to the usual Soviet faces bustling past on their way to other places.

Soviet punks are rather different from the Western originators of the movement. They are more restrained in their dress and restrict the use of safety pins to a discreet two, threaded through the ear in place of an earring. 'We are opposed to government of any kind,' they say, 'it restricts the individual.' Their philosophy of anarchy is well-formulated and they are clearly 'intellectual punks'. In the seventies, the area in front of the Kazan Cathedral on Nevsky Prospekt, Leningrad's main street, was the meeting-place for drug pushers and shady dealers. It is now the territory of the punks who meet there and sit for hours on end, for they have nowhere else to go.

The excitement is apparent outside the Palace of Culture and police vehicles patrol the road telling people to move on to the pavement, which is already full of those trying vainly to 'take tickets off others' hands'. Those lucky enough to have tickets make their way in. They are rigorously searched for cameras. Both Lenfilm and Mosfilm Studios tried to get permission to film the event – it was refused and this bag searching is to ensure that the event is not photographed or filmed unofficially. The atmosphere is one of optimism and incredulity. This is, after all, an official festival. It is possible to forget that you are in the Soviet Union, the fans here look like music fans the world over. Curiously enough it is their shoes that make it apparent that they are Soviet. While here and there black-market Adidas trainers are in evidence, most wear Soviet footwear which is clumsy, badly made and usually plastic. The foyer has been hung with a collection of modern paintings that would generally be on view only at private, underground exhibitions. It is relatively common for unofficial painters to use their homes as galleries and invitations to such 'exhibitions' are cautiously circulated. When you arrive at such a gathering the reason for the State's disapprobation of the works of art is instantly apparent. Frequently the paintings are religious and devoted to the representation of Christ in the vivid colours of the icon painter. The paintings on show at the festival today are not religious, but no more acceptable. There are a series of complicated collages using diverse materials and many of the images are from the pop world. They have little to do with Socialist Realism. The musicians have used the festival today as an opportunity to help some friends by exhibiting their work.

There is a tendency among some sections of Soviet youth to admire anything that comes from the West. Ideas in music and fashion are eagerly sought and quickly absorbed and copied. Powers of discernment are lost in the assumption that anything from the West must be better. The spectators at this festival, however, are more circumspect. The first group to play is 'Jungle', an imitative rock band. Their performance excites little interest and they receive half-hearted applause.

The second band are judged more harshly. They are found to be wholly inadequate after the first few bars. They play the sort of Soviet pop that can be heard in any restaurant, a slavish imitation of Western pop music, and, although they are competent musicians, they do not deserve a place at this festival. After the first minute, members of the audience rise from their seats and make their way to the exits. Within moments the hall is virtually empty and the unhappy band is left to play on. The audience is not angry or upset, they merely see this as an opportunity to go into the foyer, have a cigarette and chat about what is to come. Sergei Kuryokhin is scheduled to appear with his big band 'Popular Mechanics' and it is obvious that this is what everyone is waiting for.

The crowd take their seats again and a lengthy pause ensues as technicians haul equipment on to the stage and set about the business of getting it working. This gives the festival a distinctly amateur air but bothers no one in the audience. Most of the equipment is from the West and will have found its way to Leningrad by many complicated means. Getting hold of decent instruments and equipment is a problem for every Soviet musician. 'I have a lot of plans but no facilities,' says Sergei. 'I need several choirs, symphony orchestras, a circus and a zoo! I need synthesisers and many, many things which I will never have.' Certainly the equipment on the stage looks unpromising and there is as much improvisation in this area as there will be in the performances to come.

Finally, after a long wait punctuated by uncomfortable blasts of high and low frequencies as the amplifiers and microphones wheeze into life, the stage is set for 'Popular Mechanics'. Once you see the band, the lengthy preparation becomes more comprehensible. A crowd of players make their way on to the stage: string players, drummers, percussionists and saxophonists. They are all between the ages of eighteen and forty-eight. Some are dressed in conservative suits, others wear waist-length hair and dungarees. The audience laughs with pleasure. Boris appears with elaborate stage make-up and greased-back hair, and is greeted with a burst of applause. He is planning to play any instrument he can get his hands on. At last Kuryokhin appears and the audience erupts. They roar in appreciation. This is the moment they have been waiting for.

Sergei is dressed entirely in black with white face make-up and a single large black tear painted on his cheek. 'I want my performances to be worth looking at. I have always loved the theatre and I think that in my music, behaviour is always the continuation of a musical idea. I try to create a paradoxical cultural "happening" where the actions are secondary to the development of the music.'

Sergei turns to his band, pauses and then, seemingly without any effort, leaps several feet into the air and stabs at the ceiling to signal a blasting staccato sound from the brass section. The string section, at a sign from Kuryokhin, come to life and scrape their bows discordantly across their instruments. The blasts of brass and the screech of strings follow each other with increasing speed until, finally, a rhythm is established and a thumping and recognisable oom pah, oom pah accompaniment to a well-known melody makes itself heard. The audience roars with appreciative laughter at the musical joke. The music careers on, picking up ever more unlikely influences: ancient Russian chants become traditional jazz, Mozart turns into rock and even the strains of 'Greensleeves' are heard. Chekasin, of the Ganelin Trio, is on the stage and is playing two saxophones at once in perfect harmony. The behaviour of the band is anarchic, Sergei throws plates around and makes noises with whatever he can find.

This extravagant and unconventional style of performance may not be unknown to the West, but it is to the Soviet Union. For sixty years this sort of performance has not been known. However, in the years leading up to the Russian Revolution of 1917, there was a great deal of experimental activity in the Arts. A group known as 'The Futurists' came into being in about 1912. They published a manifesto, 'A Slap in the Face of Public Taste', where they determined 'to stand upon the rock of the word "we" in a sea of cat-calls and indignation', challenging the established canons of art with their extravagant behaviour.

The group was made up predominantly of writers and artists and a notable member was the Russian poet Vladimir Mayakovsky who later became the poet of the Revolution and dedicated himself to writing verse and plays about the Revolution. Disillusioned with life, he committed suicide in 1930. He is now hailed as a great Soviet poet. He and his fellow futurists repudiated the social order and turned art upside down. They dressed outrageously and Mayakovsky used to shout his poetry from rooftops and scatter posters to the crowds that had gathered urging them to attend poetry readings. Kuryokhin's artistic style, while new to Soviet society, is carrying on a tradition that was arrested by the Revolution.

The audience is enraptured; some sit with their eyes closed, smiling quietly. Others twitch to the strange half-rhythms. People are laughing, clapping and shouting. One woman is sitting in tears. She cannot believe that this is really happening. 'I would never have thought that it was possible for something like this to happen in our country. I have never seen anything like it in my life.' Her tears are of gratitude.

There is a singer on stage with the big band. Valentina Ponomaryova formerly sang with the well-known gypsy ensemble 'Romen', and now sings regularly with Sergei. Her songs are wordless and her shrieks and wails turn into melodies and again become strangely haunting sounds. She is herself of gypsy extraction. There are many gypsies in the Soviet Union and the State has always been unsure what to do about them. The 'tame' gypsies are admired and work in the gypsy theatres, entertaining audiences with the beauty of their songs and dances. Others live as they please, according to their own customs and traditions, and are generally felt to be parasites as they do not work and make their living by begging. It is not uncommon to be stopped on the street and asked for money. Sometimes, a woman clad in what can only be described as gypsy costume – bright headscarf, full skirt and golden hoops through the ears – will beckon you into a corner, produce lipsticks or scarves from her bag and try and persuade you to buy.

Gypsy influences pervade Sergei's music and Ponomaryova's singing. The music has no boundaries or rules. The musicians rely on their imaginations and daring. Kuryokhin is neither anti-Soviet nor pro-Soviet, and politics do not interest him. He is first and foremost a musician and wants only the freedom to play. 'I'm afraid that if we don't keep on playing and let people hear about us, our music will simply dry up and die.' The future is uncertain. The audience's response at the festival is ample evidence that there is a place for such music in Soviet society. Whether the authorities will recognise this and whole-heartedly sanction the work of Sergei and his colleagues still remains to be seen.

[O.L.]

Index

abortion, 22, 51
Aeroflot, 43
Afghanistan, 48, 50, 55, 60, 61
Africa, 47
agit-trains, 66
agriculture, 30, 124–35
Aiden (footballer), 142–3, 145–6
air travel, 87
Alaska, 35, 148
alcoholism, 70, 102, 120–1, 166
Alexander the Great, 61
Alik (footballer), 142, 143
Alishanov, Aziz, 138
Allakulov, Usta, 60
Allen, Woody, 87–8
Aluminium Works, Sumgait, 138, 139
Andrei (artist), 75, 76
Andrei (Rita's boyfriend), 17, 20–2, 23, 26
Andropov, Yuri, 25, 166
'Aquarium', 167
Arctic Sea, 36
Arkhangelsk, 83, 167
Armenia, 81
Artists' Union, 158
arts, 66–7, 160–71
Asanov, Anwar, 64, 70, 72–3, 77
Asanov, Nikolai (Kolya), 64–5, 72–3, 75–8
Asanova, Dinara, 64–78, 167
Association of Estonian Handicraftsmen, 118
Azerbaidzhan, 90, 136–47

Baikal, Lake, 27, 35
Baikal-Amur Railway, 16, 36
Baku, 90
Baltic, 109–23, 156, 163
bear hunting, 33
Beltsy, 96–108
Bibi-Khanum mosque, Samarkand, 57
Bible, 65
birth rate, 50–1
black market, 112–13
Black Sea, 135, 156
Blue Blouses, 66
Bolsheviks, 155
Bolshoi Theatre, Moscow, 66, 115, 162, 163
Boris (chauffeur), 79, 80, 81, 92
Brando, Marlon, 95
Bredova, Tatyana, 154
Britain, 89, 164
Bubulich, Lyubov, 96–108
Bubulich, Valera, 103, 108
Bukhara, 54, 55, 62
Bukhara, Emir of, 54

Bulgakov, Mikhail, 65
bureaucracy, 80–1

cars, 79, 92, 125, 134
Caspian Sea, 90, 136, 138, 142
Caucasus, 127, 135, 141
Central Asia, 36, 50–63
Chapaev (film), 67
Chebatar, Giorgi, 105
Cheboksary, 82–3
Chekasin, Vladimir, 162–4, 170
Chernenko, Constantin, 152
children, 12, 13, 22, 50–1, 70, 93, 97, 131
China, 12, 50, 60, 148, 152
Chukchis, 35
CIA, 47
cinema, 65, 66–78, 131
class differences, 92, 93
clothing, 52, 110–18, 121–3, 131
Club '81, 160
collective farms, 30, 124–35
Communist Party, 55, 58, 89; and the film industry, 68; and the judicial system, 97, 98, 101; and local government, 148, 149, 153; membership, 14, 94–5
Composers' Union, 162
contraception, 22, 51
Cossacks, 35, 127
Council of Ministers, 90
crime, 96–108
Czechoslovakia, 66, 112, 145

dachas, 40, 93–4
Dalintorg, 152
dances, 118–19
Danes, 109
Dearest, Darling, Beloved, Only One (film), 65, 68, 73
defections, 140
democracy, 154–5
Dinamo Kiev, 136, 144
dissidents, 105–6
divorce, 22, 70, 97, 103–4
Dnepropetrovsk, 145
Dockers' Union, 41
doctors, 85–6
Don, River, 39–40
Dostoevsky museum, Leningrad, 160
drugs, 85–6
Dzhan, Akhmad, 57–8

East Germany, 76
education, 13–20, 23–6, 62–3, 132
Egypt, 111
elections, 154–5